But What About Men?

JOHN H. MOORE

But What About Men?

After Women's Lib

ASHGROVE PRESS, BATH

First published in Great Britain by
ASHGROVE PRESS LIMITED
4 Brassmill Centre, Brassmill Lane
Bath BA1 3JN
and distributed in the USA by
Avery Publishing Group Inc.
350 Thorens Avenue
Garden City Park
New York 11040

First published 1989

British Library Cataloguing in Publication Data

Moore, John H.
  But what about men?
  1. Men. Sex roles
  305.3'1

ISBN 1–85398 014–5

Photoset in Palatino by
Ann Buchan (Typesetters), Shepperton
Printed and bound in Great Britain by
Dotesios Printers, Trowbridge, Wiltshire

CONTENTS

5   *Mind-split*

Differentiated functioning of two sides of brain/mind –
left-side programming or social conditioning, right-side
ambition for power and status as individual – public service
versus private enterprise – inter-hemisphere relationship
as reflection of inter- gender relationship – feminine-left
either in harmony or confrontation with masculine-right

6   *The weaker sex*

Myth of the male as the stronger sex – his expenditure of
energy and resources as 'a modified female', his 'fight to be
male', his vulnerability and higher mortality rate – female
constitutionally stronger and psychologically better integrated – her increasing dominance as need for male declines

7   *Masculine-right*

Male's right-brain talent for visualization expressed as
humanity's 'higher aspirations' – creative arts, religion,
philosophy/psychology – patriarchy's superimposition
onto matriarchal power (transcendent god versus goddess
of fertility) as representing spirituality versus sexuality –
present need for spiritual renaissance as traditional
belief-systems based on group-survival fall into decline

8   *Marriage on the rocks*

Traditional social and religious concepts of long-term
inter- gender relationship now under siege – sexual, procreative and economic bases of marriage contract no longer
valid as women become increasingly independent and
role-differentiation diminishes – co-operation gives way to
competition and contention as divorce rates and increases
in illegitimacy, single-parent families, homosexuality, etc.
testify

9   *The hero in trouble*

Gender incompatibility, previously suppressed for reasons
of group-survival and social expediency, increasingly
evident – male heroes no longer required – men confused as
their occupations become less fulfilling and their responsibilities less defined – dispiriting effect of the employer/
employee/unemployed syndrome – the male need to
re-establish employment of himself in creative, self-
generated, self-fulfilling occupations, especially in the
third third of his lifespan

10 *The sexual conspiracy*

Premises for male roles as lover, husband and father undermined by the liberated female – sexual interaction as competition for dominance – negation of the procreative combined with sensual licence eclipses inspirational aspect of the erotic – present emphasis on passion, orgasm and sexual dysfunction – need for restoration of compassion, respect and revitalization rather than 'mutual annihilation'

11 *So, what about men . . . and women?*

Present disillusionment giving rise to frustration and anger, anxiety and depression – drugs as escape – 'marriage of true minds' as higher purpose of long-term relationship – reconciliation of two sides of mind as prerequisite of true individuality – either continuing obsession with maximum procreativity and procurement or aspiration towards self-fulfilling vision, creativity and contemplation

Hamlet: Lady, shall I lie in your lap?
Ophelia:: No, my lord.
Hamlet: I mean, my head upon your lap.
Ophelia: Ay, my lord.
Hamlet: Did you think I meant country matters?
Ophelia: I think nothing, my lord.
Hamlet: That's a fair thought to lie between maids' legs.
Ophelia: What is, my lord?
Hamlet: Nothing.

Hamlet, Act 3, Scene 2

1 Women's Liberation From What?

Whatever men in Western societies may care to make of it, the social change known as 'the women's liberation movement' has proved very powerful and far-reaching in effect. The energy employed in its propagation during the past twenty or thirty years can only denote the collective pressure of frustration amongst women which had long been awaiting opportunity for release.

That which had previously begun as relatively few isolated voices of protest, escalated after World War II into a loud chorus of demand – for equal rights and opportunities for women. The considerable media attention given to the movement has ensured that the subsequent transformation of attitude and behaviour among women has gained it revolutionary status. This revolution has now brought about changes in almost every social institution. In particular, it has deeply affected long-established patterns of conduct within inter-gender relationships, especially those within marriage contract.

It seems that little notice was taken of the early voices of dissent. They appear to have been regarded by the majority of society, by both women and men, as amusing, eccentric, impertinent or objectionable. Most men – in what may be seen in hindsight as their insensitivity or indifference – must have considered the phenomenon as being of little significance, being mounted by a few frustrated wives and rebellious daughters at odds with their husbands, fathers or their own femininity. The import of those first protests and demands seems to have been greatly underestimated and little understood. Few could have then envisaged where the initiative would eventually lead. After two devastating wars – which were certainly catalytic in the process of emancipation – the clamour for equal rights and opportunities for women reverberated throughout urban society. Wide-ranging changes of attitude and conduct became irresistible.

Men who are now, say, in their fifties and over appear to have been taken by surprise by the speed, scale, intensity and repercussions of this revolution. Those who are younger, having grown up with it, are not so aware of the contrast with the old conventions. Liberal-minded, adult males may have come to see it as reasonable that women should have the right to the same occupational opportunities as themselves, equal participation in matters of common concern and more control in matters which affect them particularly. But men in general do not yet seem to have fully assimilated the likely longer-term effects of the revolution on their own traditional conditioning, on their domestic situations or on their relationships with women.

Furthermore, many of the older men have surely been taken aback by the bitterness and animosity evident in some of the accusations made against them, especially by the more militant, feminist[1] wing of the movement. Most men will surely not have realized that their inherited presumptions and dispositions had become so offensive. They will have taken it for granted that in the main their gender has behaved more or less as women for generations have expected and wanted them to behave. To have the entire blame for inequity and suppression then laid upon them can hardly do other than leave them at best somewhat bemused, at worst seriously offended. The great majority will not have thought of themselves as having been intentionally exploitive; simply as having willingly undertaken the responsibilities placed upon them by society as a whole.

It is perhaps because of their bewilderment at the accusations made against them, and their present preoccupation with having to cope with the repercussions of the revolution itself, that men have really said very little as to what they think and feel about what is going on. Certainly any media coverage given in this respect is vastly outweighed by the amount given to women having their say. There has been no sign of collective-male counter-demand – perhaps partly because, on the face of it, there can be no reasonable objection to women claiming their liberation and partly because the full implications of the initiative have not yet been acknowledged. In the main, men seem to have acquiesced with little resistance to women's active participation in their own right in whatever areas they have wished to engage (one exception being certain areas of the orthodox religious establishment).

There is no definite evidence to support any male claim to superior ability in any occupation where mental powers are the means to successful participation. There are, of course, certain areas in which women would usually prefer not to venture on equal footing, e.g. the military. And there are others where muscle-power still favours predominantly male employment. (But even these are now steadily declining in technologically-developed societies.) Given inclination, training and experience, women can fulfil the intelligence-requirement of any occupation just as effectively as men.

In theory, if men can bring themselves to abandon the centuries-old conditioning which has disposed them to claim exclusive right to particular power-roles, there is no good reason why women's emancipation should not be welcomed as progressive, even evolutionary. The resultant shift in power-holding is, however, bringing about an unprecedented reorganization of society, one in which old balances established in different and now no longer relevant circumstances are being replaced by new and unfamiliar ones. And, in practice, these may not prove in the longer run easy for men to tolerate.

There is also in theory no clear reason why the reorganization should result in less enjoyable and fulfilling relationships between the sexes. But here again there are radical adjustments to be made; and in practice these are certainly not proving easy for men to accommodate. The old-fashioned conflicts which gave rise to the term 'battle of the sexes' may be seen to have been caused by differentiation of roles. That differentiation – which gave each gender separate and distinct self-image – is now rapidly disappearing. But there are no signs yet that relationships are improving. On the contrary, such indicators as the rate of divorce suggest that the battle is far

from over and that casualties are not decreasing. Transformation of attitudes and expectations evidently has a
considerable way to go. It could even be that the institution
of marriage – as the custom of lifelong contract – will
become regarded by both genders as no longer desirable or
appropriate.

In a survey carried out in the U.S.A.[2] attempting to
identify the most stressful situations in modern life, five
out of the first ten heading the list were connected with
marriage. The top three in the rating were death of
husband/wife, divorce and separation. Marriage itself and
attempting reconciliation were the other two. If further
stress factors such as sexual problems, suspected or actual
infidelity, infertility, parental and family discord, etc., are
also taken into account, it becomes increasingly difficult to
sustain the conventional concept of marriage as ideal in
this day and age.

We may have reached a juncture in the evolution of
human society when it would be as well to acknowledge
that the genders are not entirely complementary. It would
be wishful thinking to suppose that they can now be in
competition as individuals and simultaneously complementary as partners. The idea that the genders are
different in nature and compatible – two halves of a
whole, as it were – is largely due to centuries of religious
persuasion which has seen long-term commitment
between the genders as the best means of ensuring social
stability (albeit, at the same time often advocating celibacy
for its own priesthood). It might now be better to recognize
that in certain respects the genders are inherently
incompatible. To do so would be to open the door to improved and healthier relationships. It would remove a
pretence which has all-too-often in the past been the cause
of considerable suppression, a suppression not of psychological benefit to either gender. There will be many, of
course, who will refute the above, claiming that people do
have long and successful marriages. If that is actually and
honestly so, then they would have a case. But are such
marriages as unconditionally happy as they are made out
to be? Do both partners retain their individuality, or does
the long-term continuation of the relationship depend on

one partner becoming subordinate to the other at the expense of his or her potential development? Feminists aver that self-denial has always been the fate of wives under patriarchal domination.

No revolution is ever entirely profitable for all affected. In the process of throwing out the intolerable and the no-longer relevant, some good features of the old convention are bound to be sacrificed. It would be naive to suppose that the current dismantling of the old social structures will be accomplished without any detrimental effect. A great deal of concern is presently being expressed, for example, about increasing levels of disorder and violence (mainly being perpetrated by men), and about such matters as the increasing intake of drugs, both illegal ones and those medically prescribed or socially acceptable.

Numerous reasons for these undesirable effects are suggested – unemployment, deprived living conditions, breakdown of moral values and sense of responsibility, break-up of family life, lack of parental authority, failure of educational discipline, and so on. Amongst all the explanations offered, hardly a voice is heard venturing that such effects might also have something to do with tensions exacerbated by the emancipation of women.

Of all the causes of social disruption, stress in the arena of sexual relationship has to be one of the most potent of precipitating factors.[3]. Despite our civilized and sophisticated veneer, we are still, like all other creatures, basically motivated by sexual energy. And there can be little doubt that the new-found assertiveness and independence of the human female may not only be seen as threatening to the male but also as threatening to the stability of inter-gender relationship itself. That threat is bound to cause an escalation of frustration and anxiety in both genders; and they in turn are likely to find their way out as aggression and escapism.

It is all very well for liberated women to throw out with enthusiasm all the traditional concepts, beliefs and attitudes about their role in society and their relationships with men. But there is surely hazard in failing to give adequate consideration to what guidelines will replace them and what the psychological consequences of a competitive free-for-all might be. It is one of the extraordinary features of the liberation movement that, throughout all the hue and cry for rights and opportunities, there appears to have been no such consideration.

And men might be forgiven for thinking that the liberated woman does not care about the consequences for them. As far as the militant feminist is concerned, they would be right, if the following quotation may be taken as typical: 'Men's spirituality is very badly mangled . . . Men don't have intuition or sensitivity . . . Women have total mind. Men's minds are not true . . . We must learn about men and their archetypes in order to put them back in their place – they are an aberration and out of control. . . Men won't exist for much longer.'[4]

Whatever the place man may eventually be destined to be put back into (if indeed, they are to have a place at all) it was suggested earlier that their response to date seems to have been a mixture of bewilderment, irritation and acquiescence. The danger must be that as the full implications of the revolution come to be worked out and men become deeply aware of what is expected of them – or, more to the point, not expected of them – it will be they who will begin to experience a serious build-up of resentment and anger.

As is already becoming apparent in some sections of the community, there is not only an increase in random violence against the person but increasing incidence of rape and other forms of assault and abuse against women. Apart from such emotional reaction, men may also take the alternative course of dissociation and withdrawal from committed heterosexual relationship. The latter course may well be suspected in the increased incidence of males who prefer their intimate relationships to be with other males. For reasons which should become apparent later in this book, the emergence of women's liberation and the public surfacing of overt male homosexuality cannot simply be coincident and unrelated phenomena.

Women's bid for greater independence is bound to have its price. Understandable in theory though their initiatives may be, and possibly also beneficial in the socio-economic organization at large, the possibility has to be recognized that in the realm of personal relationships there may be greater polarization between the sexes, not better integration and harmony. At best, women may have to forego to some degree the security of male commitment and support. At worst, if alienation increases, they may have to content themselves with only fleeting engagements or having to contend with a psychological war of self-defensive attrition.

Men will also have to count the cost. Psychologically, the likely problem for them is that they will begin to see themselves at best having to come to terms with much-reduced status, at worst having to contend with increasing redundancy, even impotency. The more the genders elide in conduct and occupation, the more difficult it will become for men to identify with and justify the biological programming through which they have hitherto been able to exercise what they have understood as their 'maleness'.

There can, of course, be no denying the physical differences between a man and a woman; nor that the child-bearing experience is exclusive to the latter. It is generally assumed, however – and actively emphasized by the feminists – that psychologically there is no difference between the genders. Both are deemed to have the same emotions and feelings, and to have potentially the same mental abilities. It is therefore upheld that existing differences in disposition – which give rise to the conventional differences in priorities, preferences, interests, occupations, etc. – are simply due to parental, educational and social conditioning. Furthermore, if such differentiated conditioning were eliminated, male and female would become psychologically the same and equal in all respects for all intents and purposes.

The male may well suspect that this contention is not in fact correct. He may, for example, like to think that there is some particular ingredient in his nature which gives him distinction as a male. Psychologists may say that this is wishful thinking and that the male's continual attempt to justify himself is simply an effort to compensate for the denial to him of child-bearing fulfilment. There may be an element of truth in that. But it could also be true that the male does in fact have some gender-exclusive, mental capacity. The trouble is that he does not seem to have been able to define what that special asset might be. If it does exist, he ought now to try to identify it (a task which in part this book attempts to do).

When pressed for justification of their conduct, men can find themselves nowadays in something of a quandary. They may claim that it has been their capacity for invention which has created all manner of technological means to enhance the prospects for survival. But, by the same token, they would have to admit that their inventiveness has also caused much suffering. Not only have men now invented weapons of mass destruction which have put human survival at risk, but technologies exploiting natural resources are also causing serious damage to the environment. As well as aspiring to the most refined and noble of human accomplishments, men have also – and arguably in greater measure – all-too-often seen fit to equate success with the satiation of any appetite, regardless of consequence.

Through their ingenuity, men may have enabled proliferation of the species (frequently at the expense of other species); but they seem to have accomplished comparatively little to ensure a happier life for those teeming millions. For all their endless promises and apparent commitment to establishing goodwill and peace on earth, they have persistently argued and found cause to fight. On the face of it, women have a good case for claiming that not only do they have the right to equal power to try to remedy this perennial situation but also that, if men are allowed to continue to exercise their power as they have done for much longer, they may soon go too far.

However, the claim made by women that having gained overall power they would not make the same mistakes but would reverse the suicidal trend has to remain questionable. If, as it is claimed, the female is psychologically exactly the same as the male, why would she not, given the opportunity, be tempted to behave in the same manner? Women can be just as vain, greedy, ruthless and exploitive as men.[5] Apart from their having in the past and in large measure condoned and actively encouraged the competitive and exploitive ambition in men, they have been only too pleased at their partners' success and scornful of their failure. On the evidence to date, women given power behave no differently from men,

Be that as it may, it is no sensible argument in favour of men being able to carry on regardless. It is surely high time the male woke up to the fact that the old parameters within which he has operated for so long are becoming increasingly tenuous. As some feminists justifiably contend, women's liberation cannot simply mean women gaining the freedom to behave just like men. It has to mean gaining the power to overthrow (what they see as) exploitive, patriarchal belief-systems. The prospect of the old systems being dismantled may at first, as already suggested, seem threatening to the male. But there is also the possibility of his waking up to the fact that the revolution is an opportunity for his liberation too. His present apparent insistence on pursuing old courses has an air of obstinacy and desperation about it, a desperation which surely masks an underlying anxiety that direction is being lost and that sense of fulfilling purpose is ever slipping away over future horizons. The feminists' crusade is largely borne along by the spirit of revolution for its own sake, its object being to destroy the old regime. Other than being determined that men will have little or no place in it, they do not say much as to how they envisage their promised land beyond. If the male does have a gender-exclusive mental capacity and that capacity (as will be explored later) has something to do with creative vision, then it must now be time for him to exercise it. Men badly need to liberate in themselves a new vision of themselves if they are to avoid obsolescence.

For such a positive and constructive vision to emerge, men will have to undergo a revolution of belief and attitude. This will require not only a radical overhaul of traditional conditioning, but also a transforming of the terms in which they have been for so long used to seeing justification of motivations and fulfilment of ambitions. Inevitably, at the heart of such far-reaching reformation, there will have to be radical appraisal of their assumptions about women, especially their expectations as to what roles women are supposed to play in their lives. There are signs that this is happening to a degree. But the aforementioned incidence of violence, separation and dissociation suggests that it tends to be happening as much through force of events as through intelligent response.

The adjustment required of the male is certainly a formidable challenge, and not likely to be at all comfortable. The dislodging of well-embedded assumptions inevitably involves disillusionment; and the revealing of misconceptions tends to undermine confidence, invoking in its wake anxiety and resentment.

In the realm of beliefs about sexual conduct, for example, the male might once have been complacent in the notion that the female is not naturally promiscuous and that he could therefore assume her to be likely to be satisfied by and faithful to the one man in her life. Of that notion, in the wake of women's liberation, he may well now be disillusioned. Women have been awakened to the fact that their appetite for sensual pleasure is just as great as the male's has always been reputed to be. Publicity promoting the entitlement of women to satisfy this appetite – and encouraging them to pursue and demand such satisfaction – has resulted in a major shift in their attitude and behaviour in matters sexual. That may or may not be a welcome disillusionment for the unattached male in search of sex; it certainly is not a comfortable one for husbands.

The above is just one example of current assault on the male's self-confidence. Gradually, he is having to concede that he has no exclusive rights or privileges in any respect where his sexual relationship with the female is concerned. Conceding equal rights to take initiative is one thing; the possibility of losing the initiative – or, even worse, becoming impotent – is quite another. The male may try to reassure himself that at least in one respect he is indispensable. He is the one who provides the seed to enable conception and thus he may assume that he is essential to the female's natural desire to bear children. Beyond that, he may also presume that a woman will prefer to commit herself to a particular man not only because she sees him as an ideal father for her children but also because she will want to rely on him to provide support and security for her and the children whilst they are growing up.

These assumptions may still commonly coincide with popular expectation and practice; but they are nothing like as well-founded as they used to be. Women, if they so wish, do not now have to abide by such convention. An increasing number are giving preference to career over lifelong commitment to being wife, mother and house-keeper. And an increasing number are prepared and able to have children without entering into marriage contract. Even if they do make such commitment and then the relationship fails, they are not likely to fear divorce as a threat in social and economic terms to anything like the degree that their mothers and grandmothers did. The stigma previously attached to being a divorcee or an unmarried mother has virtually disappeared. Not only are single women more likely to be capable economically of supporting themselves and their children, but divorce settlement nowadays favours them where entitlement to share of marital assets and continuing contribution by the ex-husband are concerned.

All these factors encourage the female's sense of independence whilst further eroding the male's self-image. If all the above were not intimation of dispensability enough, the male now even has to face the fact that his vision of himself as potential father, as an essential and desirable provider of semen, is not totally inviolable. The existence of sperm-banks and modern techniques of artificial insemination mean that it is possible for a woman to have children without having to rely on sexual intercourse with any particular man.

The implication of all the above has to be that the more independent-minded and assertive the female becomes, the less likely it will be that she will commit herself with confidence to the prospect of a lifelong, binding rela-tionship. She will not countenance obedience to a dominant male partner; she will not respect a subservient male partner; how then can a relationship flourish with both partners exercising equal right to authority? Some may argue that the presently increasing divorce rate is due to modern legislation which makes divorce easier to obtain. But that does not negate the point being made; rather, it endorses it. Not only does the legislation reflect popular demand but it also indicates that the disposition to resort to divorce is already there, whether or not it is made easier to effect.

If more and more women and men decide that a one-to-one, lifelong contract is inappropriate in modern circumstances, that it is an undertaking which is bound to affect adversely the longer-term progress and development of each partner, that it is an arrangement in which the price to pay for a degree of mutual pleasure, ease and security is too high, and so on, then what might the psychological and social consequences be if the practice is increasingly abandoned?

If more and more children are not going to be growing up in a traditional family context – i.e., with the regular and continuing presence of a mother and father performing recognizably and conventionally differentiated roles in a single, shared home – what might the psychological effects be on them? Will it matter to them that their parents become, functionally-speaking, indistinguishable from each other or that they may experience little or nothing of the presence and influence of one parent?

Statistics show that single-parent families, predominantly mother-only, are steadily increasing.[6] So is the incidence of children having to adjust to 'temporary fathers', foster parents and second-marriage step-parents, usually step-fathers. Is it not most probable that such children will grow up with undermined confidence in the marriage concept, a predisposition which will not only increase their reluctance to enter into it themselves but also, if they do, will increase the likelihood of their abandoning it if the relationship becomes difficult?

If the more militant, feminist wing of the women's movement has its way, the custom of long-term, mutual commitment between heterosexual adults will certainly disappear. As touched on earlier, some feminists advocate no less than a humiliating demotion of the male; even, as far as the real hardliners are concerned, total ostracism of him. It is (hopefully) unlikely that the majority of women, including those who see themselves as liberated, will be converted to such an extreme viewpoint. That majority may welcome the prospect of equal rights and opportunities, but it would not envisage a total takeover. Neither, presumably, would it relish with confidence the prospect of women's lives being lived in relationship with other women only.

Nevertheless, if that majority does not want to find itself caught up in the most uncomfortable of confusions and stressful situations, it has some serious thinking to do about the future conduct of its relationship with men. And it would do no better for a start than to ask itself just what it thinks women are being liberated from. By what or whom have they supposedly been imprisoned?

A feminist would quickly answer, in so many words, 'From men and their oppressive, patriarchal domination.' A more moderate, liberated woman might say, 'From the traditional conditioning which has confined women to child-rearing and domestic occupations.' Whatever the answer, either explicitly or implicitly men are all-too-readily targetted as having been to blame for causing the situation. From a man's point of view, it would be reasonable to suggest that, due to the technological progress made by men over recent decades, women have now become able to liberate themselves from their own conventional image of themselves.

Meanwhile, men also have some serious thinking to do. And they would do no better for a start than to ask themselves, 'But what about men?'

Women's liberation and all that it implies as a gaining by the female of self-confidence and independence cannot help but have a cumulative effect on the male's evaluation of himself. How is he to adjust to the fact that the centuries-old patriarchal systems and their authority which enabled him to establish his status and power-holdings and which moulded the form of his relationship with the female are now fast falling into disrepute and decline?

Whether men care to admit it or not, they have rendered themselves (ironically, due to their success) increasingly redundant and impotent. Given that the effects of women's liberation are irreversible, men would be well advised to see if they ought also to liberate themselves from their conventional image of themselves. To do so will mean having to trace back to see where such images came from in the first place.

Male and female self-images are the product of conditioning. And that conditioning is not just the result of all we learned from our parents, teachers and the particular social environments in which we happen to have lived. It goes right back to the biological roots via which we evolved to become human beings. Changing social systems, patriarchal or otherwise, will not eliminate features of behaviour deeply embedded in our genetic inheritance, passed down to us from the most ancient, ancestral origins.

2 Men's Dilemma

It is one of the main planks of the feminists' platform that longstanding bias in patriarchal systems has allowed men to take the power-roles in society and to assign to women roles which have systematically denied them power, limited their freedom and prevented development of their potential.

That in some respects, contexts and eras this situation has prevailed cannot – on the face of it and from the viewpoint of today – be denied. What is questionable about this charge are the implications that women have been continually discontented with this state of affairs, that the annexation of power by men was sought entirely in order to satisfy their vanity, greed, lust, etc., and that they set out deliberately to oppress and exploit women.

Certainly there is plenty of evidence in historical record and contemporary report to substantiate the claim that, having acquired the power for themselves, men have often abused that power, behaving irresponsibly and sometimes downright destructively. And clearly women have often suffered as a consequence. But men have also consistently – and surely in far greater measure? – used their powers directly and fully, as best they saw it, in support of social well-being in general and women in particular.

The trouble is that the credit side of men's contribution tends to be taken for granted and dismissively left out of account. Their misdemeanours and crimes have always been, and still are, more newsworthy than their dedicated services.

The point to be made is that the powers which men have traditionally held were surely not originally appropriated simply in order to subjugate women? Unless, perhaps, at some juncture in social history it became necessary for men to counteract what had become an intolerable imposition of matriarchal power upon them?

Whatever the case, all that past history has been passed down to us and the gist of it will be present in the social conditioning we received in our own upbringing. That conditioning – or programming as we might call it in this age of the computer – will to some extent have been selective according to gender, the extent being dependent on the social context into which we happen to have been born. It is this selectivity which feminists maintain as being responsible for men assuming certain power-holdings which have operated to women's disadvantage. Though men are held to blame for such inequity, the fact that it is the mother who is the primary influence in the childhood of both boys and girls suggests that women have to take some blame for having perpetuated it.

Arguments as to which gender is to blame for such inequity can go round and round in vicious circles of charge and counter-charge; and that cannot be beneficial for anyone involved. It would perhaps be more helpful to go back to beginnings to see if it is possible to trace a reasonably objective account as to how we have ended up in this contentious situation.

Accounts of beginnings tend, of course, to be hypothetical and speculative, since there are no contemporary records. Nevertheless, ever since man conceived the notion of passing time he has been intrigued to explain the origins of his own existence. Such attempts at explanation gave rise to numerous creation myths, a central feature of which is the 'sudden' appearence of ready-made Man and Woman.

For example, there is the familiar story of man's origin in the Hebrew tradition.[7] As translated into the English biblical account, the almighty, patriarchal deity first created an instant human male called Adam and put him in a garden where there was plenty for him to enjoy.But then the deity decided that it was not good for Adam that he should be there alone so, whilst Adam was asleep, the deity created an instant female from a piece of his body.

Adam, who had previously been given to naming all creatures in the garden, woke up to find this 'help-meet' before him and said, '. . .she shall be called Woman because she was taken out of Man.' Because these first two humans then displeased the deity through disobeying his orders (at the instigation of the woman), the deity punished them, declaring amongst other things to Adam, 'And I will put emnity between thee and the woman, and between thy seed and her seed . . .' And to Eve, the woman, he said, 'I will greatly multiply thy sorrow and thy conception; and in sorrow thou shalt bring forth children: and thy desire shall be to thy husband and he shall rule over thee . . .'

A bit steep for eating an apple. And plainly not a good start for humanity. The scenario cannot be said to have promised well for inter-gender relationship. It is certainly not a set-up which would commend itself to a feminist . . . who would undoubtedly condemn it as a blatant piece of patriarchal propaganda, as a result of which millions of women have subsequently suffered.

This is not the context in which to consider what the myth might mean symbolically (even though it may be saying something about the inherent, psychological incompatibility of the genders referred to in the previous chapter). Few in this scientific age are in any case likely to take the story literally. But it cannot be denied, as the feminists maintain, that such age-old myths have had, and continue to have, subtle psychological effect. Particularly through their perpetuation in modern culture, they insidiously promote notions of male precedence and female subordination, especially when they are told to the young.

Gender bias in creation myths apart, modern society is far more likely to look to scientific disciplines to provide less imaginative and prejudiced accounts of human origins. Whether such explanations, elaborate and soph-isticated though they may be, are in the long run any more satisfying than the myths remains questionable.

Palaeontologists are generally agreed that anthropoid species have existed on earth for several million years but there is some uncertainty and debate as to the evolutionary sequence which eventually gave rise to Modern Man/Woman.

One theory is that a species of *homo erectus* emigrated

northwards out of Africa about a million years ago. This precursor is thought to have given rise to the presence in Europe of Neanderthal Man, a hominid who died out, for reasons unknown, some thirty-five to fifty thousand years ago. He was superceded by Cro-Magnon Man who is generally regarded as having been the immediate ancestor of Modern Man. At one time, Cro-Magnon Man was thought to have been a direct descendant of Neanderthal Man; but that now seems unlikely. There would not have been sufficient time for the skull formation and heavy bone structure of the latter to evolve into the larger, differently-shaped cranium and much more slender bone formation of the former. It is therefore suggested that there must have been a second migration from Africa of another hominid species, one which originated from ancestors different from those who gave rise to Neanderthal Man.

Whatever the truth about these events long ago, in one significant respect the genesis of *homo sapiens* must surely for ever remain a mystery. Research into that distant past is limited to making extrapolations based on physical data only. Through investigating fossilized skeletal remnants, it is possible to establish the form of skull and pelvis-leg structure. And through using ingenious dating techniques, it is possible to estimate when those beings were alive. Assuming certain genetic mutations along the way, the scientific mind might then be satisfied that it understands the evolutionary steps which produced the human being. This exercise, however, only accounts for the *homo* element; it still leaves the *sapiens* factor a mystery. No laboratory technique could ever trace the evolution of psychological experience and how we have come by that power of comprehension we call 'wisdom'. It could never explain how the human being was able to become conscious of itself and objectively conscious of its environment, capacities which proved crucial to the survival and success of the species.

The applying of the label 'homo sapiens' to ourselves, along with the scientific labelling of all the phenomena we perceive about us, is not, when objectively considered, a far cry from the situation in the aforementioned creation myth when the deity brought all creatures 'unto Adam to see what he would call them; and whatsoever Adam called each living creature, that was the name thereof.' The only difference is that we have taken to naming dead things as well.

We may have accumulated a great deal of man-contrived, scientific information over the ages but we will never be certain of the cause and nature of the mind-shift which distinguishes us from our evolutionary precursors. All we can do is deduce from residual traces how that shift modified behaviour and, hence, how the intelligence behind that behaviour enabled our ancestors to survive, proliferate and 'gain dominion' over all other species.

However many millennia ago Modern Man/Woman may be reckoned to have emerged from less-wise ancestors, we have recorded account of his/her activities over only the last half-dozen or so. For our picture of earlier times, we rely on the painstaking efforts of scientists in various fields of investigation. Archaeologists, through their study of long-buried artefacts, deduce a certain amount. Anthropologists, through their study of societies whose present way of life are closer to those of the distant past, make their contribution. And biologists, through their study of other life-forms, from the most primitive to the most complex, add their share. From the total framework of scientific exploration – all based on physical data and the notion of continuous, chronological sequence – a picture emerges of constant struggle to survive. The human species is seen to be like all others, subject to the same evolutionary principles – such as adaptation to changing environment, survival of the fittest and specialization of function. The last-mentioned – as applied, for example, to the survival strategies within colonies of ants and bees – could well be called 'role differentiation'.

It is thus right back at the most primitive, instinctive levels that we may find the origins of role differentiation. Hence the beginnings of differentiated programming or conditioning of the genders.

Pragmatic survival-strategy is then passed on to succeeding generations as social conditioning. But, where the behaviour of other species is concerned, we do not speak, say, of some kinds of female spider 'satisfying their sadistic lust' by consuming their male partners after copulation. Neither do we speak of the queen bee as 'despot of a totalitarian matriarchal state' subjugating her 'harem' of drones in order to satisfy her 'ego and vanity'. Nor do we accuse the tiger of being a 'chauvinistic rapist' because he only seeks out the company of the tigress 'to have sex' with her or of being a 'psychopathic murderer' because he may try to kill and eat her cubs.

We may, from our civilized viewpoint, look upon such behaviour as extraordinary but accept that in some bizarre way it must be advantageous to the survival of the species concerned. We do not judge such goings-on in the natural kingdom as evidence that one gender is attempting to dominate and exploit the other. If we did choose to make such anthropocentric judgement on Nature's tactics, then it would be fair to say that she usually gives the male a harder time than the female. What is more, she often sees to it that the genders are kept well apart, sometimes being hostile to each other, only allowing them to engage with each other when necessary for species survival.

So that we do not assume ourselves too complacently to be a species apart and not naturally subject to such programming, it would be as well not to overlook the fact that our own physical organisms – the bodies we refer to as being us – are themselves complex, programmed societies of cells governed primarily by survival instinct. And each cell has its own specialized function.

Each person, of either sex, begins as a single-cell ovum fertilized by a single spermatazoon. During gestation, that original cell, by a process of multiple division, generates billions of other cells. By a miracle of in-built programming, intelligence within each cell nucleus 'tells' that cell its location and function within the total organism. It could be said that no cell has a choice as to which one of hundreds of possible functions it is to perform. It has no say, as it were, in whether its role is to be a superficial, short-life skin cell or a long-lasting, sophisticated brain cell; or as a cell in a male or female organ.

We assume that no cell, whatever its assignment, considers itself oppressed, exploited or denied equality. It gets on with its allotted task within the total survival system. Day after day, all those cells are involved in feeding, killing, regenerating and dying processes; our being depends upon them.

One exception to the above is the cancer cell – a cell which through 'self-will' opts out of its role-responsibility to the well-being of the whole organism, thereby threatening to destroy it. We may think of the cancer cell's behaviour as bizarre and barbaric (whilst it may think of itself as being 'liberated'); but it serves to remind us that we have not transcended the fate of all living creatures and that we have little or no control over our fundamental programming. By changing the fabric of society, we are not going to alter the essential nature of the structure upholding it. Civilization does not eliminate the primitive, for it is founded upon it.

The scientific picture of human evolution cannot but be an outline sketch of changing form, diversification of function and behavioural adaptation to changing circumstances. We can hardly begin to comprehend with appropriate awe the astounding, supramundane intelligence which over millennia brought each one of us to our present experience of being human and alive, here and now. A sobering scientific analysis published some twenty years ago assessed that the average person – you and me – is comprised of 'eleven gallons of water and £1.17s.6d worth of chemicals'. Out of such cheap and commonplace material, there are formed 'some two hundred different bones, two hundred joints, five hundred muscles and four billion brain cells.' As if that were not miracle enough, out of that physical constitution there arise such phenomena as the experience of feelings and emotions, and such mysteries as memory, intelligence and imagination. Above all this, as a kind of crowning touch of magic, there arises the most mysterious and elusive phenomenon of all – consciousness; that which permits us to know that we are.

Within the limitations of the physical view of evolution, we may still pursue the progress of the mortal human responding to the everyday challenge to survive, existentially. The scientific accounts demonstrate that for many thousands of years after his emergence Modern Man was fully occupied with that task only. And we may deduce three principal aspects of this endeavour, in the success of which exercise of intelligence will have played a crucial part since man could be said to have been otherwise more poorly equipped than other creatures in several respects.

Firstly, there would have been the necessity to cope with adverse climatic conditions. In many parts of the world, this challenge will have stimulated his powers of visualization and inventiveness – in the finding and constructing of shelter, the controlling and use of fire, the devising of protective clothing and coverings, and so on. The essence of this aspect of survival could be called the provision of comfort.

Secondly, there would have been the necessity to defend himself against other threats to survival, mainly other creatures. Apart from the speed and strength of limb permitted by his upright structure – not necessarily powers equal to those of his adversaries – he did not have formidable in-built weaponry such as fangs, claws, poisons, etc. These disadvantages would again have been incentive for his mental powers to devise artificial weapons. The essence of this aspect of survival was the ability to defend/attack.

Thirdly, there would have been the necessity to obtain adequate supplies of water and food. The former would not necessarily have been difficult to find, although its availability from time to time and place to place will have influenced his movements until his powers of visualization and inventiveness enabled him to devise the means of conserving it and transporting it. Provision of food, however, will have required much greater and more sustained effort, either to find it in edible plant form or to hunt for it in the form of meat. In the latter case especially, the exercising of his powers of visualization and inventiveness will have been crucial. The essence of this aspect of survival could be called procurement.

The three survival imperatives – comfort, defence/attack and procurement – may seem obvious enough. What seems to escape the notice of Contemporary Man, who involves himself in all manner of sophisticated occupations, activities and diversions is that the same aspects of survival directly or indirectly underlie almost all of them. Fundamentally, nothing has changed other than form, as anyone who cares to analyse why most people are doing what they are doing most of the time will appreciate. Our primary motivations in life are all connected with existential survival, i.e., the security, stability and continuity of both the group and the individual.

How then may our distant ancestors have seen the purpose of their existence, other than simply to survive from day to day?

We cannot, of course, presume to imagine how they may, from time to time and from place to place, have understood their purpose in life – even if we may even presume that such considerations crossed their minds. But, like all sexual species, they will have been well aware of the physical differences which brought the genders together in the act of copulation.

Because some anthropologists have observed that primitive peoples do not necessarily realize that copulation is linked with the subsequent birth of offspring nine months later, we cannot assume that our ancestors copulated in order to procreate. Presumably the desire to perform the act arose from the pleasure of it, at least as far as the men were concerned.

Whether the connection was understood or not, women became pregnant, gave birth, and their maternal instinct ensured that the offspring were fed and looked after. Inevitably, procreation or reproduction became a central focus of human cohabitation and, whether or not those ancestors thought of it as such, beyond the day-to-day task of surviving the begetting and raising of offspring will have become their main purpose in life. Apart from any other benefit, they will eventually have realized that maximum reproduction via the female was the key to the tribe's strength and continuity. Hence the undeniable power-base of matriarchy in human society. Despite the later superimposition of patriarchy, that power-base has remained undiminished through the ages. It is thus one of the revolutionary and paradoxical aspects of present-day women's liberation in modern, developed societies that the female now seems increasingly willing to abandon it.

As far as early social organization is concerned, there is no evidence to suggest that man has ever been a herd animal in the sense of there being one dominant male who, having proved supremacy over all other males in the vicinity by defeating them in combat, thereby gained exclusive power to pass on his superior genes to all the females he could acquire. There may be intimations of such practice in later patriarchal times, when chiefs, emperors, sultans and the like acquired large numbers of wives and concubines. And there will most likely always have been an element of competition between the most powerful males for the most desirable females. But in the main the human species did not adopt this system common amongst other creatures. Nor did it adopt the practice of other species where male and female only come together for the purpose of mating, living independently the rest of the time. (Could we now, however, in the wake of women's liberation, be moving in that direction?)

It can be deduced from such evidence as exists that the first humans, to ensure the best chance of survival, did as we in the main still do – lived throughout their lives in mixed-gender groups, all members participating if possible in the need to reproduce. Codes of conduct for sexual relationship have varied considerably from one society to another through the ages, but the underlying priority will nearly always have been maximum reproduction. In that interest, there have often been sexual customs which might now be regarded as immoral, promiscuous, exploitive of women, and so on. Closer to our own time, the vast majority of societies, whatever the gender ratio within them, have adopted the arrangement of committed relationships and thus defined family sub-groups within the total group. This arrangement best ensures such benefits as reduction of conflict between males, deterrence of incest, avoidance of the undesirable effects of close inter-breeding and male commitment to family support and group welfare in general.

From earliest times right through to the recent past, men's commitment to serve the group will have been crucial to survival. The emphasis for the male will always have been on the need to compete and to take initiative and risk. And in large measure his efforts to ensure the group's survival will have been indistinguishable from his desire for self-survival.

The clear implication of all the above is that, in the interests of group-survival dependent on female reproduction, the male is the gender which has had to be more disciplined and conditioned. He has become far more akin to the male bee or ant than the tiger or bull.

By whatever trial-and-error processes human beings came to adopt the social arrangement which is so familiar to us and which we take for granted, it certainly proved advantageous for the species. One of the chief features of that advantage was that the arrangement allowed specialization of function or role-differentiation between the genders.

Obviously the female is equipped to enable the nine-month carriage and gestation of the foetus, to give birth and to feed the offspring during the first months of life. Over the ages, all manner of factors will have influenced frequency of pregnancy but, in principle, it will have been seen as the female's responsibility to group survival to be as-near-as-possible continually pregnant during her fertile period. There is no avoiding the intent of Nature that propagation of the species should be the primary, time-consuming occupation of the females of all species. The human female has been no exception, until recent times.

Meanwhile, the male's role in this respect is clearly not a time-consuming occupation. He has only ever needed to spend a fraction of his time in the act of initiating the process. Given therefore the female's heavy commitment to long periods of pregnancy and the continuing task of rearing the children, and given the male's disposition to stay with the group and support its welfare, it was inevitable that he should take responsibility for virtually all other requirements, especially those of procurement and defence/attack.

In the times before plant cultivation and domestication of animals, procurement of food meant random gathering and hunting. It would be reasonable to assume that this task was usually as time-consuming for the male as child-rearing was for the female. As it happened, male physique lent itself better than the female's to taking on this more active occupation, though some might argue that it was pursuing the task which produced the stronger physique. Whichever way round it was, his longer limb, more streamlined shape and greater muscular development gave him superior speed and strength to improve chance of success.

Hunting and gathering required the male to range widely in search and pursuit. Although fluctuations in the availability of food may have caused the group to move periodically, there would always have been the tendency for the female – often pregnant, carrying the newly-born or shepherding the young – to settle as much as possible whilst the male continued his efforts to retrieve. It logically fell to her therefore to take on as many as possible of the home-based tasks such as food preparation and provision of comfort.

The above scenario suggests that the differentiation of roles between the genders was originally simply the outcome of trying to meet survival requirements in the most efficient manner. There is no question here of one gender deliberately seeking to oppress or exploit the other; both co-operated in their common interest.

Apart from his competitive role as procurer, the male's greater speed and strength, and his developing skills with weaponry, must have led, as already mentioned, to his taking on responsibility for defence/attack. Threat to survival will have meant the hostility of other creatures but gradually, as human population increased, it will also have meant increasing chance of collision between groups. Competition over food supply, for example, will have led to contention over territory. With no mutually-agreed boundaries and rights of ownership, resolution of this threat could only be through combat. Since such combat meant close-quarter fighting, muscular strength and skill with weapons multiplied by the number of males on each side dictated the likely outcome.

Three factors (important for this theme) emerge from the above. First, the probability that whilst the female's roles remained virtually constant, the male's gradually changed

in form, complexity and emphasis. Second, the requirement that he should develop strength and skill to procure
more effectively became compounded by the increasing
need for that prowess to be used for fighting and killing
other human beings as well as animals. And third, in a
situation where there was no commonly-recognized right
of land ownership, defence and attack were more or less
synonymous.

Group survival thus much depended on a social
conditioning which endorsed the male's instinct to be
competitive. And in areas where increasing populations
meant the likelihood of competing groups, it also
encouraged him to become aggressive and combative. Yet
again, it has to be said that this conditioning was primarily
instigated in the interests of group-survival. The current
feminist charge that the male is wilfully aggressive seems
conveniently to overlook the fact that for millennia the
female must have condoned his being so . . . for her own
matriarchal interests depended on it.

The above is not to say, of course, that group encounters
were inevitably hostile. Especially in later times, when
groups were less nomadic and more settled in defined
territories, there was increasing incidence of friendly and
co-operative liaison between them. But usually there
would have had to have been some common interest or
mutual advantage, such as trade, for such relationship to
become stable and lasting.

Anyone conversant with what is going on in the world
today between all kinds of groups cannot but reluctantly
admit that, for all the technological progress and sophistication of lifestyle, nothing has fundamentally changed;
only contexts and scales have changed. Despite centuries
of hope for the triumph of such human virtues as goodwill
and reason, the basic and ancient motivations of survival
prevail when all the talking is over.

Out of the incidence of groups in conflict in those earliest
times, there emerged a further development. Anthropologists generally agree that the need for maximum reproduction was dealt with within particular groups on a
pragmatic basis according to circumstance. Customs of
inter-gender relationship may have varied considerably,

but underlying them all was the need for cohesion and expansion. In groups with equal numbers of males and females, monogamous relationships would have been the most sensible arrangement – though not likely in the long-term, formalized sense as instituted in later civilizations. However, apart from the fact that gender ratio within a community could fluctuate dramatically, evidence suggests that a preponderance of females was a more common situation.

There are probably several reasons for this excess. One of the major ones will have been the higher mortality rate of males due to the greater danger to which their procuring and defence/attack roles exposed them. Given the principle of optimum reproduction, and therefore the desirability that no female should be left childless, the obvious solution to this excess was for the males to take as many partners as was necessary to make sure that every female was catered for. Polygyny thus became more common than monogamy.

However such arrangements were managed within a given group – i.e., whether they were dictated by the women or the men or by mutual agreement – and regardless of whether the males looked upon such arrangements as a pleasure or an obligation, the point is – apropos of the feminists' charge that the male is exploitively promiscuous – that the practice of the male having more than one sexual partner originally had its roots in survival necessity.[8]

In comparison with polygyny and monogamy, polyandry – as a longer-term social arrangement quite distinct from the possibility that a female might for some reason have sexual relationship with several males – appears to have been extremely rare. That rarity would most likely be accounted for by the aforementioned usual excess-of-females/shortage-of-males factor; not by some innate disposition in the female to be content with only one partner. Apart from which, whereas the male could well serve and provide for more than one female, the female only needed one committed partner to keep her more or less continually pregnant.

However, given the more common practice of polygyny,

it is not difficult to envisage a further development – one which does begin to have connotations of male exploitiveness. Having coped with the occurrence of an excess of females in the group, and assuming there were no other constraints on the number of females a minority of males could support, the temptation would clearly have been there to increase the number of females if possible.

The competitive male may well have seen this objective as a justifiable means of further enhancing the strength of the group; but he may well also have come to see it as a means of gratifying his desire for pleasure, status and power. And one obvious way of bringing such increase about was to acquire additional females from other groups.

Collision and conflict between groups inevitably resulted in the maiming and death of males on both sides. The winning side's remaining males would not have seen it as sensible (honourable?) to abandon the losing side's bereft females. It would therefore abduct them with a view to assimilating them into its own group. One might surmise that by today's standards such a practice would not have been a welcome one for the women concerned. It is difficult to tell; but certainly the practice became commonplace and it seems that such women did adopt their new parent-group readily enough and continued to bear offspring by their new partners.

However the practice may be judged in its origins, it would be fair to say that it set a precedent the legacy of which is still in some measure with us in the customs of arranged marriage, of the marrying daughter accepting adoption of her husband's family name, of inheritance and title passing through the male line, and so on. Although the women's liberation movement (and other factors) may be steadily undermining such residual practices themselves, it is the male assumption of such privilege that the movement is most at pains to see removed.

The age-old practice of female 'abduction' (not at all uncommon in the animal kingdom) may have been justified originally as a group-survival strategy; but that brief too readily lent itself to all manner of subsequent abuse. Perhaps worst of all, where residual attitudes are concerned, it gave rise to the male's tendency to regard and treat the female as an asset to be acquired and possessed. Male conditioning all-too-often encouraged men to look upon women as pleasure-objects, status symbols, begetters of sons; needless to say, viewpoints which helped men to fashion their image of themselves as the superior gender.

What should not be lost sight of in this development, however, is that the female, whether or not she resented her situation, continued through her more resolute sense of purpose to obtain the support she needed for her procreative fulfilment. The male, for all his attempts at self-gratification and self-justification, has always had to accept that the female's loyalty as a mother, if put to the test, is likely in extreme to be stronger than her loyalty as a wife.

Why did the male's initiatives on behalf of the group escalate from provision of need to exploitive greed? One answer must be that the role assignments he became heir to also opened up for him opportunities for self-development. At the same time as he became conditioned to commiting himself to the support of the group's survival, he also discovered the rewards of personal ambition. From this juncture onwards in the evolution of human society, the male in particular found himself driven by potentially conflicting motivations – serving the group versus self-gain. Obviously, after the passing of millennia, that problem is still as acute as it has ever been.

The limitations placed on women due to their physiology and their naturally-ordained roles as child-bearers and -nurturers led them towards adoption of the more passive, domestic roles (which is not to say that they were not continually occupied with work). The nature of their undertakings tended to be repetitive and unchanging, being regulated by such recurring cycles as menstruation and pregnancy and by continually repeating daily and seasonal tasks. Such commitment required continual dedication, tolerance and patience – all those qualities requiring surrender of self-will and traditionally attributed to the female nature. They had little time or opportunity for personal ambition outside the home.

This situation has changed little over the ages for most

women, persisting in society after society, however primitive or civilized. Even when women were later expected to take on tasks outside the home, in agriculture for example, and even later in industry and commerce, their work still tended to remain repetitive and serving. Such tasks were not conducive to the gaining of status and power; nor could they be said to have offered much in the way of opportunity for self-development.

Meanwhile, the procurement and defence/attack roles of men required the development of quite different talents – which eventually led to quite different consequences. Apart from having to be more active and mobile, men's ability to succeed in their roles presented them with a continually-changing challenge. Their mental powers were exercised in ways quite unnecessary for women in their roles. They needed to be enterprising, adventurous and willing to take risk. They had to observe and study their environment in many ways, learning all the time from their varied experience. They had to acquire and remember all kinds of information – about seasonal changes, locations, routes, plant properties, animal behaviour, hunting techniques, combat tactics, and so on. They had always to be on guard against threat, learning how to deal with unexpected difficulties, always endeavouring to improve their skills and their abilities to foresee and plan.

This continuous challenge must have stimulated particularly the specifically-human powers of imagination and visualization. Although women may have been involved to an extent in some aspects of the challenge, the onus would have been predominantly on the men to visualize the means to reduce unpredictability. The more accurately they could anticipate in advance, the better the chances of success. Observation and memory gave men the power to visualize; visualization gave them the power to invent tools, weapons and techniques; invention gave them the power to improve performance and succeed. Hence the emergence of the male's power-base: the control of technology.

It would then have been logical and sensible for the men to pass on their knowledge and skills to the sons who would eventually succeed them and take over their responsibilities. Likewise, the women would have passed on their expertise to their daughters. However, due to the difference in nature of their appropriate roles, there would inevitably have been a considerable difference in the conditioning of those sons and daughters. The challenge conveyed to the former would have been one emphasizing the need to improve still further and succeed still better, whilst the responsibility passed on to the latter would have been mainly one inviting continuation of established practice. Out of this tradition surely came the adage that sons strive to emulate their fathers whilst daughters seek to simulate their mothers. Once again, this is yet another tradition being thrown overboard in the wake of women's liberation.

This traditional, differentiated conditioning gave rise to the social attitudes and expectations which have persisted through generations. Based on the original, pragmatically-devised differentiation of roles, societies have perpetuated the notion that women are content to fulfil themselves through a predictable and unchanging participation in society's affairs, whilst men need to be continually striving, competing, succeeding, and all the rest of it. This is not to say that women are not naturally competitive. In other species, they frequently are so. It is simply that in the human case they have not needed to be. They may have seen fit to compete with other women for men, but not usually against men. The fact that they do now wish to compete against them in many respects runs totally counter to thousands of years of social situation and convention.

Evidence to reinforce the idea that, conditioning apart, the male is already naturally disposed to be competitive can readily be drawn from the behaviour of males in other species. For example, the report of a research project on the behaviour of squirrel monkeys makes a significant observation about male competitiveness.[9] It was found that the male monkeys often performed aggressive sexual displays when in the company of other males, no females being present. This display evidently denoted male rivalry because, although the ritual involved the flaunting of erect penises, it could not have been sexual exhibitionism intended to impress females – as indication of potency or readiness to mate.

The researchers then found that by making a lesion in the male monkey's forebrain they could eliminate the erotic display behaviour without eliminating reproductive ability. The conclusion therefore reached was that, although the male's display had indirect breeding con-notations, its primary purpose was to signal challenge to other males. In other words, display of the aroused male genital organ had less to do with desire to copulate, more to do with ambition for status. As in the monkey, so in the human being.

Here we may see a strong link with the point made earlier about the emergence in the male human being of divided motivations – that whilst conditioned to serve the female and the group's survival prospects, he also experiences personal ambition for status and power. The above research findings clearly demonstrate that male competitiveness primarily indicates desire to gain status-success amongst other males rather than desire to possess and dominate females. Which is not to discount the fact that the latter may prove to be the reward for achieving the former.

That instinctive urge in the male to gain power and status also begins to answer the earlier question as to why male initiatives tended to escalate beyond provision of immediate need to an open-ended pursuit of self-gain. There is thus a strong connection in the male between his sexual potency, his erotic arousal, his status, his ambition and his appetite for all manner of self-gain – the motiva-tion behind all of which may or may not be in the im-mediate interests of female procreativity and group welfare.

By extrapolation, the present bid by women to gain rights and opportunities to achieve success in hitherto exclusively-male arenas cannot help but invite certain conclusions: that their 'liberation' indicates the releasing in them of qualities and characteristics hitherto thought to be specifically male (but presumably suppressed in the past due to their traditional role assignments); that the emancipation process will therefore make women more masculine (in outlook, attitude, behaviour, etc.); and that women's present initiatives cannot be read as other than direct challenge to the male for status and power, a challenge in which the intent is to dominate. There should be no mistake here. The power of biological programming being as it is, ideas such as negotiated power-sharing are likely to be about as lasting and stable as a cloud of dust in a gale.

This development represents, of course, a totally unfamiliar challenge for men. It is one thing for the male to be naturally competitive with other males; quite another for him to face the prospects of competing with females as well. His biological and conditioned brief is to compete with other males for and on behalf of the female. If he is now to find that what he was competing for is competing against him, whence his motivation? In yet other words, the male has always sought primarily to dominate other males (hence the hierarchical structures of patriarchal institutions in which authority is exercised over subordinates). If he now finds the female competing against him, he can only respond on the basis that in effect she is seeking to dominate him. He will surely then begin to think that he is being forced into competing for and on behalf of no one but himself?

Even though some of the foregoing may sound far-fetched, it is well worth spelling out because, although women understandably resent what they now see as increasing aggression and hostility by men against them, the over-simplistic accusation by feminists that it is all due to innate flaws in the male constitution is no less far-fetched. Those flaws – if that is what one wishes to call motivations within our genetic inheritance – are equally as likely to be present in the female's genetic make-up as in the male's. Unless, perhaps, as will be considered later, there is an 'unnatural' reason for them being there, a reason which the male in particular has been at some pains throughout human history to discover.

In natural, unthreatening circumstances, male aggression is not directed against the female. The reason for the present escalating incidence of male physical or psychological abuse of the female cannot sensibly be explained only in terms of some in-built, anti-female vindictiveness in the male constitution. It can be better explained in more subtle terms connected with the male instinct to combat threat. Thus, if a man does assault a woman, the reason will have more to do with his instinct to eliminate what he perceives as threat, real or imagined, to dominate him, than with the fact that the target happens to be of the opposite sex.[10]

Apart from male competitiveness being in line with Nature's strategy to ensure the passing on of the most effective survival characteristics – with its reciprocal, the lesser need to ensure the selection and passing on of any particular female characteristics – there are other psychological ramifications in the typical male's quest to gain status.

The desire to gain status is closely linked with the desire to hold and exercise power. In whatever context the exercise of power may be expressed, success or failure in the gaining or losing of it can only be publicly registered in relation to the lesser or greater command of it held by others. Thus, the only way of testing the measure of one's power is by competing with others and the only means of being able to claim possession of it is by the conceding of it to oneself by others. It does not exist in a vacuum – though some, as a means of self-defence and -justification, will sometimes delude themselves into believing they have it when in fact they do not. The principle is that power can only be held by one who in a certain context succeeds in having influence on others. No matter what the apparent motive of the wielder – service to those others or self-gain – the ambition to have influence is at root self-generated and thus unequivocally self-promoting.

In the earliest times, power was most obviously associated with muscle. Later, it came to be held by those with tools, weapons, techniques and skills. Finally, it came to be held by those with the best-developed mental powers – of memory, logic, intellect, visualization, foresight, imagination – i.e., the most intelligent.

Therefore, given the validity of what has been proposed thus far, the roles which fell to men eventually proved more conducive to the gaining of governing power in society than the women's did. Whilst the women's unchanging, serving roles required them to be continually self-effacing, the men's, despite some compensating veneer of altruism, encouraged them to be self-promoting.

But now, the revolution. Women have had enough of their self-sacrifice and have become eager to promote themselves. They want status, power and identity in their own right. Apart from the fact that their purusit will mean abandoning in some measure their procreative and nurturing roles – a step which probably the female of no other species has ever taken before – their initiatives are bound to disrupt increasingly all the practices and balances of inter-gender relationship, the bases for which go right back to the dawn of human history.

All of which leaves men in something of a dilemma.

Should they try to carry on as they have always been conditioned to do – though now treating women as competitors rather than complements? Should they now adjust their attitudes towards women, and their expectations of them, so that they will need to regard them as just like themselves? Will they then possibly therefore have to settle for fleeting engagements and uneasy alliances?

Or should they surrender to what would otherwise seem inevitable – a gradual decline in their status and power, and a conceding in the process that, if they do not submit to the revival of matriarchal power, they will be alienated and held to ransom?

Neither horn of the dilemma looks comfortable; and neither will do much for men's customary image of themselves.

3 Male Redundancy

Men's dilemma is compounded by the fact that the women's liberation movement coincides – though the two phenomena are surely closely-related – with a juncture in their story when their traditional contributions to society are running into difficulty. Alongside the challenge of increasing female independence, there is the challenge of increasing male redundancy.

As far as the survival requirements mentioned in the previous chapter are concerned, it is not difficult to appreciate just how dispensable the male has now become, paradoxically through his having largely succeeded in his tasks rather than failing in them. Whilst the underlying nature of his traditional roles – hunter, gatherer, procurer, warrior, father, inventor, etc. – have remained more or less constant, he has so extended his power beyond the limitations of his muscle by the development of intelligence that those tasks could now be said to have been almost fulfilled. Beyond that, the main threat to human survival becomes man himself.

Men would claim that the majority of their endeavour over the ages has been in the interests of their parent-groups – sometimes, in more recent history, for the benefit of humanity as a whole. In some measure, however – usually through ambition for identity, status and power – they have also endangered group-survival and, again in more recent times, the survival of humanity itself. Either way, they have pursued the brief inherent in the divided motivations of their biological programming very effectively.

Being continually stimulated by the challenges of circumstance, the male particularly has been encouraged to develop his powers of observation, memory, visualization, imagination, logic, deduction. Having realized the power of knowledge and having devised the means of communicating information, and having learned the means of translating and applying that information (science and technology), he has on the whole been able to improve the prospects of physical survival.

Broadly speaking, all the credit for scientific and technological advance has been given to male enterprise – at least until modern times. There is perhaps no justification for this attribution other than the fact that evidence for female participation does not appear in historical record. We are simply left with the impression that the female has all along remained committed, willingly or otherwise, to her procreative and home-based responsibilities. Whether or not that is a fair view, history is littered with the names and exploits of men who have gained fame for their enterprise, discovery and invention. Whether they have then become celebrated as benefactors or malefactors has largely depended on the source of the record and the judgement of historical consensus.

What is therefore extraordinary about this present juncture in the human story is that, alongside the unprecedented phenomenon of women's liberation, there is now growing doubt whether the male (and the liberated female, for that matter) ought sensibly to be allowed to procure and exploit in the unbridled manner of the past. To put it another way, there is mounting concern that modern enterprise is showing signs of becoming more of a threat than a benefit to human welfare.

It would be worth considering briefly what has happened in those areas of survival requirement which were mentioned previously as having traditionally been male responsibilities.

The original quest for the comfort and security of shelter – as protection against cold and wet, excessive heat and hostile predators – resulted in people living in caves or constructing simple dwellings from stones, dried mud, timber and other available plant materials. Gradually, especially in the more inclement climes, there developed the building of more durable and spacious dwellings, enabled by the excavation and preparation of other suitable materials. From crude beginnings, technological advances permitted the construction of more and more complicated and capacious buildings, designed to house a growing diversity of activities, occupations and possessions. Settlements became permanent, being organized to facilitate increasingly sophisticated lifestyles.

Of all survival requirements, shelter is the one most likely to have involved participation by both genders in earlier times. Gradually, however, as retrieval of materials and constructions themselves demanded increasing use of muscle-power, men tended to become more occupied with the building and women with the comforts of the domestic interior. It was thus men who had the incentive to invent technologies of construction. Even though such technologies improved over the centuries, there still continued to be considerable demand for manpower. Now, however, modern techniques and materials and the use of machinery have steadily reduced that demand.

Discovering the means to make, control and use fire has to have been one of the principal factors which enabled man to survive and prosper. It gave warmth, shed light, frightened off hostile creatures, permitted the cooking of otherwise indigestible foods and, later, allowed the processing and working of metals to make tools and weapons. In other words, it helped him in all aspects of survival – comfort, procurement and defence/attack.

As the use of fire increased, so did the need to retrieve fuel. In earlier times, when such retrieval will have meant the gathering of timber and other suitable plant materials, both genders are again likely to have been involved in this day-to-day task. But the constant demand for fuel eventually led to the discovery of other sources of considerable potential, but more difficult to procure. This again threw onus on male muscle-power, and again led to the invention of technologies to make retrieval easier, more efficient and less dangerous. Now we have vast industries of fuel extraction, processing and distribution.

Not only were men responsible for inventing all manner of fuel technology but the whole enterprise was (and still is) entirely staffed 'in the field' by a male workforce. And,

over the centuries, they have assumed the right to exploit
fuel resources to the feasible maximum.

This century, however, there have been warning signals
– about eventual exhaustion of fossil fuels, about environmental pollution, about national economies being too
dependent on the fuel market, and so on. Such signals spur
on the advocates of nuclear energy, but that enterprise has
raised even greater concern. No matter what the immediate advantages, there is growing suspicion that there may
well be short- and long-term counter-productive consequences. Apart from the fact that large-scale introduction of
nuclear energy will increase male redundancy in the fuel
industry, there is widespread unease that science and
technology are here engaged in an enterprise which will
not necessarily improve the prospects of human survival;
on the contrary, it may in the longer term increasingly
endanger it. We have come a long way since our earliest
ancestors realized the potential of a flickering flame. We
now stand to get a lot more than our fingers burnt through
playing with this kind of fire.

The nuclear initiative found its first application, of
course, in the context of defence/attack, i.e. as a weapon. It
represents the ultimate in what had begun thousands of
years before as the discovery of the means to kill other
creatures, a vital necessity in the human bid to survive. We
imagine the earliest weapons as having been crude
instruments of wood, stone and bone. After the hand-
wielding of percussive weight and sharp edge, it must
have revolutionised prospects when ways were devised to
strike accurately at a distance. Apart from the advantage
that it became less necessary to get to close quarters with an
adversary, there was the chance also of keeping out of
range of the other's weaponry. Visualization and craft
resulted in the development of increasingly lethal objects
being propelled with increasing accuracy at increasingly
longer range. The eventual ability to work with metals and
the discovery of explosives led to a catalogue of deadly
weapons. After guns and bombs, we arrive at the ultimate
– the in-flight-controlled, long-range missile of mass
destruction.

One effect of all this ingenious 'progress' is that, whereas the defence/attack strength of the group once relied on male muscle-power, we have now arrived at a situation where push-button technology has rendered the warrior-hero virtually redundant. Whereas at one time all able-bodied males in a society would need to be prepared to fight, in developed countries today only a relatively small number are trained to do so; and even fewer are ever called upon to translate that training into practice. And whereas at one time not so long ago a male might well have seen the warrior role as a means to gain identity and status, such prestige is now scarcely feasible in a world where strength is measured in machines.

Where the procurement aspect of survival is concerned, similar historical developments apply. Due to the continual necessity in earlier times for the male to expend energy in finding food supply – the availability of which was frequently uncertain – the pressure to discover means to establish regular, stable and more-easily retrievable supplies will have been considerable. Improvement of hunting weapons and skills will have helped enormously. But the real breakthrough came about through those who visualized and developed ways of cultivation and animal husbandry. These were the initiatives which totally transformed prospects for human survival and proliferation. The story from then onwards is one of ever-increasing efficiency and productivity in those societies whose members had the intelligence to develop the science and technology of food production.

Except where adverse climatic conditions have prohibited or periodically intervened, and except in those parts of the world where production has proved insufficient to meet the demand of population, human society as a whole has considerably reduced both the unpredictability of food supply and the amount of physical exertion required to obtain sufficient quantity. Especially in the technologically-developed areas of the world, the hunting and gathering which once occupied most of the group's muscle-power and time has been replaced by an agriculture making extensive use of machinery.

Mechanization of agriculture led to increasing redundancy on the land. Other technologies, however, opened up a whole range of other industries which for a while could occupy all the male workforce. Food procurement became 'earning a living' – i.e. working to purchase food instead of producing it – in a considerable variety of ways. Muscle-power could be usefully applied in a diversity of specialized functions, some more creative and competitive than others but still generally-speaking providing for the male's sense of usefulness and status.

But science and technology marched steadily onwards. The continuing invention of increasingly ingenious machinery for use in industry, trade and commerce gradually reduced the need for manual labour. Emphasis in qualification for earning a living shifted inexorably from muscle to brain. The male became more and more out of touch with the physically-demanding powerbase on which his gender-exclusive, traditional roles had been founded. Thus began erosion of the mystique and authority upon which his self-image and status had for so long depended – an erosion now compounded by female competition in nearly all the occupational territories remaining available to him.

The dismantling of male prestige is then even further compounded by the tendency for the nature of his work to drift increasingly towards sedentary, non-creative, non-constructive, servicing roles in large, amorphous organizations – e.g., in finance, administration, trading, marketing, leisure industries, communications, etc. Although there may be some room for competitiveness and enterprise in such occupations, they are not conducive to fulfilment of male status in the virile, adventurous, physically-demanding outdoor, risk-taking ways which once challenged and inspired him. A lifetime of pressing buttons, of shuffling pieces of paper and talking in offices is a far cry from wielding a sword or making a ploughshare.

It may be thought that those employed in the many fields of science and technology might still find their desire for adventure, discovery, enterprise, status, etc., met through pioneering research and development. Apart from the fact that such work nowadays can be extremely tedious, unproductive, tenuous and frustrating for various reasons, growing public concern, reservation and resistance to what is going on in and coming out of laboratories these days cannot help but diminish the scientist's image of himself (or herself).

It would not be an exaggeration to say that there is virtually no field of research and application over which there do not now hang gathering clouds of public doubt and disquiet. It seems that for every faction claiming future benefit from scientific initiatives there is an equally vociferous faction – often of other scientists – questioning and opposing the claim, or doubting the wisdom of pursuit.

No one could seriously dispute the fact that the discoveries of science and their technological applications – in the broadest sweep of knowledge gained and applied to useful purpose since the emergence of *homo sapiens* – have enabled tremendous advances in the interests of human survival. Visualization and invention account for man's success in meeting and surmounting threats and difficulties to such good effect that he has been able to proliferate with growing confidence.

But now there are serious warning signs; and growing suspicions that longer-term back-fire consequences are beginning to outweigh short-term advantages. Perhaps scientific initiatives are reaching limits of benefit. Thus there is increasing demand that the activities of scientists need at least to be subject to greater scrutiny and assessment; even further, to be subject to constraint or curtailment. What is more, that monitoring and control needs to be carried out by people without vested interest in the research and development activity. Research work is now extremely expensive and needs the backing of investment on which there will be profitable return. Apart from the fact that much of the research is aimed at counteracting the unforeseen and adverse effects of previous scientific innovations, specialization has become such that scientists expert in their own field may well not understand what scientists in other fields are doing. Meanwhile, the public at large comes increasingly doubtful, suspicious and disquieted.

Change of direction and policy is being called for by environmentalists, ecologists, naturalists, conservationists, consumer protection groups. Other groups protest about the dangers of nuclear energy; about the exploitation of other creatures and natural resources and amenities; about the pollution of land, sea and atmosphere; about interference with foodstuffs through the use of chemicals, hormones, radiation, preservatives; about the drug industry, genetic engineering, medical practices, etc., – in brief, a considerable lobby of opinion which sees the incentives to scientists of commercial gain and of finding short-term, quick-impact solutions to be at best suspect and probably counter-productive, at worst downright irresponsible and dangerous. The scientists' self-prescribed brief to pursue unconditionally any research and its applications that they and their paymasters think expedient is beginning to lose credibility in the world at large. 'Progress' is beginning to lose meaning, and to become a tarnished word inviting doubt; 'advance' arouses apprehension. 'Progress' and 'advance' . . . towards what?

The pros and cons of future research and development apart, the fact remains that science and technology have in the end led to male redundancy. The roles of hunter, procurer, warrior and inventor are not what they used to be, being now so diluted as to be almost inapplicable. Male confidence, self-image and status have, as a result, come increasingly under siege. What then of the fathering role? On present trends, prospects look no more promising.

In parallel with human success in developing techniques for survival, so procreative prospects also improved. In accordance with divine ordinance, man did 'go forth' and multiplied. Thus, the advance of technology over recent centuries has permitted a dramatic growth in population. And that population is presently increasing at a prodigious rate, not only due to acceleration of birth rate in some areas of the world but also due to extension of life-expectancy in others.[11]

World population is estimated to have been about one billion about a century and a half ago.[12] In other words, there could be a few alive today who can remember people who were alive then. Today, world population is estimated to have reached four-and-three-quarter billion. Projection of the current rate of increase suggests that the total could be around nine billion in thirty-five years' time. India's present population alone is reckoned to be greater than the world's population two centuries ago.

To express the recent explosion in another way: if the total history of humanity is represented by a year, then the population has multiplied fourfold during the last two or three days of the year and will double again tomorrow.

The relatively-recent expansion of population is daunting enough in several respects, but particularly so where food supply is concerned. The fact that demand could increase by at least twenty percent by the end of the century has to be alarming. Many doubt whether there is enough fertile land to provide for such an increase. As it is, current demand has already caused impoverishment of millions of acres through intensive farming, a deterioration which can only be retarded by the application of vast amounts of artificial fertilizers. Millions more acres have been lost due to ecologically unsound practices such as deforestation.[13] It seems at present to be task enough to maintain levels of supply sufficient for existing populations; to cater for an open-ended further escalation has to be inviting disaster.

War, famine, disease and other catastrophes (such as earthquake and flood) have always taken their toll of human life and will no doubt continue to do so. But in view of the probable exponential growth of population predicted, it would take some horrendous intervention to make any serious impact on the population-food-supply problem in many parts of the world. No matter how the problem is tackled in the next few decades, there has still eventually to be a limit to growth. The finite resources of this planet, no matter how efficiently re-cycled, cannot provide for indefinite human proliferation. Either a halt will be forced through catastrophe[14] or there will have to be an intelligent change of mind and course.

In view of the probable ninefold multiplication of humanity in only two hundred years, one aspect of such change of course is obvious: reduction of the rate of birth to at most a one-to-one replacement level.[15] Again obviously, such restraint calls for human conduct running counter to both the biological programming and thousands of years of social conditioning which have urged maximum proliferation. The change of mind required is thus 'unnatural' and revolutionary. It is unlikely that any other creature has ever before been faced with having to curb its reproductive instinct instead of pursuing it to the best of its ability.

In developed societies, there is already a tendency for birth rate to decline[16] (although total populations have not due to increasing numbers living longer). One reason for this decline has to be the economic factor, i.e. the cost of supporting and educating offspring. But it may well be women's liberation factor (alongside male redundancy and homosexuality) which will in due course be seen to be having an equally-powerful curbing effect.[17].

Whatever the changing circumstances affecting birth rate, the underlying factor which has made restraint possible has to have been the invention of contraceptive (and abortion) techniques. Yet again, it was (presumably) male initiative in the realms of science and technology which produced effective mechanical means of preventing conception (and terminating pregnancy). Undoubtedly, cultures throughout history have discovered more or less successful ways of avoiding conception (or inducing miscarriage); but not it seems on a significant scale. It was the scientist of the modern world who opened the door to mass-production of cheap and readily-available contraceptive devices, an access which has proved to have far wider repercussions than simply the ability to avoid conception.

It would be difficult to claim that the motive behind the invention of widely-available contraceptive devices was primarily to reduce birth rate, even if that was and is an indirect effect. One may be forgiven for supposing that the motive was to gain maximum sexual pleasure without incurring the responsibilities of parenthood. Although such prospect no doubt appealed to the male, it may well not have occurred to the male inventors that they would at the same time liberate the female and her sexuality. And even less likely did they anticipate what the repercussions of that would be.

Whether or not contraception has been the unqualified blessing it was intended to be has to a large extent to be a matter of personal opinion. Certainly, it has permitted greater sexual licence; and indirectly it must certainly have had considerable effect in restraining birth rate. Out of this twin-aspect, a strange paradox emerges. Apropos the population-growth/food-supply problem mentioned above, it may turn out in the end that the invention of reliable contraception will prove to be more important to human survival than it has ever been a success in the pursuit of pleasure-gain which motivated its invention.

But to the more immediate point made above concerning contraception and the female, women being freed from the fear of unwanted pregnancy is one thing; their ability to decide whether or not to become pregnant is quite another. The latter has given the female an authority which she never truly had before. From an original situation where group-survival required her to be continually pregnant from puberty to menopause, and to be subject commonly to male sexual initiatives, her access to contraception has opened up for her a quite different prospect. Whilst her life was dominated by the demands of her physiology, and that in turn largely determined her roles in society, she had little opportunity to broaden her horizons. Through contraception, she can now not only control pregnancy and enjoy her appetite for sexual pleasure but is enabled also to pursue whatever career or interest she chooses.

What is more, contraception has allowed the female to alter the power-balance in sexual relationship in her favour. Once in a position to take initiative herself, she inevitably took a degree of it away from the male. In fact, it could be said that he has lost all his prerogatives in this respect. Bearing in mind the male's biological programming and traditional conditioning, this turn of events is psychologically very difficult for him to accommodate.

Thus, to the aforementioned increase of redundancy and impotency for the male in many of his conventional roles, and the need now to compete with the female in many of those remaining available to him, there now has to be added his loss of initiative in sexual relationship and the loss of his erstwhile prerogative to father offspring as and when he found it desirable to do so. The economic, population-pressure and liberated-female factors all contribute to male redundancy in his role as father with all its erstwhile trappings of paternal authority.

Adding together the whole catalogue of decline mentioned thus far, one is tempted to wonder what, if anything, is left to shore up the male's image of himself? Whilst the female is relishing her new-found powers and opportunities, and moving in directions novel and stimulating for her – in her own right and regardless of any male disquiet, disapproval or resistance – the male may well begin to ask himself what is now worth striving for, and what purpose and incentive remain for him. In brief, whether he is of any further, particular use and whether there are any grounds remaining on which to found the status of his gender.

For a while, he will no doubt continue to bluff and bluster along well-tried paths. He may have to settle for less, and persuade himself that he can retain self-respect in supportive roles. Even here though, he will have to lower his sights and accept that his excursions will be far more circumscribed and his occupations far less fulfilling. And all this in the knowledge that he is not now indispensable. As mentioned earlier, he cannot even claim that he is at least indispensable in the act of fertilization – a loss once again due to his own ingenuity in the research laboratory.

For various reasons – one of them being increasing male (and female) infertility, another the insatiable appetite of scientists for challenging the ways and decisions of Nature[18] – techniques of preserving semen in sperm-banks, of artifical *in utero* insemination and of implantation of ova fertilized *in vitro* are being increasingly used. Although the immediate justification for such techniques may seem reasonable enough, potential is simultaneously created for quite other possibilities. For example, since the techniques enable a woman to conceive without having sexual intercourse, it is but a short step – given the social acceptability and necessary legislation – to a situation where women could choose to have children without having any direct involvement with men at all.

Beyond that, as it were, 'half-way' stage of the female's

being able to dispense with male participation – 'half-way' because it still requires access to a source of sperm – scientists envisage the possibility that reproduction of the species might be feasible without any male contribution. Techniques of genetic engineering could lead to the ability to fertilize the ovum of one female with genetic material from the ovum of another female[19]. This would give rise to the generation of female offspring only. However, by repeating the technique, the species could continue as female only, the male becoming extinct. Present experimentation in this field is being conducted with other species, presumably on the grounds that its applications may in some way improve efficiency and volume of food production. But there is clearly no reason to suppose that it could not be applied in the human case also (a possibility that could well commend itself to the militant feminist). And it might be worth adding that, of course, there is no possibility of a male-only option.

Yet even further, it is also not impossible that some form of artificial triggering of ova *in vitro* could be successful in inducing them to develop. By then implanting a 'stimulated' ovum back in the womb, something very near parthenogenesis of 'virgin birth' could be achieved. Parthenogenesis is common enough in less-evolved species; some once-sexual species are known to have reverted to it as an evidently-preferable survival strategy. And scientists are apparently curious to find out whether it is possible in the case of higher vertebrates, even in the human. If that strikes the lay-person as sheer science fiction, then he or she cannot have read reports of successful implementation of the triggering phase. In this particular case, a human ovum was allowed to develop into a three-day-old embryo before being 'aborted'.[20]

Clearly, such scientific 'advances' are still very much in their embryonic stage. Much less clearly is it evident where such advances are supposed to be beneficially leading. In principle, it is well understood by biologists that such female-only or cloning prospects can invite considerable drawbacks and dangers. Not only is it extremely easy to upset and damage genetic material when manipulating it – as a number of ante- and post-natal aberrations have already demonstrated – but female-only reproduction tends to eliminate the capacity of the species to adapt to changing circumstances. Characteristics become 'fixed', thus increasing vulnerability to external threat and denying any possibility of evolutionary mutations.

Whatever the ostensible reason for all this research into the mechanics of reproduction, could it – unbeknown to those scientists involved – be preparation for a situation as yet unforeseen? Apart from the fact that a deadly and incurable venereal disease (such as AIDS) could negate sexual reproduction, the idea that the female should countenance the distancing and dissociation of herself from the male may again sound like the stuff of science fiction. Yet is not the initiative of women's liberation, by implication and already to some extent in practice, a bid by the female to go it alone? If the problems of regeneration of the species via the female only are resolved, why should she not choose to do so if it suits her? Perhaps the evolution of the human species has gone as far as it can go? If so, there will be no further need for genetic mutations. Given that the species is well and truly established, it could adopt asexual reproduction. And the male, if considered more of a liability than an asset, could be dispensed with.

Amongst the principles involved in survival instinct, there is not only that of survival of the fittest but also selection of the fittest. There is thus a deeply-seated instinct in the female of all sexually-reproducing higher vertebrates which urges her to select and be receptive to the fittest male she can find to father her offspring. According to circumstances and opportunity, a woman will ideally have the choice of a number of men and signal willingness to partner the one with qualities and attributes she judges most likely to be beneficial to her children and likely to provide best for her and those children whilst they are dependent on support.

What then if we arrive at a situation where women no longer see paternal attributes worthy of being passed on and no longer need male support for themselves and their children? In other words, their instinctive judgement may tell them that men have become less and less fit to father and less and less necessary as husbands.

Male response to the above may be one of astonishment and incredulity. Men may well, for example, have thought of themselves as the ones who do the selecting. In which case, they would do well to examine such assumption, carefully consider the above and then see if they are quite so sure. The awe-ful truth (for the male) is that his pretensions are founded on self-projected illusions. He has only been supported in them by the female because it either suited her to do so or else she had no other option . . . until recently.

However successful a woman may have been in selecting her partner, she had no guarantees as to how things might later turn out. If, through error of judgement or bad luck, her partner proved to be a failure or disaster, she had little option but to suffer the consequences and manage as best she could. That was a risk that the modern woman would understandably prefer not to have to take; and now she is less and less obliged to do so.

The male should be under no illusion that freedom for the female simply means his allowing her greater scope to amuse herself. Liberation means what it says – freedom for the female to lead her own life in her own right. She can obviate the risk of male failure by becoming self-supportive or by relying on public welfare support (the latter being an option that more and more women are taking).[21] And that economic independence helps obviate the risk that she might find herself trapped in an unsatisfactory or damaging relationship. The rights she now enjoys in the event of separation or divorce have increasingly protected her custodial and financial interests.

Even further, if committed, contracted relationship to a particular male looks to be far too hazardous a prospect, the female may well prefer not to take such risk at all. In such distancing or dissociation from the male, she would not necessarily, as touched on earlier, have to deny her desire to have children.[22] The fact that (in the U.K.) one in five births are 'illegitimate'[23] suggests that this option is becoming increasingly common.

This tactic, however, can invite attendant and conse-quent complications and difficulties, especially if the father pursues unwelcome rights of access, etc. A preferable and, in some ways, safer option might be her ability to obtain semen from a sperm-bank for artificial insemination or self-impregnation. In this case she could not only avoid any personal and sexual relationship with a known father but could also possibly select semen from donors with qualities and attributes which she would have difficulty in obtaining in her social environment.

Once again, such an option may sound preposterous. But, far from being some science-fiction fantasy, the practice already exists in the United States. Private agencies for sperm supply issue printed catalogues in which the listed male donors (who get paid for their 'donation') remain anonymous but their important characteristics are given in some detail. Such information includes physical description – race, height, build, colour of eyes and hair, etc. And, since other qualities are likely to be important to the kind of American women taking this option, evidence is also provided of the donors' 'success-ability' – their qualifications, status in society and occupational field, IQ rating, attainments in academic and cultural fields, and so on. The better the quality, the more expensive the consignment. Even the semen of Nobel prize-winners is offered, at a price. In other words, what the woman is buying – and can if she wishes have delivered to her door in a deep-freeze canister – is the means to have 'fatherless', successful children.

Bizarre as this enterprise may presently seem, it has to be admitted that from a liberated women's point of view it has advantages. Having become economically independent, she can fulfil her maternal instincts without having to get involved with a man. It gives her complete control over when she has children and how many. If she does have more than one, each of her children may have a different father. (Biologically, this is apparently what the female naturally and ideally prefers.[24]) And further, instead of having to enter into a potentially hazardous, or perhaps tedious, long-term commitment to one man, the practice leaves her free to have as many relationships with men as she desires on whatever basis she chooses; or to avoid them altogether.

Needless to say, all such scenarios for the emancipated female leave the male very much out on a limb. There is no way he can hope to establish independence to such radical degree. The individual male during his lifetime may prefer not to enter into intimate relationship with women, as in the cases of the religious celibate and the homosexual. But the bottom line has to be that though the male may opt out of the fathering role he has to have a mother.

To the formidable array of factors presently being stacked against the male, there should be added yet another – one that has the potential to become the final straw. Sexually-transmitted disease has often in the past been both a hazard in sexual relationship and a deterrent to promiscuity. In relatively recent times, scientific enterprise has greatly reduced the hazard through producing effective treatment for the common venereal diseases, thus reducing their deterrent effect also. However, in the wake of an era of greater sexual permissiveness, there has now emerged the particularly virulent, sexually-transmitted disease called AIDS.

The disease has been described as 'an unexploded time-bomb' because, beyond the degree of lethal damage it is already doing, its potential for future destruction is formidable. The insidious nature of the virus involved is such that it may be carried in the bloodstream of an infected person for a long time before actively attacking the body's defence system; it may even be carried for a lifetime without attacking the carrier at all. Nevertheless, during its quiescent period it can be transmitted. The chances are that it is so doing and that therefore the tens of thousands of carriers of today will become hundreds of thousands 'tomorrow'. The possibility of containing the spread of infection by screening millions of people to identify the carriers and then to dissuade them from sexual activity has to be a non-starter. Apart from the scale of the screening operation required, it could not be mounted fast enough. And human nature being as it is, it is hardly likely that all identified carriers would even then desist from sexual activity.

Meanwhile, the prospects for medical counter-measures are not promising. It is thought likely to be a matter of several years before safely-effective antidotes will come out of the research laboratory and be manufactured on sufficient scale. Even then, there are not likely to be once-and-for-all-time preventative and remedial solutions. The nature of the virus is thought to be such that it will have the ability to mutate rapidly and frequently. The battle against it will therefore have to be a continuing one for the foreseeable future.

With no proven medical counter-measures on the horizon, the only option left to social authority is publicity – a campaign to broadcast the danger and advise against certain practices. Appeal to common sense combined with fear of consequence may well bring about a degree of containment. But since one is dealing with an easily-transmittable, very 'patient', long-living virus propagating and spreading itself via the most popular of human activities, it must be realistic to view the self-discipline tactic as likely to have only limited effect. Scare and persuasion are difficult to sustain; as time passes, they tend to fall on increasingly-deaf ears.

In trying to dissuade people from leading immoral or promiscuous sex lives, the present anti-AIDS campaign understandably promotes the virtues of long-term, single-partner relationship. For reasons already described, such exhortation runs against the tide of present trends. In view of the implications of women's liberation – especially that of her bid for independence – it has to be admitted that, far from encouraging re-integration of the genders, AIDS may well have the opposite effect.

Although, at the moment, the disease in Western societies mainly afflicts male homosexuals and drug-users, it is well-established that heterosexuals of both genders are equally at risk. And one of the most insidious aspects of the disease where women are concerned is that a virus-carrying mother can transmit it through her bloodstream into the foetus in her womb so that, when the baby is born, it is already a carrier. A woman's fear of contracting the disease may thus be at least doubly compounded. The idea of sperm-banks and artificial insemination begins to seem less bizarre, especially if it can be guaranteed that the genetic supply is not only of good quality but free from disease also.

Psychologically, the female will see herself as taking the greater risk. In sexual encounter, she will increasingly see the male as potential threat and will become far more circumspect in dealing with his approaches whether casual or serious. In his turn, psychologically, the male will feel himself to be continually on probation. He is likely to find himself increasingly kept at arm's length and his embassis thwarted, no matter how sincerely made. This distancing between the genders can only exacerbate his sense of alienation. To the decline of the male role as father, there will have to be added that of lover (if that pursuit may be called a role).

It may well be thought by those steeped in conventional conditioning that male redundancy in traditional roles and gender-polarization are bad news, surely indicating that things are going badly astray in modern society.

Most of them may also like to think – probably more in hope than with conviction – that in due course all will be sorted out and everything will return to normality, i.e. as it used to be. Regardless of whether such reversion would be desirable, it hardly looks feasible. It may be possible to engineer semblance of worthwhile employment for most males for part of their lives (on average perhaps only a third). Much less likely would it be possible to reverse the trends of women's liberation, let alone its already-penetrative effects. The social repercussions might be negotiable and forms of accommodation may be reached between the genders in due course; but that will do little to ensure stabilization of the psychological shifts that have taken place.

As intimated earlier, women's liberation may, on the face of it, seem a reasonable, justifiable and potentially progressive initiative which men cannot fault on intellectual grounds. What they may instinctively or intuitively suspect is that that liberation has also unleashed an awesome and primitive power deeply embedded in the female psyche (one which their forefathers several millennia ago had managed to suppress). Men fear that power for a very simple reason. They may or may not fear occupational redundancy; usually they are resourceful enough to overcome that threat. Far more deeply, they fear impotency. The modern female may not have the prospect of literal castration in mind (even though, as Freudians have suggested, she might be envious of and subconsciously wish to appropriate the male's genital apparatus). But, translated into terms commensurate with the evolution of intelligence, she may (albeit again subconsciously) wish to emasculate the male psychologically (thereby hoping to gain for herself a male-exclusive mental capacity which she does not herself possess).

For the female to attempt to appropriate from the male what she wants from him, she must first overcome her propensity to admire the male's power and gear herself up into a state of provocation. In other words, if the male is unwilling or unable to give her what she desires, she has (perhaps against her better judgement), to provoke him (and herself) to the point where she can wrest it from him (shades here of Adam and Eve, demonstrating that biblical stories are not as naive as is usually supposed). Translated into sexual analogy, the female has to arouse the male to desire to penetrate her if she wishes to conceive.

Such profound psychological issues have their roots right back in the most ancient parts of the brain. Here we will find that deepest of survival choices – survival of the species versus self-survival. The latter is paramount; it can only be countermanded in favour of the former by ages of conditioning. For reasons which will become apparent later, it has generally been easier to condition the female to sacrifice herself (usually in favour of her offspring) than to likewise condition the male. This, as we shall see, is because the male is less committed to survival of the species, more to self-survival (in other than regenerative terms in the human case).

Thus, the male cannot ignore or lightly dismiss the hostile accusations and sometimes vitriolic animosity expressed towards him by the feminists – the vanguard of provocation. He may complacently consider such aggression to be some kind of hysteria on the part of a few unsufferable women with sexual hormone problems. To do so would be to underestimate the depth, and the import, of what is being demanded . . . of him.

To the previous feminist quotation (p. 6) here follows another:[25] '. . . It must be understood that as women have less power than men, and that as men are prepared to reinforce their power with murder in order to maintain their superior brutal position, women cannot be held accountable in the same way. If the penalty for successfully thwarting destruction, i.e. removing men's power, is death – and men will kill for less – then all of us women have to learn the hard lessons of how to survive.'

This is obviously a particularly aggressive and uncompromising stance, introducing an ultimate, life-or-death option. The majority of women, whatever their degree of liberation, would probably consider such outburst as excessive. But, in order to be in public print at all, it has to be recognized as symptomatic of a very deep, and probably widely-felt frustration in the female state. She has come to the point of holding the male responsible for her present predicament, he now being accused of having perpetrated offensive prejudice against her. Though most women may still be fairly deaf to such provocative outburst, some will be impressed and persuaded by it; and many more will be subtly influenced and infected by it. The female inexorably becomes more sensitive to and suspicious of male behaviour; thus becoming increasingly capable of being triggered into hostility at any moment by his apparent offences against her.

The male may in turn be offended by such animosity towards him. He is more than likely to regard it as an unfair condemnation, as a deliberate, typically-female, negative attitude designed to pressure or demote him. His vulnerability is such that, despite all the efforts he has made, and despite all the instances of harmonious and enjoyable relationship he has had with her, he is forced to concede that it is the female's survival and that of her offspring which in the end counts for the most. Whether the male of today consciously feels innocent or guilty about the male's treatment of the female in the past, he must surely be more aware now that he is on trial. He may even begin to suspect that he has been pre-judged and that he cannot expect verdict in his favour.

Whether or not it could ever be objectively and conclusively proved that the male has been unfairly exploitive, he must surely now realize that he has lost the grounds on which his sense of status and prestige formerly depended; and that now it is his turn to feel dominated and exploited (as, in fact, many males always have been). It is thus not surprising that there is now a growing anger and resentment in the male, expressing itself as blame on the female as being the cause of his increasing impotence. The danger of this reaction is that he may behave belligerently and destructively – as the growing incidence of male violence in general, and against the female in particular, surely indicates. Unfortunately, the more the male adopts such tactics, the greater the likelihood of further alienation.

Although the growing alienation may be explained in terms of released female competitiveness and ambition, and/or her reaction to past male oppression and exploitation, the deep psychological factor now surfacing as female animosity towards the male is at root related to the most primitive instinct – self-survival. Male competitiveness and aggression towards other males has always been based on this instinct. The currently-overt emergence of these characteristics in the female is no different. Hence, what we now see as increasing discord between the genders is primarily due to each gender trying to defend itself against the challenges of the other – as anyone who has observed marital conflict will recognize. Self-defence begins to take precedence over co-operation.

It could be claimed that the longstanding human social arrangement of cohabitation in groups of more or less equal numbers of males and females has stood the species in good stead where survival and procreation are concerned. But it could also be argued that such an arrangement has always been uneasy. Biologically-speaking it is a less-than-common survival strategy which requires the male to discipline his ambition and channel it into group support, i.e. to give precedence to being a contributing group-member over his ambitions as an individual. Now that the female is herself becoming competitive and ambitious in her own right, the arrangement is showing signs of considerable stress.

As described earlier, science and technology have enabled human success as far as providing for the basic necessities for survival is concerned, a success which has permitted proliferation of the species. But that success has in turn now led to increasing male redundancy and impotency in his traditional roles as a group-member. In other words, many of the features of human society which held the genders in co-operative relationship have become, or are becoming, irrelevant. As result, the power of female self-survival and ambition, regardless of the fate of the male, emerges with formidable force.

In view of this overall decline in male status and power, one may well wonder what the longer-term fate of the male might be. It would be heartening to suppose that he may find ways in which to re-direct his energy, initiative and talent – perhaps into channels less familiar yet more fulfilling. This might constitute for him a revolution no less impressive than the women's liberation movement is proving for the female.

If this is to be the case, the male will need to recognize clearly that present female suspicion of him and hostility towards him really constitute a demand upon him. He is being provoked to wake up and to come up with some positive, constructive and creative ideas. And if he cannot restore her confidence in him, she may well prefer to do without him.

The question is, in what direction should he look for such vision?

All commentary thus far has been on behaviour and relationship at the level of the human being simply as a biologically-programmed creature in a socio-economic setting. Although this is basically what we are (and how science largely prefers to view us), it might well be asked what purpose is served by the human's experience of 'higher' feelings and emotions – love, compassion, admiration, gratitude, respect, awe, wonder, worship, and so forth. This will be considered later but let it suffice for the moment to say that such experience is not dependent on committed, heterosexual relationship.

Neither has anything been said of what might be called the human's 'higher' aspirations – in such realms as the arts, philosophy and religion. These again will be considered later. But let it again suffice for the moment to say that such aspirations contribute nothing directly to the business of physical survival and procreation.

However, it may be in such realms of 'higher' nature that the possibility of male redemption resides. To give substance to such flight of imagination requires some consideration of human brain evolution – to see not only what it may signify in itself but also what differences in development there may be between the genders. It is here that we may begin to find clues to the direction in which the male may need to look in order to fulfil that redemption.

4 Brain Strain

The foregoing sketch of human survival strategy is drawn from the findings of archaeologists, palaeontologists, anthropologists, social historians – all those who investigate the past and the links between that past and the world as we know it. There are certain 'gaps' in these accounts, and new theories replace disproved beliefs as different disciplines and their schools of thought seek to establish a coherent picture, especially of the developments which gave rise to *homo sapiens*.

Despite some areas of uncertainty and disagreement, there is sufficient firm ground for us to be reasonably sure of the principal events which enabled man to become the dominant species on the planet. And we may further take it that there would now be no serious dispute over the factors which moulded human behaviour patterns – in particular those which governed conduct between the genders and the adoption of distinct roles. In principle, these seem to have changed little since the dawn of human history.

But what the evolutionary purpose of this human success might be – other, that is, than sheer survival and proliferation of a particular species – is still anyone's guess. However, in the findings of the neurophysiologist there may be some significant clues. Developments in the human brain seem to suggest a moving away from the biological imperatives which dominate the behaviour of all other species. Could it be that the evolutionary purpose of the human being is eventually to transcend them altogether?

Biologists have given us a picture of evolution which begins with primitve, unicellular organisms and ends with higher vertebrates of great complexity. This is a story of progress from small size, simple construction and limited function to large size, complex construction and considerable variety of function and ability. Running right through this evolution, over hundreds of millions of years, there are always the survival requirements already mentioned – food procurement, defence/attack and reproduction.

The ability of a species to cope with and if necessary adapt to changing environmental circumstances fundamentally dictates its continuing success or eventual demise. Where food procurement is concerned, competition between animal species is ruthless. Linked with defence/attack capability, survival means attacking in order to eat and defending in order to avoid being eaten. Such competitiveness has given rise to an amazing diversity of creatures with an extraordinary variety of attack/defence techniques. In parallel with this complexity, strategies for successful reproduction are no less diverse.

As complexity of construction and function increased, so did the necessity for an increasingly efficient, internal system for overall control and co-ordination. Or, it could be argued, development of the latter enabled the former. Whichever promoted the other – or if they took place simultaneously – increasing intelligence was the outcome.

In the earliest forms of life, communication between a certain and limited number of cells with simple function could be effected by short-range, biochemical 'messages' across cell walls. But, as organisms became larger and specialization of cell function increased, there came the need to transmit more complicated signals over longer distances. Hence, the development of nerves, nerve-centres and networks.

On the evolutionary ladder, the first creatures with ability to travel far were worm-like invertebrates. To progress from that stage, we surmise that Nature had a problem. To increase mobility, energy production and information-gathering capacity meant larger organisms with more complex, specialized cell functions. How were such larger bodies to gain sufficient rigidity and strength to maintain form and yet retain sufficient flexibility for ease of movement? The problem was solved, of course, through articulated structures of bone. At the same time, this skeletal framework could serve another useful purpose, as a protective housing for the vital central nervous system. Hence the emergence of the vertebrate: at first in the buoyant medium of sea water in the form of fish.

Development of more and more complex nerve systems gradually became the vital key to survival. Intelligence became more important than sheer speed and strength. Thus, whilst the spinal cord of the vertebrate could house all the main nerves responsible for the body's more automatic functions – such as digestion, excretion, blood circulation, breathing, reproductive mechanisms, etc. – it became increasingly necessary to develop capacity for information processing and overall control. Hence, evolution of the brain.

The brain began to develop at the front end of the spinal cord – 'front' being defined by direction of travel. It presumably developed there because the increasingly effective information-gathering equipment was also located at that end. Information – about prey, threat, sexual opportunity – could be more efficiently dealt with if the intelligence unit responsible was closely connected to the sensory organs. They themselves, in the best interests of their functions, were in position to discover what lay ahead – rather than relate what had already passed by. (Thus, psychologically, the evolution of our mental potential favours discovery of future prospect rather than dwelling on past event.) Meanwhile, other organs nd systems relying more on muscle-power were more sensibly located further astern.

Brains first began as swellings of proliferating nerves. The most primitive parts - such as the medulla oblongata and cerebellum – came to be known collectively as the hindbrain. This section, a direct extension of the spinal cord, is mainly responsible for co-ordinating movement in the interests of self-survival and reproduction (i.e., survival of the species). It also looks after such basic functions as control of blood circulation, temperature and respiration – in brief, control of all those life-sustaining functions that still go on whilst we are asleep.

After the first primitive fish, on the evolutionary ladder, there came more intelligent creatures able to live out of the water. In front of the hindbrain, further rudimentary sections developed which came to be called midbrain and forebrain. Bearing in mind that whales and dolphins are mammals who surface for air, the highest intelligence achieved by the fish-brain is said to be that of the shark. One would expect there to be slightly greater incentive for the hunter than the hunted to improve intelligence. Attacking tactics would always need to keep an edge of advantage over defence strategy for a species to be able to survive and prosper.

As the evolutionary story unfolds, more intelligent creatures, with more highly-developed parts of the forebrain, appear 'on dry land, in the open air'. One of the significant features of this process is that when amphibians, reptiles and, later, land-roving creatures appear on the scene, their brain development has taken place as an enlarging of or an adding to the original component parts. In other words, as more intelligent species emerge, they do not dispense with any part of the primitive brain. Those parts are extended or have modifications superimposed. When we arrive at mammals, primates and then the human being, the original, basic systems are still there, even though the sizes and shapes of the hindbrain, midbrain and forebrain differ greatly from one species to another. That is to say that the human brain still contains the same primitive components as the fish, amphibian, reptile, etc. (Redolence here of the observation [p. 21] that civilization does not eliminate the primitve, but is founded upon it.)

The human brain contains, for example, a hind/midbrain area sometimes called the R-complex which, since we share it in principle with the reptile, has origins dating back several hundred million years (Again, does not the intimation of serpent-level intelligence in the biblical creation myth then seem a good deal less fanciful?). In this ancient part of the brain, there are some interesting behavioural features – interesting, that is, as far as their projection into human pyschology and behaviour is concerned.

This region is described as being responsible for competitive behaviour, aggressive display and ritualistic performance. These interlinked tactics have interlinked purposes – e.g., to establish dominance and claim territory. Obviously they operate at the level of physical survival.

But they are also, of course, projected into human social interactions and we would recognize them as often being present in the mind when communicating with others. Desire to dominate and claim to personal 'territory' frequently underlie our most civilized conversations; they are always evident in debate and argument ... having been translated into the desire to be right and to extend power and influence. In our sophisticated, modern world, we are not likely to admit that our motives stem from our reptilian past.

As far as the genders are concerned, there is no evident distinction in this part of the brain between male and female. Both have the R-complex and both are therefore capable of competitiveness, aggressive display and ritualistic performance. That is to say, both experience the desire to win, dominate and claim territory.

It would be reasonable to suppose that, after the emergence in human history of role differentiation, the male's hunter-warrior commitments gave him far better opportunity for the expression and exercise of these primitive motivations. That would neatly account for the male's having gained the reputation for being the competitive, aggressive and exploitive gender. But that overtly manifested behaviour of the male should not be allowed to mask the fact that the female, denied such exercise by her more passive, procreative commitments, nevertheless employed the primitive motivations, but in more subtle ways. She may not have had access to public arenas; but she certainly held her own behind the scenes.

Thus, the feminists' claim that there are no psychological differences between male and female would surely be correct at this primitive level. What those same feminists do not seem to realize is that they are admitting by implication that, once liberated, they are likely to unleash those motivations in themselves, and to do so in no less a measure than the male has been used to doing. In other words, she is likely to become just as overtly competitive and aggressive as the male has ever been[26] ... as is already becoming apparent in Western societies today.

In connection with this ancient part of the brain, another and no less significant factor emerges in the context of sexual activity. An example of competitive, aggressive display and ritualistic behaviour was given earlier in the case of the squirrel monkey. Erotic male behaviour was observed by researchers as being a bid for status in the hierarchy rather than an indication of desire to copulate with a female. Although this was a particular case, there is no reason to suppose that it is not a general rule, especially among the higher vertebrates.

Behavioural, as well as neuroanatomical evidence, points consistently towards strong connection between sexual display and the desire to dominate. Again, there is no reason to suppose that this does not apply in the human case, given that the human central nervous system contains the same component parts as all other higher vertebrates. And, as in their case, the nerve system serving the parts of the anatomy aroused by erotic stimulation is quite separate and distinct from the system serving the reproductive elements, in both genders.

There are therefore substantial grounds for saying that human eroticism has more to do with the desire to dominate than it does with the desire to procreate. From this a perhaps-unexpected – certainly not commonly-acknowledged – fact arises: that sexual intercourse, though entered into from time to time with mutual intent to conceive offspring, contains in its erotic aspect not just the desire for sensual pleasure, but also the desire to dominate.

This disposition must be present in the erotic experience of both genders; but there is a subtle distinction between them. The female can be fertilized during copulation without her necessarily becoming erotically aroused. On the other hand, the male, in order that he can participate in copulation for reproduction, has to be. Therefore, although he may not be aware of it, his erection followed by penetration and thrust carries with it strong connotations of aggressive attack and the desire to dominate. Although the male may thus have gained the reputaiton of being the lustful pursuer and dominating exploiter in matters sexual, a certain conclusion cannot be avoided: that, if the male did not behave in that manner, procreation of the species through sexual intercourse would cease.

Meanwhile, because her procreative fulfilment did not

depend on it, the female may well not have traditionally given such priority to the erotic aspect of sex. But that fulfilment must always have necessitated her encouraging it in the male; even deliberately arousing it. Through provoking desire in the male to dominate her, she gained what she wanted. In this reciprocating situation, balance of power becomes less easy to determine. It becomes questionable as to which gender is really dominating the other.

Two brief asides result from the above. First, women reputedly dress and make up more in order to please themselves than to attract men. That would be correct in that it accords with the motive behind ritualistic behaviour, namely to enhance sense of status. The competititive element emerges where a woman presents herself with deliberate intent to compete with other women. When she deliberately uses adornment to draw attention to her sexuality, however, she is signalling desire to dominate . . . either gender. Second, men's penchant for pornographic material is generally regarded as perverse, and often exploitive of women. In fact, it is an attempt by the male to overcome his sense of impotence. By erotically arousing himself, he seeks to restore his power to compete with other males and rekindle his desire to dominate others . . . of either gender.

Observers of the behaviour of other animals often describe courtship and mating in the natural world as being akin to combat – in view of the amount of grabbing, grappling, wrestling, mauling and aggression which often occurs. The female frequently gives the impression of suffering the act or of trying to resist it, whilst the male struggles to have his way. It is suggested by some biologists that in fact neither gender in most species gets any pleasure out of mating; sex for pleasure seems to be confined to the human (and possibly certain primates such as the chimpanzee).[27] Even in the human case, within the passion and ecstasy of making love people often experience the desire to inflict pain on their partners. One possible explanation for this apparent paradox must be that, at the same time as the genders are drawn into the reproductive act, they also experience the desire to dominate and the fear of being dominated; hence the combat effect.

A further, interesting aspect of mating activity in Nature is that all species except the human being regulate their sexual encounters in accordance with the female's menstrual cycle. In other words, males and females in other species only attempt copulation when ovulation in the female ensures that the act can be reproductively viable. If the male should attempt intercourse at any other time, the female will actively resist it.

Not so in the human case. Although women have their monthly cycle and there are only a few days within it when fertilization can successfully take place, they do not involuntarily broadcast when that optimum period is, i.e. when they are 'in season' or 'on heat'. Biologically-speaking, women are described as being 'continually receptive' or as having 'hidden ovulation'. Whereas in the animal kingdom a male can tell for himself (usually by scent) whether his sexual embassies are likely to be tolerated or rejected, the human male has no such guidance. He could be described as having to be 'continually available' or 'continually demanding'.

There is some divergence of opinion amongst biologists as to why this should be so; but those opinions generally concentrate on the probability that it is in some mysterious way a species-survival tactic. In view of the human female's willingness to copulate when fertilization is unlikely or impossible, such a tactic sounds highly improbable. In default of a plausible explanation along that line of thinking, may the phenomenon have something to do with the evolution in woman of an increasing appetite for sexual pleasure: and, beyond that, or linked with it, increasing desire to dominate? If that is so, then the implications for men, vis-à-vis women's liberation, take on a further, threatening dimension.

Unlike the females of other species, the human female experiences desire for sex independently of her desire to conceive. A feminist claim arising from this is that women have as much right to pursue sexual pleasure as men have always reputedly done. Such liberated women may find, however, that – given the biological differences mentioned above – their demands will prove to have counter-productive consequences. (That is to say, as far as heterosexual encounter is concerned; female homosexual activity would not be affected.)

For, although the male may be able to accomodate female competition in many areas of his life, when he is confronted with female advances in sexual matters, he may find himself unable to meet her expectations. Especially when older, he may have difficulty in rising to the occasion. Willingness to respond to the prospect of mutual pleasure is one thing; unwillingness or inability to respond, especially for the male, is quite another. Whereas the female can if necessary feign responsiveness, the male cannot; there can be no disguising failure to erect.

And that, in turn, can undermine the male's confidence in himself. He is likely to become anxious about his potency. And likely to feel threatened because, whether he is aware of it or not, loss of status means the danger of being dominated. In the short term, he may be able to rise above such a failure to meet the challenge; but, if he fails to do so repeatedly, he may in the longer term find himself in a vicious circle where he is continually thwarted by anxiety.

A further factor arising from the above developments is their possible threat to that most fragile of human states – that of being in love. For present purposes, let us regard this state as a disposition of mind in which there is unconditional willingness to devote oneself to the well-being of another. Whatever the experience of being in love may be in evolutionary terms, there can be little doubt that such a disposition will be put severely to the test where sexual relationship becomes competition for dominance under the guise of a right-to-pleasure free-for-all. Being in love may be an ephemeral and transitory condition in which intimate exchange plays an important part; under pressure of demand, it soon blows out of the window.

In speaking of such matters as love, we move away from the relatively straightforward motivations of the primitive hindbrain and midbrain. We move from the hard facts of physical self-survival and continuation of the species into the less well-defined arena of emotions and feelings. We regard our experience of them as being important to our sense of being human. Some may even suppose that they are what set us apart from all other creatures. That may be so where 'higher' feelings and emotions are concerned. But probably not so in their more primitive manifestations because we share with other higher animals the part of the brain from which they originate.

The seat of at least the more primitive emotions is the limbic system, a region of the forebrain for which evidence suggests origins at least one hundred and fifty million years ago. This area includes such important glands as the pituitary, thalamus and hypothalamus. Association of this part of the brain with emotional states – attributable to levels of secretion and changes of balance within the endocrine system – has been established through observation of the effects of glandular malfunction and of the effects of accidental or deliberate intervention. Such interventions can precipitate extremes of anger, hostility, frenzy, fear, anxiety, depression, sentimentality, etc.

Although most of these expressions of feeling and emotion might be described as 'negative' and closely associated with reaction to threat to survival, the limbic system is also thought to be responsible for altruistic behaviour. In other words, in its 'positive' aspect, it generates emotions and feelings which dispose the subject to act in the interests of others rather than itself. In the case of humans and other higher vertebrates, it is here, for example, that impulses to protect, care for and feel affection for offspring arise.

It is strange (almost perverse) that the chemistry of this part of the brain can produce such apparently conflicting and contradictory effects; almost as if we have here an innate split in motivation. On the one hand, it generates our concern for the welfare of others; and, on the other, our extremes of self-interest behaviour, even impulse to attack and destroy others. Although the disposition to destroy is built into this part of the ancient brain in all creatures – because self-survival, even if only in the aspect of food procurement, is bound to involve the killing of other life-forms – it is probably true to say that only the human will kill a member of his/her own species through the emotion of sheer hatred. As a reciprocal to the willingness to murder, it is probably also true to say that only the human will commit suicide through extreme depression or sacrifice his/her life in the name of love. In other words, it is as if the human has pushed the dichotomy of the limbic system to its limits – killing and dying through extremes of feeling and emotion.

Damage to this part of the brain can result in effects which counteract the instinct and ability to survive – loss of certain categories of memory, loss of interest in self-care, loss of interest in sex (i.e. desire to compete and dominate), loss of consistent intent, loss of motivation to procure, and so on. These may at first seem like a catalogue of disparate effects; but in total they amount to a kind of opting out, a kind of discontinuation of oneself. It is as if the means of being able to continue into the future have broken down. In the overall sense that this part of the brain might be called the base of the will to survive, it is also likely to be the source of its opposite – the impulse to self-destruct. It must surely be an area much affected by those drugs which cause feelings of exhilaration and invulnerability, and those of utter desperation and desolation.

It is also strange to think that all these crucial and intense human experiences can be brought about by relatively slight chemical changes, i.e. of glandular secretions in the endocrine system. There are no (known) constitutional differences in this part of the brain between the genders, though clearly differences in volumes of hormone secretion affect typically-male and -female behaviour patterns. Furthermore, differentiated roles are likely to reflect and endorse such differences. And that, in turn, would give rise to what we would commonly recognize as typical differences between the genders in expression and display of feelings and emotions.

If that is the case, current role-changes in the wake of women's liberation will have an affect on hormone secretion in this part of the brain. One might expect, for example, the female to exhibit more typically-male emotion at the expense of her typically-female feelings. In response, the male would then be likely either to exaggerate the typically-male or become more typically-female within himself. (Women have usually tended to give precedence to their feelings over their emotions, claiming that guidance by them has served them well.)

Finally, in this sketch of brain evolution, we come to the development of the forebrain which, in the case of the higher vertebrates, has most obviously taken place as the relatively large extension called the cerebrum. For the great majority of vertebrates, with horizontal spine, the forebrain is described as being in front of the midbrain. With the evolution of the primates and the lifting of the spine into the vertical, it is more appropriate to speak of the forebrain surmounting the midbrain.

Some biologists suggest that the probable evolutionary reason for the transition from quadruped to biped, from horizontal to vertical spine, was to produce a structure which would be able to support the carriage of a relatively large cranium without having at the same time to develop the size of body which would have been required to carry such weight horizontally. The process of becoming upright also, of course, permitted restructuring of the forelimbs so that they could develop useful manipulatory functions, instead of remaining committed to their increasingly less important propelling function. Of great importance also, upright head and neck allowed the development of the complex sound-forming mechanisms which enabled development of language – a capacity which played an enormous and crucial part in the success of the human species.

The vertical reorganization which permitted carriage of a large skull on a relatively small frame leads to a principle generally upheld by biologists – that brain mass alone is not indicative of intelligence, but that the ratio of brain mass to body mass is. By this criterion, *homo sapiens* comes out at the top of the intelligence table (followed by the dolphin – which, due to its living in the medium of sea water, did not have the same weight-carrying problem).

At birth, the weight of the average human brain is an exceptionally high proportion of the total body-weight – around twelve percent – compared with other creatures. After birth, the brain, especially the forebrain, grows rapidly during the first three years, i.e. during a period of rapid learning. By the age of six, it has already reached ninety percent of its adult size, long before the body has reached anything like that degree of maturity. In the fully-developed brain, the cerebral hemispheres occupy about seventy percent of the total volume.

On average, the fully-grown male brain has a volume of about 1375 cubic centimetres, whilst the average female brain is about 150 ccs smaller. Nevertheless, it is generally agreed that the larger male brain does not indicate his having greater intelligence than the female. By the brain-mass-to-total-body-mass-ratio principle, male and female work out as having equal intelligence due to the average female having a smaller body than the average male.

Otherwise, the only difference between male and female brains seems to be that the latter tends to have a notably larger corpus callosum.[28] This feature is the dense network of nerve fibres which connects the two cerebral hemispheres of the forebrain. It appears that there is no known physiological significance in this fact; but perhaps, as will be suggested later, it could have psychological ramifications.

Since the human central nervous system contains component parts which we have in common with other creatures whose evolutionary origins can be traced back hundreds of millions of years, it is in the relatively-recent and extraordinary expansion of the forebrain that the exceptional features of human intelligence are assumed to lie. All evidence points to that conclusion.

It was obviously not easy in the past to obtain information about the living human brain. Many of the early discoveries resulted from observation of the effects of brain damage, caused either by accident or combat. Surgical interventions of last resort in serious cases of illness, both physical and mental, later provided further information. But it was the development of technology which could monitor brain activity from outside the skull which produced an explosion of information during recent decades.

As might be expected, much of the data and its interpretation corroborates what had already been deduced

simply by observation of human experience and
behaviour, and by comparing that with the observed
performance of other creatures. As in the case of scientific
information about man's physical evolution, the great
majority of brain research, and the reporting of its
findings, is confined to a view of the human as being
simply a highly-advanced and ingenious animal.

Mention is scarcely ever made – and, when it is, only in
passing, as if it were of no particular significance – of the
phenomenon called 'consciousness'. Perhaps this is
because it is not a physical or mental function which can be
directly monitored, located or investigated by laboratory
techniques.

However, until quite recently, psychologists – who also
seemed to regard the human being as little more than a
behavioural-response mechanism – paid scant attention to
it either. It was generally referred to as if it could be taken
for granted and as if it was, again, of no particular
significance. The general inference has been that 'consciousness' is a useful word which can be used to denote
that a mental function is working with intent. Beyond that,
it is simply employed to imply that a creature is fully alive
and, hence, that its being 'unconscious' describes some
half-way condition between being alive and being dead.

Yet, surely there is no more important a factor to be taken
into account than consciousness when attempting to
understand not only the distinction between our
behaviour and that of other creatures but also, and far more
importantly, the complicated nature of our own experience
and conduct.[29] Consciousness, especially the degree of it
accessible to the human being, has to be the 'crowning
glory' of evolution. Without it, there would be no 'higher'
feelings and emotions, and no 'higher' aspirations in the
realms of art, philosophy and religion (none of which are,
of course, of professional interest to the laboratory
scientist; nor do they fit easily into the models of
behavioural psychology). Quite apart from considerations of man's 'higher' nature, the consciousness-factor
played a crucial part in the triumph of the human being as
a species.

Though there are several levels or states of consciousness

recognized by traditions and disciplines outside those of mainstream science and psychology, four simple and easily-understood definitions will serve the present purpose. Firstly, 'ordinary consciousness': one is awake and aware but totally involved in what is going on around one. Secondly, 'self-consciousness': not in the limited sense of being shy and embarrassed but simply conscious-ness of oneself as an entity separate from all around one. Thirdly, 'subjective consciousness': attention being given to thoughts and images in the mind, cut off from all that is happening around one (e.g., 'absent-minded'). And fourthly, 'objective consciousness': here there is an absence of self-consciousness; and fully-aware but detached observation of all that is happening in that moment (quite distinct from ordinary consciousness when one is fully involved in the present experience).

We ordinarily move in and out of these different states many times a day; and they all no doubt serve their purposes. But it is the fourth one, objective consciousness, which deserves particular consideration for the moment. Whatever other advantages evolution of the brain bes-towed on the human being, it is this state of consciousness which played a crucial role in ensuring the success of the species.

The ability to observe consciously and objectively implies that there is a capacity within the mind to disengage and detach (oneself) from that which is under observation. That in turn means that power has been gained to become more than simply an automatic, sensory-response mechanism. Thus, the human being evolved as (probably) the first creature which was not entirely a slave to the preordained programme written into its genetic inheritance; or to the automatic-reaction tactics dictated by the ancient parts of the brain. There appeared in *homo sapiens* what could be described as a *deus ex machina* – a god-like power which could override the biological machine.

The human being gained, or was granted – depending on one's view of the source of human will – the ability not only to control and modify response to external influences but also to contemplate and consider in abstract the nature and activity of the world at large. He or she could choose where to direct attention to advantage.

Because man had the 'mind-space' to consider future action, and could if he wanted intervene between sensory stimuli and automatic response – e.g. 'fight or flight' – he could consciously select from memory relevant past experience and by extrapolation visualize alternative courses. He could avoid past mistakes and improve previous successes. Other creatures could of course memorize; what they could not do was visualize future action intended to bring about different results.

Having focussed on objective consciousness as being the key factor underlying typically-human mental powers, it is not surprising to find that, physiologically, all the brain regions associated with those powers are located in the greatly-developed forebrain. The cerebral hemispheres are responsible for recognition, logic, deduction, reasoning, anticipation, prediction, planning, imagination, visualization, perception, insight – all the cognitive powers. And all dependent on the power of objective consciousness.

Another well-established, and perhaps unexpected, faculty associated with the forebrain is the exercising of caution. Of course, other parts of the primitive brain are activated by warning signals of immediate danger, signals which put the whole system on alert. And such defence response can, if necessary, trigger equally-automatic escape or avoidance measures. But the fact that caution is also a factor in cerebral activity suggests that objective consciousness can be involved and therefore that we are here talking of caution in the sense of self-defence, carefulness, tact or discretion. A capacity such as visualization permits the foreseeing of undesirable as well as desirable consequences. Although the cognitive powers are usually employed in the business of fulfilling desire, they also permit awareness of potential threat. Although such foreknowledge is, of course, frequently useful, it also presents us with problems with which we may well prefer not to have to contend.

A number of these apparently-adverse effects will surface later, but one, the most fundamental, will suffice for example. Self-consciousness – as awareness of oneself as a physical organism – combined with knowledge born of objective consciousness that all organisms inexorably die, gives rise to the formidable realization that one will eventually die oneself. Foreknowledge of certain, eventual death has an enormous, if usually underlying psychological effect on human conduct.

Anyone who contemplates the fact cannot help but marvel that out of the mass of fibres and fluids inside our skulls we experience not only a miraculous world but also ourselves as witnesses of it. Nevertheless, the wonder of it tends to become obscured and overlooked because we have to devote so much of our mental activity to resolving problems. We may well ask ourselves sometimes why life has to be so difficult.

Researchers of the brain tell us that, even under non-threatening, benign conditions, or even when we are asleep, the brain is continuously active. When stimulated, the nerve networks carry wave upon wave of electro-chemical discharges which we experience as dreaming, thinking, imagining, etc. We well know that the brain/mind can become tired through continual working. The mental tension and stress involved can leave us feeling exhausted. When asked to account for all the thinking we do, we are apt to put it down to 'the pressures of modern living', or some such blanket explanation. People are frequently heard saying that they are concerned about this or worried about that, frustrated by this or angry about that. Why such strain on the brain?

Perhaps it has something to do with Nature's strategy for brain evolution, namely that of developing it by extending or modifying earlier versions, or adding to ancient parts bit by bit. This may have served the evolution of increasingly intelligent forms of life well enough in the past. But when it came to man (and introduction of the consciousness-factor), perhaps certain flaws in this strategy started to become apparent – paradoxically to man himself.

What we may be having to contend with, and be becoming painfully aware of, is that some of the constituent features of our programming do not necessarily or consistently co-ordinate and co-operate with others. Ancient and modern may be somewhat at variance, just as they can be in other historical contexts. The difference is that whereas we can, say, drop outdated beliefs and practices, we cannot dispense with the ancient parts of our brains. We have to cope with their continuing intrusion into the more modern parts of our psyche. Of course, their activity is crucial to physical survival; but often they interfere with the aspirations of our higher nature.

This suggests that some of the later modifications of the brain may have introduced motivations and dispositions which can be in contention with earlier ones already established and perhaps appropriate to different circumstances. What is more, establishment of the latter takes place in the development of each human being before the former develops to maturity. In other words, we are all primitive before we start to become civilized. We are instinctively selfish before we can learn to become altruistic – and that battle is likely to go on right through each lifetime.

As another example, our deeply-embedded reaction to fight or flee in face of threat may well find itself at odds with forebrain intelligence telling us that neutral response or attempt at negotiation would be more advantageous.

If development of brain capacity by accretion created certain in-built problems, then these will surely have been compounded by Nature's more recent tactic. Although we might have suspected it through observation of our experience, neurophysiologists have in recent decades well and truly put it on the anatomical map. The two cerebral hemispheres have different functions. This differentiation in the forebrain is apparently known to occur in only one other creature – as one might guess, the dolphin[30] (p. 72).

The scientific explanation for this development is a logical one – that it was more expedient to increase brain-capacity by dividing the existing and more-than-ample volume provided by past, near-spherical expansion than to expand even further. Such a development would have required an enlarging of the skull, which in turn would have required structural reinforcement of the whole skeleton to cope with the additional weight. As it is, it is not until several months after birth that the baby gains sufficient muscular strength to control its head in an upright position.

Bilateral differentiation of forebrain function amounts in effect to differentiation of role assignment in the two sides of the mind – a fact which, as we shall see, may have more than coincidental parallels with role differentiation between the genders.

Given harmony and co-operation between the two sides of the mind, unilateral specialization should benefit the system as a whole through providing increased intelligence capacity. But, as in the case of male and female relationship, it also allows the possibility of contradiction, discordance and non-co-operation. Even worse, one side may become dominant and exploitive of the other, or seek autonomy and dissociation (as may be apparent in the extreme in the case of schizophrenia).

Constitutionally, male and female brains are the same right through from hindbrain to forebrain. But, as it was suggested earlier that role differentiation may be linked with gender-typical activity in the limbic system, so we may find gender-typical differences in hemisphere balance.

5 Mind-split

Given that we usually assume brain to be more or less synonymous with mind, we might expect the realms of the neurophysiologist and the psychologist to be simply and clearly interrelated. In fact, it proves difficult to bridge the divide between physical phenomena and the mental experiences associated with them. To speak, for example, of electro-chemical discharges over nerve synapses as evidence of brain activity seems a world apart from our experience of thinking.

Furthermore, we vaguely assume that consciousness is in some way a product of biochemical activity in the brain. After all, it can be lost through a severe blow to the head. But neither physiologist nor psychologist can say how it arises, where it is precisely located or what it is. Neither you nor I, no matter how well-informed, will ever be able to compare our experience of being alive with what it is like to be a corpse. As far as we are concerned, being conscious is being alive; if we lost consciousness, we do not exist to ourselves, whether or not the body is technically alive or dead.

What the neurophysiologist has been able to do in recent decades is to locate accurately areas of the brain where certain mental functions and processes take place.[31] The psychological implications of such findings are far less certain. However, since we are talking here of mental processes common to us all, we do not have to be scientifically qualified to be able to observe and analyse what goes on in our own minds. Although some of the following account is not to be found in current textbooks on the subject of brain/mind, anyone contemplating their own social and mental experience can recognize for themselves whether it rings true or not.

The basic functions of the brain are the processing of

information, and instruction to act. As the continuous flow of sensory signals is transmitted via the nervous system to the brain, it is monitored and interpreted. If action is required as a result, the brain instructs accordingly. The majority of this activity is connected in both obvious and subtle ways with physical survival. Much of it takes place automatically and so rapidly that we are rarely conscious of its happening. The maintenance and regulation of physical function, carried out by the more ancient and instinctive parts of the hindbrain and midbrain, is done spontaneously and uncompromisingly without our being aware of it (unless something goes wrong). The same applies in the case of the more primitive response-to-threat mechanisms.

We do not 'think twice' – or even once, for that matter – before leaping to avoid an oncoming vehicle which would otherwise hit us (though there are occasions when extreme fear can paralyse the system completely). Apart from all such instinctive activity and behaviour, we also do not have to think about a great many of our daily actions. Once we have learned a technique – how to walk, talk, ride a bicycle, open a door, peel a banana – the brain is programmed to repeat the task automatically. In other words, our survival interests are, or become, largely served without our having to employ the cognitive powers of the forebrain.

What is interesting about these powers housed in the more modern and superimposed part of the brain is that they do nothing to make the ancient parts function more efficiently; but they can interfere with that functioning and make it less effective. For example, it is now being more widely recognized by Western medical science that malfunction (illness) in the body can be precipitated or aggravated by detrimental activity in the higher mental processes. Or, to put it another way, recovery from illness is much dependent on the mental disposition of the patient. In extreme, someone who has given up the will to live is more likely to die.

It is in this far-reaching area of psychosomatic effect that we may see evidence for the earlier suggestion that Nature, by adding new brain development to old, created

problems as well as advantages. There can be no doubt that
the modifications did enable the human species to survive,
proliferate and gain dominance over all other species; but
those superior cognitive faculties may now be becoming
more of a hindrance than a help. Unless there is a purpose
other than survival success to which they should be
applied? Perhaps there is some 'unnatural' but significant
'higher' purpose in the bifurcated and specialized functioning of the cerebral hemispheres?

The functions of the left side of the brain (in most people)
can helpfully be thought of as akin to those of a computer.
It receives (input) and memorizes (stores) information
(facts) from external sources via the senses. In other words,
it learns about the outside world in much the same
way as the commputer is programmed, though we prefer to
speak of ourselves as being educated and socially conditioned.

The left side can then retrieve appropriate information
from memory (data bank) and process it in relation to some
task that needs performing. Its working-out methods are of
a linear, sequential nature and its choosing (selecting) of
relevant information is carried out on a simple, binary,
accept/reject basis. This can be verified through considering how we make simple, day-to-day decisions. If I have
learned that I like oranges and someone offers me one, I
will reach out to accept it; if I do not like them, I will refuse
it. This information processing starts as soon as we are
born. The baby quickly learns to accept the pleasurable and
reject the uncomfortable.

Once a preferred procedure has been learned, the left
side of the brain can be relied upon to continue performing
it without our needing to think much about it. Such
functioning may be considered logical in the sense that
incoming information is dealt with in a consistent and
predictable manner within the parameters which have
been established by past conditioning and experience. At a
simple level, our personal likes and dislikes – of oranges,
for example – are of little importance. But our conditioning,
of course, goes far beyond such matters. We pick up far
more subtle information which serves to build up our
beliefs, attitudes, prejudices and opinions.

The great majority of our social and educational conditioning is of a nature which ensures that we become conventional and conforming members of the group we happen to belong to. Emphasis is such that if we do have personal ambitions, they must not be anti-social; if they are to be pursued, they must be channelled into activities which will contribute to the welfare of the group. And once that conditioning has become established – during, say, the first quarter of a lifetime – it can serve the rest of that life without being fundamentally changed.

The left side cannot on its own generate actions to bring about results other than those which can be predicted from previously assimilated data. It can only mechanistically attempt to reproduce what it has done before. Once modes of dealing with recurring situations have been established, the left side will automatically adopt habitual procedures. Thus, familiar tactics which have proved effective for self-survival in the past will be repeated on the assumption that satisfactory results previously obtained can be achieved again by taking the same actions.

Having faith in being able to predict consequences is of course based on the expectation that everything in the outside world will continue to conform to recognized laws and patterns. This we may safely do at the physical level most of the time. I sit down on a chair, for example, happily assuming that it will support my weight as satisfactorily as it did the last time I sat on it. Such policy is not foolproof; accidents happen now and again. On the whole though, we get away with it. But such procedure becomes a good deal less reliable when we use it at more subtle, psychological levels, especially in our transactions with other people.

For example, if we note in memory that someone behaves in a certain way in a particular circumstance, the left side of the mind will expect that person to repeat the behaviour pattern if similar circumstance repeats. We tend to make friends with those whose habitual patterns of behaviour we approve of and enemies of those whose offensive behaviour we assume will be repeated against us. Anyone who has been party to a longstanding personal relationship will recognize establishment with the other of familiar and mutually-pleasing interactions. Such habitual ritual assuages fear of the unpredictable.[32] The familiar is comforting whilst the unfamiliar is potentially threatening. Bias in favour of the left-side mode of dealing with life tends to increase with age. Hence it is common to find that older people are more inclined to cling tenaciously to old habits, attitudes and opinions, and thus to resist innovations.

The overall effect of left-side learning and conditioning is that the person comes increasingly to rely on it for sense of continuity and certainty. The more I can safely predict, the more consistent and less threatening my environment seems to be. The less my fear of discontinuity, the greater my sense of stability and security.

Obviously, the conditioning process during the first years of our lives is crucially important. The assimilation of as much useful information as possible enhances the likelihood of survival and success, not only of the individual concerned but also of the group of which he or she happens to be a member. Most of the content of early learning, usually conveyed by the parents, is directed towards self-survival, i.e. learning to look after oneself. This initial period is traditionally followed by a period of formal education outside the home. Here the emphasis is on learning how to behave in the world at large and how, in due course, to be able to contribute to society, i.e. earn a living. The fact that in parts of modern society formal education tends to place less emphasis on group-responsibility and more on self-gain does not detract from the principle that the former is essential for stable and civilized society.

Although the group's educational process provides to some extent for individual development, the overall purpose of left-brain induction is preparation of the person to fulfil group requirements and expectations. Whatever the methods employed and the content conveyed, and whatever the opportunities made available to the individual, left-brain conditioning is primarily intended to achieve one aim – survival of the group. Success or failure of the group-member is predominantly measured in terms dictated by the group. Ultimately, the fate of the individual is of little account compared with the importance of the group's security and continuity.

What then of the right side of the brain/mind?

The right side has what may be described as a more subtle, more wide-ranging and less easily defineable role. One immediate key to appreciation of this role is that it involves exercise of the powers of visualization and imagination. From the ability to use these powers, a great deal follows.

As suggested earlier, objective consciousness permits detached viewpoint and contemplation, an ability not to be involved in what is happening. This distancing introduces the possibility of modifying habitual, reactive behaviour. In other words, it allows some perspective on the established left-side processes of linear, repetitive thinking. That perspective enables the visualization of unfamiliar patterns and permutations, and thus different possibilities. Whereas the left works on the basis of predictable continuity through historical time, the right brings in a spatial dimension in which new ideas, inspirations and revelations can stimulate new initiatives and directions.

Consider any particular daily habit. Because it is performed frequently, it requires very little attention, being almost automatically carried out by left-brain programming. If that habit is to be changed, there has to be a conscious and deliberate intervention by the right side. Through being able to visualize the whole sequence of actions involved in the habit, the right can envisage either a change of sequence or introduction of a new feature (or even dropping the habit altogether). The right side's purpose will be to achieve the previous result more efficiently, to achieve an improved result, to eliminate undesirable consequences, and so on. Such intervention is the equivalent of modifying the programme of a computer.

Or consider, say, the answering of a question; this may or may not require active employment of the right side of the mind. If the question is simply asking for information which is readily available in memory, it is only a matter of retrieval; the answer does not need thinking about. If the question is of a more complicated nature – say, asking for advice – there may well be need of a mental pause in order to give a considered reply. That means that the right side needs to distance itself in order to visualize the best way of expressing response. That 'thinking about' requires perspective, or 'mind-space'. (Appropriately enough, the word 'consider' is thought to have come from Latin roots: *con* meaning 'before' and *sidus* meaning 'star'; hence, clear connotations of space.)

An analogy to give further indication of the different natures of left and right functioning could be taken from a game such as chess. First, the left brain has to learn about the playing area of the board, about the powers and movements of the pieces, and about the rules of the game. This could be likened to education about the nature, laws and customs of a society, and the powers and roles of its members.

If the game is then to be played, moves have to be made. This requires visualization of strategy and the tactics needed to carry it out; and then modifications required to counter the opponent's play: hence, the employment of right-side powers. This would represent the individual's need to determine the strategy and tactics of his or her own life. This in turn means needing to visualize options and thinking ahead into an unknown future. The object is to win the game – or, at least, not to lose it.

The game analogy cannot be taken too far; the rules are not so clearly defined in life itself. But it serves well enough to convey the nature and character of the right side of the mind. It is the side which experiences the desire to compete, achieve and win, i.e. to attack, gain and dominate. Whereas the left-side motivation is to maintain continuity and security – thus favouring a solid, defensive strategy – right-side motivation is geared to gain status and power through vanquishing – thus favouring an adventurous, offensive strategy. The left will be cautious through fear of making a fatal mistake; the right will take risk through desire to succeed. The left is conditioned to conform with the expectations and requirements of the group, motivated by fear of disapproval. The right is self-generating and strives to fulfil personal ambition, motivated by desire for individual status.

Anyone can observe this dichotomy or twin-motivation in their own experience. Where decision has to be made, one side of the mind advocates the safety of familiar and proven course; the other will promote the taking of risk in order to achieve better result. Sometimes one side prevails, sometimes the other. Sometimes the two sides co-operate harmoniously and decision is easily reached; sometimes the two sides are equally weighted, leaving the mind in a state of indecision and perhaps stress.

A particular feature of the right side is that its powers and talents need to be stimulated, encouraged and exercised; they develop through actual or self-generated opportunity for expression. They cannot, like left-side powers, become effective simply through learning from externally-induced influences. Thus, though left-brain education can ensure that the majority of group members will become useful participants in society, it cannot guarantee the emergence of right-brain innovators and achievers. Having learned all manner of information and law, and having been introduced to a spectrum of occupations, it is up to the individual – if the spirit is there – to visualize goals best suited to innate right-side talents. (Of course, if left-side capacities are limited, so right-side talents will have less prospect of development.)

Whilst left-side qualities such as perseverance, consistency, caution, obedience, etc., can be to some extent established by social conditioning – either by extolling their virtues or threatening retribution if ignored – there is no certainty of outcome where development of right-side ambition is concerned. Capacity for initiative can be used constructively and creatively, or exploitively and destructively. The group may benefit or suffer accordingly.

Whereas the left is concerned with public service, the right is concerned with private enterprise. The dynamics within any group – from family to nation – much depends on its valuation of individual initiative. Balance has to be struck between necessity for conformity to ensure cohesion and the need to allow enterprise to improve prospects. If the group suppresses the latter through fear of disruption, it stands to lose the benefits of innovation – and will invite decline because established programmes eventually become moribund. On the other hand, undisciplined opportunism can undermine the stability of the group. And the same applies in principle within the individual as he or she experiences changing balance between the two sides of the mind. Ideally, neither side should become strongly and continually dominant. An over-dominant left leads to lack of initiative; an over-dominant right can lead to irresponsibility. A healthy balance means good judgement – sometimes being cautious, sometimes taking risk, sometimes persevering, sometimes changing course; and so on.

From the above, it follows that inequality between group members is inevitable. Although all may be deemed equal in their left-side responsibility towards the group, and though the group itself will ideally seek to ensure that all members have equal rights of opportunity and receive equal social benefit, right-side talents and the desire to exercise them vary greatly from one individual to another.

In the left-side sense, as group-members, all may indeed be born equal; in the right-side sense, as individuals, clearly they are not. For example, intelligence is a factor highly dependent on right-side powers. And intelligence is said to be 'eighty percent inherited, twenty percent acquired.'[33]

Any group which does not encourage development of right-side talents is heading for trouble; if it ignores or actively discourages them, it is surely doomed. After all, initiative, enterprise and creative talents have been responsible for the success of the human species. It may even be that the whole purpose of evolution has been to see such powers manifest in *homo sapiens*. The group, however, in the interests of its own survival, has always been biased in favour of right-side talents being used primarily for group-prescribed benefit. Their use to enhance the wealth and welfare of the group is welcome; their selfish misuse is not. The group thus exercises collective judgement in its approval or disapproval of the enterprises of its members.

Whether or not the individual is heedful of public approval or disapproval, there can be no doubt that the individual's ambition is bound to be the gaining of identity, status and power – whether they be in terms of public recognition or self-assessment. The gaining of them is what is important to the right side of the mind; not whether the gaining of them attracts fame or notoriety, or goes unrecognized.

Thus far in this commentary on brain-hemisphere differentiation, clear distinction has been made between the two sides of the brain/mind for ease of description. Left and right are convenient shorthand for indicating the nature of polarization (and, as it happens, they turn out to be extraordinarily apt). In fact, the two hemispheres are normally closely interrelated and exchange across the corpus callosum takes place continuously, so that most of the time we feel psychologically integrated, unified in our sense of selfhood. That there are functions exclusive to each side has been scientifically established; but, apropos of the reservation made earlier about possible psychological implications, it has to be said that the lateral division of motivation, disposition, etc., is not scientifically proven (and perhaps never will be). The important and indisputable fact is, however, that we do from time to time experience the mental dichotomy as described, no matter how such divergence may be physiologically located. What is more, that divergence of standpoint does reveal some compelling coincidences.

There are striking similarities in the terms in which it is appropriate to describe the evolution of role differentiation between the genders and those appropriate to describe differentiated functioning of the cerebral hemispheres.[34]

The three basic requirements for survival, as outlined earlier, are procurement, defence/attack and reproduction. For pragmatic reasons, prime responsibility for the first two fell primarily on the male and the third on the female.

Traditionally, the female's procreative role is unchanging, repetitive, predictable, 'automatic', consistent, programmed, reproductive, etc. Its motivation is essentially continuity of the species and its furtherance is best served in conditions of stability and security. These are all characteristics typical of and sympathetic to the functions and dispositions of the left side of the mind.

Meanwhile, male procurement and defence/attack roles are competitive, aggressive, questing, acquisitive, challenging, exploitive, unpredictable, continually changing; and they require enterprise, risk-taking, initiative, innovation, invention – in all of which the power of visualization is crucial for success. Exercise of talent enables the individual to gain recognition within the group and is therefore conducive to the gaining of identity and status. Although traditionally such male endeavour is conditioned to serve the group in general and the female's procreative role in particular, it is nevertheless motivated by personal ambition. All these typical requirements of the male in his roles correspond with the nature and powers of the right side of the mind.

Therefore – bearing in mind that the role assignments of male and female were dictated in the first place by survival tactics in hostile circumstances – a significant coincidence emerges in which traditional female responsibilities align with left-brain functioning and the male's with right-brain functioning. The left side of the mind could be said to be 'feminine' in nature and the right 'masculine'. Although it may then be appropriate to say that the typical male is right-brain-dominant and the typical female left-brain-dominant, it is by no means the general case, especially in modern times. Both genders have feminine-left and masculine-right sides of the mind, and balance can vary in either gender, from person to person and from time to time throughout phases of a lifespan.

Leaving aside for the moment considerations of typical gender bias, we all of us have brain-hemisphere differentiation, or split-motivation, which can be represented thus:

Feminine	Masculine
LEFT	RIGHT
Stability	Identity
Security	Status
Continuity	Power

Anyone may test this division of the psyche in any number

of contexts. For example, as mentioned earlier, all will have experienced situations in which the left side of the mind advocates taking a safe and familiar course, versus the right side which desires to be adventurous and to take a more self-rewarding but hazardous course. Caution versus risk; being like everyone else versus trying to be original; the juxtaposition of alternatives with the above character-istics enter into so much of our decision-making.

The outcome depends on the relative strengths of the two sides of the mind, one immediately or eventually over-ruling the other. Sometimes decision is easy and there is little or no internal debate. Sometimes decision is difficult as the two sides are in conflict and neither can readily gain authority over the other. As one might expect from what has already been said, need to make a decision arises because the right side takes initiative in coming up with a proposal; the left side then concedes or resists.

In a state of indecision, we speak (accurately) of 'being in two minds', and of not being able to 'make up one's mind' – as if the mind is split. And sometimes, when the right has visualized a proposed course of action but is not pressing to put it into effect, we may say we have 'half a mind (to do something)'.

The interplay of feminine-left and masculine-right with-in the mind is readily projected into outer relationships, especially into inter-gender relationship. Both male and female can alternate between taking typically dominant-left or dominant-right stances, being motivated by left or right bias. Traditionally, it has usually been a case of the male being dominant-right (taking the initiative) and the female being dominant-left (conceding or resisting the initiative). Whatever the context of encounter, the under-lying principle is that one needs to gain authority over the other (otherwise the situation will result in 'stale-mate'). In other words, whether in the mind of the individual or between two people, the need to make decision always invites the possibility of confrontation and conflict.

The left side fears and dislikes confrontation because it threatens continuity and security. We prefer states of harmony and co-operation because they are more comfort-able. In general, we favour the belief that the two sides, or genders, ought to be able to work together for mutual benefit. However, there is a catch. Because of the underlying dominance principle mentioned above, co-operation inevitably means that one has to work on behalf of the other. For action to be feasible, there has to be a singular purpose, and therefore one side's disposition has to defer to the other's. Thus, the give-and-take in personal relationship tends to imply alternation between being dominated and being dominant.

The twin-motivations are inherently incompatible. For instance, it is not possible to be left-cautious ('better safe than sorry') and right-adventurous ('nothing venture, nothing gain') at the same time. As projected into the business of investment, it is a case of either better security and lower yield of interest or greater risk and possible higher dividend. So in life; we cannot have it both ways.

Consensus and conditioning tend to favour security over risk because group stability and continuity – focussed traditionally on female procreativity – take precedence. Thus, right-side initiatives are persuaded into co-oper-ation with left-side priorities. This bias can be seen, for example, in the political arena. The nature of the left side aligns with left-wing ideology and the right side with right-wing ideology. But right-wing enterprise is more likely to have to acknowledge social demand than left-wing socialism is likely to champion the importance of private enterprise (especially at the communist end of the spectrum). What is more, since the bid for political power and leadership aligns with right-side motivation, ambi-tion in that respect fits more comfortably into right-wing philosophy than into left-wing philosophy (which no doubt gives rise to the notion that right-wing government is more 'natural' than left-wing). Right-wing leadership can become insensitive and over-reach itself; but left-wing leadership carries within it inherent contradiction and can easily become self-confounding and ineffective.

In the context of the individual, feminine-left condition-ing through parental influence and education is usually dominant. The left side of the brain is inculcated with a programme which will ensure that the person will beocme a co-operative and conforming member of the group.

Concession to right-side initiative is made on condition that it is employed in the group's interest. It thus becomes easier for the individual to fail than to succeed – in his or her own terms. However, it is easier for the female to concede than the male; he is the one more likely to be troubled by failure to succeed (though the more liberated the female becomes, the more likely she will also become exposed to the threat of failure in her enterprise).

The characteristics which are appropriately ascribed to the functions of each hemisphere of the brain reflect the nature of the split-motivation which runs right through our experience of relationship, especially as evident in sexual relationship between the genders. At base, the juxtaposition of feminine-left and masculine-right is epitomized in the act of fertilization. The female carries the passive, mature ovum, full of potential for reproduction; but that potential cannot be realized without the active, penetrative initiative of the questing, male sperm. However, whereas the female is traditionally satisfied by the procreative fulfilment of the act, the male's motivation – as described earlier – carries desire for pleasure and ambition to dominate. The dualistic nature of this fundamental interaction is in principle carried right through into all areas of encounter in the world at large.

If inter-hemisphere relationship corresponds so closely with inter-gender relationship, what might the implications of women's liberation be, given that it is an initiative to gain independence? Might increasing polarization of the genders indicate increasing dichotomy in the brain/ mind? Or perhaps it is the other way around: that increasing mind-split is being projected into and being reflected back by a growing split between the genders? Conflict in either causes conflict in the other.

Whether or not this is the case, two tendencies seem to be on the increase as longer-term heterosexual relationship becomes more difficult. First, the male becomes more confused and frustrated the more opportunities for right-side exercise in fulfilling occupation diminish, i.e. as he becomes more redundant and impotent. Second, and simultaneously, the more liberated the female becomes the more she gains opportunity to exercise her long-suppressed right-side powers, taking initiative to pursue status and power *in her own right* in areas hitherto denied to her.

As the genders dissociate – particularly as the female becomes independent of the male – and at the same time compete in their occupations, a paradoxical effect becomes apparent. As the female's disposition moves towards the right and she becomes more 'masculinized', the male's disposition is pulled towards the left and he becomes more 'feminized' (emasculated). (Or else he is forced further right and becomes despotic.) The general effect of the shift is that the sexes become less distinguishable. Society becomes more 'unisex' as its members become less distinctly male and female in occupation, interest, appearance, conduct, attitude, etc.

I recall asking a male homosexual how he regarded women. His reply was to the effect, 'Well, I don't think of them as being sexual at all. They are just other people with whom I sometimes have social but not sexual intercourse. . .' Is this self-defence; or a sign of the future?

Perhaps we have entered a phase in human evolution in which inter-gender relationship will become less and less sexually-based. If so, it would seem that the male cannot help but become increasingly redundant and impotent – not just in the occupational and sexual senses already covered in previous chapters, but psychologically also. His right-side powers of competitiveness and ambitiousness will decline (or be diverted into trivial pursuits), not so much because there will be decreasing scope for exercising them but more because the female, instead of inspiring and encouraging him as she has done in the past, will not only be preoccupied by her own ambitions but will be competing with him also.

Well, it could be argued, perhaps such competition will spur the male to make even greater effort? Apart from the fact that male competitiveness loses its impetus if the sexual factor is removed, male attempt to compete with the female is doomed to failure. As should become apparent in the next chapter and later, there can be no doubt in such contest which is the weaker sex.

6 The Weaker Sex

Popular myth has it that the gentle female is the weaker sex. Whether the male in his vanity invented it on account of his superior muscle-power – biceps, quadriceps, phallic, etc – or whether the more shrewd female promoted it to flatter the male into compliance with her wishes, the physiological and, in certain respects, the psychological evidence is overwhelmingly in favour of the opposite – that in reality the male is the weaker sex.

The male may have gained greater dynamic strength through development of muscle; but that muscle is built through expenditure of energy, traditionally through competitive performance of hunter-warrior-procurer roles on behalf of group-survival. The female meanwhile expends less energy (hence, less muscle), conserving it instead for self-preservation and for her traditionally less energetic procreative and nurturing roles. (The fact that modern women are often to be heard complaining how arduous and demanding domestic roles are – despite the aid of a formidable array of appliances – probably has more to do with frustration, boredom and attitude towards the tasks themselves than with the actual expenditure of energy involved).

Muscle-power apart, there is no lack of scientific evidence to substantiate the view that the male is both more profligate in his expenditure of resources and constitutionally weaker in several respects.[35]

To begin where we all begin – in the event of fertilization. In any single ejaculation, the male discharges at least 250 million sperm, probably as many as 350–400 million. In the not-too-distant past, that would theoretically have been an amount of genetic material in one emission sufficient to fertilize the entire female population of the world. Even today, it would be enough to serve, say, about ten percent of the fertile women on earth. Given adequate recuperation time, one man within, say, the period of one month's menstrual cycle, could theoretically father an entire new generation of humanity. It could even be that one virile male in one full lifespan can emit as many sperm as the total number of human beings there has ever been.

Theoretical potential is always, however, a quantum jump away from practical realization! The point is that the ratio of genetic expenditure between male and female is greatly biased in favour of the latter. The human female produces – from an original potential of a quarter to half a million ovarian follicles – somewhere between 200 to 500 mature ova in a lifetime. Even if a woman has several pregnancies, the vast majority of her ova, a good ninety-nine percent, will be wasted. Her success rate, however – given that she has at least one child – is of the order of one in hundreds. In comparison, the success rate for male sperm must be of the order of one in hundreds, if not thousands, of billions. The number of sperm wasted is astronomical.

In a single conception, a woman will use one two-hundredth to one five-hundredth part of her lifetime's genetic potential. In that same conception, only one part in several hundred million of the genetic potential of one male emission will be used. Male expenditure of genetic material in the interest of reproduction is thus enormously greater than that of the female. Where the ratio of successful to unsuccessful seed is concerned, Nature is remarkably extravagant; nevertheless, she sees to it that the female is able to conserve her resources far more efficiently than the male. What is more, in the human case, a proportion of male emissions will be totally lost, even when there is intent to fertilize, due to the human female's 'hidden ovulation'.

Once a month, during the short fertile period of a woman's menstrual cycle, a mature egg cell – occasionally more than one – leaves one of the ovaries and travels a short distance into one of the Fallopian tubes where it awaits possible fertilization. If sexual intercourse takes place (and there are no contraceptive barriers), several hundred million sperm set out in attempt to reach that one ovum.

In relation to their size – one five-hundredth of a millimetre long – the sperm have an immense distance to travel – from the vaginal passage through the cervix and the uterus to the Fallopian tube. (They are certainly not met anything like halfway.) They have to undertake the journey with some urgency because their energy resources for swimming are very limited. As if this twenty-four hour marathon were not challenge enough, the sperm have to run the gauntlet – incredibly perverse though it may seem – of an initially hostile environment. The vaginal fluid first encountered is acidic and, though the sperm have some antacid protection, it soon wears off. More than ninety-nine percent are killed even before they reach the cervix; only about one million get through to the uterus. Of these survivors, which then have to battle their way against fluid currents, only about a thousand succeed in gaining the upper end of the womb (and presumably fifty percent of these may then attempt the wrong Fallopian tube). Very few – approximately one hundred – actually reach their target. With what strength remains to them, those few then have to compete with each other to be the first to penetrate the protective wall of the ovum. Finally, only one of the original hundreds of millions can succeed in fulfilling its task.

If a single image were required to demonstrate the male's need to be competitive, then this account of the odds-against-success embassy of the sperm would suffice. On the other hand, the militant feminist would no doubt regard the image of the sperm's invasion and assault as typical of the male's aggressive disposition to exploit and rape. So much depends on point of view when judging who is doing what to whom and why.

Although it could be argued that all the above implies that the male must be the stronger in order to sustain such disproportionate loss of 'vital substance' and in order to mount his more active and demanding role in the whole process, it could be countered that it is really the innate strength and dominance of the female which ensures that the male will expend his energy and resources – and if necessary exhaust himself – in order to fulfil her potential.

As we shall see later, psychologically the latter viewpoint is more convincing. Certainly a biologist would affirm that Nature consistently gives priority to the female's procreative interests in all species; the male is always comparatively surplus to requirement and more expendable.

In the process of conception, chromosomes (genetic material) contributed by the sperm complement an equal number of chromosomes present in the ovum. In the human case, there are normally forty-six in total, twenty-three from each parent. Of the twenty-three pairs, twenty-two are called autosomes, and they are concerned with the general development, maintenance and functioning of the body whether it is destined to be male or female. The twenty-third pair, called the gonosomes, will determine gender and hence all the physical characteristics associated with each gender.

The gonosomes are of two types, called X and Y. The mother's ovum always carries an X type; the father's sperm carries either an X or a Y. If the successful sperm carries an X – thereby making a complement of XX – the embryo will become female. If the sperm carries a Y gonosome – thereby making a complement of XY – the embryo will be disposed to become male.

Whilst there can be a fertilized ovum without a Y component, there cannot be one without an X. The mother with her X-only gonosome is, as it were, predisposed to continue the female line – to have daughters only. Or, to put it the other way around, she could be said to be biased against having a son. The father on the other hand is not so 'prejudiced'. His gonosome will determine the sex of the offspring but he is equally well-disposed, statistically, towards begetting either a daughter or a son. In a sense, survival of the male gender depends entirely on the male. He has to intervene and over-rule the female's predisposition to beget her own gender only. It would seem unlikely that such a biased set-up would have no psychological consequences where parental relationships with sons and daughters are concerned.

An ovum without a female X gonosome cannot develop at all; but an ovum without a male Y gonosome can do so. This indicates quite forcefully that male development is a modification of the female fundamental.[36] Logically, there ought to be the possibility of three genders: XX, XY and YY. But whereas there is an XX ('double-female), there is no such gender as YY ('double-male'). The second gender, the male, is XY ('half-female-half-male'). Again, it would seem most unlikely that there are no psychological implications in this arrangement.

The clear biological (and surely psychological) bias in favour of the female is compounded by further factors which we will come to below. But it can hardly fail to be appreciated already that in the matter of survival of the species the female factor is primary and the male secondary. As described earlier, it is not impossible that through genetic engineering the human race could survive as female only; it would be totally impossible as male only. The only advantage in having the male at all is that as a modified-female he allows the possibility of genetic mutation.

In view of the secondary yet demanding role assigned to the male in reproduction, it seems rather unfair that some biologists should describe the male as 'parasitic'.[37] This arises from the fact that the male, in pursuit of reproducing himself, only provides the female with genetic material, the sperm being nothing more than 'a gene-bearing torpedo'. The female in contrast not only provides the other half of the genetic material but supplies all the resources required for development after conception. It is thus said that the ovum constitutes 'a desirable resource' which the 'parasitic' sperm seeks to 'exploit'. This so-called 'parasitism' of the male seems to overlook the aforementioned matters of expenditure ratios, biases in favour of the female, and so on; it also fails to take into account what follows.

The X chromosome is larger than the Y. An XX combination has some four percent more genetic content than an XY. This fact has given rise to the speculation amongst geneticists that the greater investment in the female XX may account for her longer life-expectancy. Furthermore, the XX combination is thought to confer other advantage. For the potential female, any defects in her mother's X gonosome are likely to be cancelled out by

the father's X gonosome, or *vice versa*. But in the case of the
potential male, any X gonosome defect from the mother
cannot be cancelled out by the father's Y. Thus a mother
can pass on abnormalities – particularly blood disorders –
to her sons but will not be likely to do so to her daughters.
Likewise, the mother will not rectify defects being passed
from father to son.

Allowing for possible congenital disadvantages taken on
board by the male at conception, one might suppose that
from then onwards there would be more or less equal
chance of survival for male and female. Not at all.

For some twelve weeks after conception, the embryo
develops without showing sign of sex differentiation. In
fact, the embryo could be described as being androgynous
during this period since the rudimentary reproductive
organs and ducts formed at this stage can become either
male or female. If the embryo is to become female, the
hitherto uncommitted gonads develop into ovaries and,
whilst potential male ducts disintegrate, the female ducts
develop into Fallopian tubes, uterus and vagina. The
potential penis remains as the clitoris. If the embryo is to
become male, a more or less converse process of
disintegration and development takes place, the gonads
becoming testes, the ducts becoming vas deferens,
ejaculatory duct, etc.

There is, however, a remarkable – and for this theme,
significant – potential disparity in this apparently equally-
balanced sex-differentiation process.[38] Embryological
experimentation has demonstrated that if, at an early stage
after differentiation has taken place, the ovaries are
removed from a female foetus, that foetus will continue to
develop as a female. If, on the other hand, the testicles are
removed from a male foetus at a similar stage of
development, the foetus will revert from being male and
become female. There could be no clearer indication than
this that, biologically, the female takes precedence over the
male.

Biological explanation for this bias in favour of the
female demonstrates yet again the need of the male to be
competitive. The key factor for becoming male – a factor
which implies that the embryo would otherwise auto-

matically become female – is the triggering by the father's Y gonosome of the uncommitted gonads to become testes. The testes then secrete a hormone which absorbs the part of the reproductive system which would have become the womb in a female. The testes then need to secrete testosterone to ensure continuing male development.

There are clear intimations here of the underlying supremacy of the female and of the male's need to intervene if the gender is to survive. One research commentator speaks of male hormone activity 'suppressing the under-lying tendency to become female'. Another speaks of the hormone 'attacking and destroying the potential womb'. In fact, after reading so much commentary characterizing the male as parasite, interloper, oppressor, exploiter, attacker, destroyer, etc, one begins to feel that the male is a total disaster and that men ought to apologize for their existence. Perhaps the male's only defence in the end is to point out that he had no choice in the matter. Be that as it may, the fact is that biologically the male does have to 'fight to be male'. And the odds must be that psychologically he has to do so for the rest of his life (evidence for which follows below).

A relevant aside may be mentioned here. Testosterone secretion in the foetus controls male development and could thus be said to be crucial to future 'maleness'. Adrenalin in the mother's bloodstream is known to affect testosterone secretion, tending to suppress it. Increase of stress in the mother during pregnancy increases the amount of adrenalin in her bloodstream, hence tending to suppress testosterone in the foetus if it is male. This has given rise to speculation that there may therefore be a connection between stress during pregnancy and later inclination in male offspring towards homosexuality[39]. In a survey carried out in Germany involving some five hundred subjects, it was found that twice as many homosexuals were born during the six years of World War II than in the six years preceding the war and the six years following it. Connection between stress, hormone-balances during pregnancy and long-term after-effect is very difficult to establish. Apart from the enormous task of accurate monitoring on a large enough scale, there could be any number of other factors affecting the results. If, however, there is a biological connection between maternal stress and homosexuality, it would give substance to the possibility of connection (as suggested earlier) between the emergence of women's liberation and the overt surfacing of male homosexuality over the same period. In brief, the more that women are diverted from giving full attention and care to their maternal role through becoming involved in other, stressful occupations, the greater the likelihood that male homosexuality will increase.

Apart from 'the fight to be male' during the sex-differentiation period of foetal development, it is then evident that the bid for maleness continues and that it has to be made and consolidated before predisposition towards femaleness overtakes and becomes dominant. As in the case of sexual development, hormone activity seems to be the key determinant in all respects, not least that of the relative growth-rates of the brain hemispheres. In this matter, there is much speculation amongst scientists because it is a relatively new area of research and therefore one in which little is known for certain.

One report[40] suggests that testosterone (the principal male hormone) present in the blood of both the mother and the foetus is responsible during the fifth month of pregnancy for inhibiting the growth of the left hemisphere. (That a male hormone should inhibit the left side accords with earlier suggestion that the left-side function is 'feminine' in nature.) In the context of the report, the word 'inhibit' conveyed a sense of negative restraint. However, in view of what has been said about the male need to establish maleness in defiance of preordained proclivity towards femaleness, it would seem to be important for the male that the strength of the feminine-left is positively restrained. The implication must be that restraint of the left prevents its becoming too dominant over the more slowly developing masculine-right hemisphere.

Obviously, developmental problems will arise where there are excesses. An excess of testosterone would cause over-inhibition of the left hemisphere's growth (just as excesses in typically-male behaviour in ordinary life can threaten the welfare of the female). On the other hand, a deficient level of testosterone will mean less restrained growth of the left hemisphere and thus a tendency towards left-brain over-dominance. The latter situation would again accord with the possible connection between the mental state of the mother and its effect on hormone activity in the foetus. If the mother is under stress and secreting an excess of adrenalin, testosterone secretion will be inhibited to an extent where there will not be appropriate inhibition of feminine-left-brain development in the male. This will not prevent continuing development of the foetus; but it may mean improper balance between left and right sides, at the expense of the latter – in effect, a 'mental emasculation' of it.

It has also been found that, in younger people who have suffered accidental, left-hemisphere brain damage, the right side of the brain can take over responsibility for lost left-side functions.[41] A well-recognized example of such changeover can occur when left-side damage deprives the person of speech. In learning to talk again, it can be the undamaged right side which undertakes the task, one with which it is not ordinarily concerned.

It is further suggested that when there has been excessive inhibition of left-hemisphere development during pregnancy the right side will tend to take on some responsibility for functions which the left side is failing to develop as it should. This principle of the right being required to make up for retarded development of the left – in which concession it will need to sacrifice some of its own potential – appears to confirm the natural and conditioned dominance of the feminine-left over masculine-right. It seems that the latter, if the former is for some reason deficient, must to some extent abandon its own interests. This is understandable given that ability to survive as a group-member must take precedence. (In any case, the right side's own talents cannot be expressed if the left is malfunctioning.) As we shall see, this tendency for the right to defer to the left continues psychologically throughout adult life. Personal ambitions and aspirations are always subject to the pressures and demands of social responsibilities.

The suggestion that the right hemisphere may have to support or take over functions of an under-developed left hemisphere has been cited as a possible cause of left-handedness.[42] Left-handedness is more common in males than females, and the former are more prone to mental difficulties such as dyslexia and autism – both indicative of inter-hemisphere liaison difficulties. Left-handers are also twice as prone to migraine as right-handers.

It would be reasonable to infer from all these observations that some confusion and possibly conflict arises, especially for the male, when degrees of imbalance occur in the relative strengths of the brain hemispheres during gestation. The activity of a hormone such as testosterone is clearly crucial; both too much or too little of it can have long-term consequences after birth. It could be that increasing prevalence of left-handedness, dyslexia, migraine, schizophrenia, etc, could be connected with stress during pregnancy. And, as intimated earlier, such increase of stress could be connected with the repercussions of women's liberation, i.e. competition in the mother between maternal responsibility and personal ambition.

Generally, the left hemisphere develops in advance of the right in both genders. But there is a difference between them in the rate of advance. In the female foetus, the left develops faster. Five months after conception, the female's left side is two weeks in advance of the male's. At birth, it is as much as four weeks ahead. Given that gestation takes nine months, this advanced strength of the left in the female constitutes a comparatively large left-side advantage over the male. In other words, she is potentially far better equipped at birth to assimilate conditioning influences. At the same time, the male's right side is relatively stronger than the female's.

At birth, the neural connections between the two hemispheres are not fully established. This suggests that, at this juncture, there is still a degree of autonomy in each side. This is borne out by observation of preferences adopted in the baby's learning to manipulate (bearing in mind that the left side of the brain operates the right side of the body and *vice versa*). For four to five months after birth, the baby tends to favour use of the left hand. For the next two months, it becomes ambidextrous. And then, up to the age of eight, the child becomes very much committed to use of the right hand. (The phases are typical of the natural right-hander, about six out of seven.)

Interpretation of these preferences would indicate that for a short period after birth, the still-autonomous right hemisphere can take precedence and initiative. This would accord with the notion that the masculine-right must make its bid for exercise and expression before the feminine-left can become dominant. It is as if, during those early months after being ejected from the confines of the womb 'into space' and relative independence (cf. evolution of creatures from the medium of water to dry land/open air), the baby's first interest is spatial exploration. And its first concern – through use of tactile and auditory senses – is to find food. As described earlier, exploration and food procurement are typically-male role-assignments.

That initial, brief period – though to the baby it is 'timeless' because its left side has not developed concept of passing time – is followed by the shorter period of ambidexterity which suggests that the two hemispheres are in balance and learning to co-operate as the inter-hemisphere connections become established. Perhaps significantly, this is the period when the two eyes, which have previously been 'wandering about' independently, begin to co-ordinate and focus. The outside world becomes visually integrated. Although the newly-born baby responds to light and dark, it is several months before it responds to seeing things without hearing them. As the two eyes and the two hemispheres learn to work together, what had hitherto been an experience of random sounds and tactile encounters, of periodic light and dark, starts to become a continuous totality. And what had been a dimensionless chaos forms into a finite, three-dimensional world of connected objects with definite meaning.

Projected into its implications for later psychological development, this co-ordinating (or 'marrying') of the hemispheres, and their relative strengths at the time, becomes very important. It would suggest, for example, that concentration of attention and balanced view – the equivalent of the eyes co-ordinating and focussing on a single point – depend on the state of balance and harmony between the two sides of the mind. Likewise, when applied to personal relationships, the implication must be that co-operation between two people much depends on their having a focal point of mutual interest, i.e. a common purpose.

After this transformative interval – when a world of random stimuli becomes a meaningful continuum – growing emphasis on continuing use of the right hand as the actively manipulative one indicates increasing dominance of left-hemisphere functions and motivation. The next seven years are ones of maximum sensitivity to external environment, of rapid learning and conditioning within the social ethos. Whilst the left brain is assimilating a prodigious input of information and instruction, the right will be doing its best to explore and test means to gain pleasure and power. Its embassies are always up against inculcated pressure to conform, to forego selfish behaviour in order to meet external requirements and expectations.

After this seven- to eight-year indoctrination, the connection between left and right hemispheres is fully established in most children. Where it is not so, there will be what are regarded as socially-unacceptable problems. The great majority will have developed sufficient co-ordination to move on to further education and eventually to become contributing participants in society; but there will be varying left-right balances from one individual to another. Up to puberty, and especially through adolescence, there will be considerable variation in how individuals experience and express their right-side talents and ambitions, whether it be in their interests, occupations or their relationships, especially sexual. Nevertheless, all such bid for individual identity, status and power is likely to be disciplined and channelled into compliance with the group's need for stability, security and continuity.

The group's continuity, as previously described, is in effect focussed on female procreativity; and traditionally this requires male co-operation and support. In past times, the upsurge of sexual power at puberty would have been directed easily enough straight into this priority. Girls will have been immediately initiated into their maternal role and boys into their procurer-warrior roles. As societies developed technologically and became more sophisticated, however, the educational process took longer and, since economic independence also took longer to establish, the procreative aspect of sexuality had to be postponed. Inevitably, this curb on left-side motivation could not easily be counterbalanced by equally-effective restraint of the right side. That side was bound to experience increasing frustration. And that in turn shifted emphasis towards coping with the erotic, pleasure-gain aspect of sexual energy. As has been evident in recent decades, the social consequences have not been easy to manage. To try to repress the energy is to escalate the danger of aggression and violence; to give it licence is not only to increase problems of unwanted pregnancy, venereal disease, etc, but also, more significantly, to undermine the basis of the social structure. The only alternative is to encourage direction of the energy into ambition for material gain, status and power. Needless to say, due to disparity between individuals, this can lead to divisiveness in society because of the tendency for the stronger to exploit the weaker.

After puberty through to young adulthood, there is usually a masculine-right surge of initiative and enterprise in both genders (until recent times more evident in the male than the female). During this phase, the individual experiences self-generated desire to explore, to be adventurous, to be independent, to prove oneself to oneself, to gain status, to succeed, and so on. The emphasis here is on self-development. It may well involve rebelliousness, wanting to change the group ethos, even to opt out of it altogether. But, in due course, such diversion is likely to evaporate and there will be a falling in with mainstream social expectations. Left-brain dominance will reassert itself. For many, psychologically, it may be the end of 'the fight to be male' since, from then on, masculine-right initiatives will always be overridden by feminine-left fears, responsibilities and obligations. (Though, for some, there can be a resurgence of frustration and rebelliousness in mid-life.) The quest for individuality has to be pursued in the group's terms, not in one's own; or abandoned altogether.

Though in principle the above applies to both genders, there is in effect difference between them. The inter-hemisphere co-ordination takes place more rapidly, more substantially and more effectively in the female than the male. This is where we may find significance in the fact (p. 73) that the corpus callosum – the network of nerves connecting the hemispheres – is more extensive in the female. By extrapolation, this physiological fact would suggest that the female experiences less polarization and, hence, less contradiction, between the two sides of her mind. It would mean that her right-side powers co-operate better with, and are more committed to, her left-side motivation and disposition. In other terms, she is more strongly drawn by fear of insecurity and discontinuity than she is stimulated by desire for status and to exercise power. In the male, where the inter-hemisphere connection is less strong, the balance of priorities tend towards the opposite – favouring risk in order to achieve ambition. It should hastily be added, however, that in the wake of women's liberation, this traditional difference between the genders is rapidly diminishing. As the female's procreative commitment for one reason and another decreases, so emphasis shifts towards her masculine, right-side ambitions.

One commentator on brain differences between the genders states: 'The clear implication is that women . . . are less lateralized (in their thinking) . . . Reduced lateralization has both a good and a bad effect on mental abilities, which may well explain some of the classic differences between men and women.'[43]

What the 'bad effects' may be should become apparent in due course. The 'good effects' are best appreciated in the context of the female's greater proclivity to commit herself to the persuasions of consensus and her generally-superior ability to come to terms with circumstances as she finds them. (If she cannot cope, she will be inclined to surrender rather than contend.) As indication of her better integration, she usually learns to speak, walk and read earlier than the male. And as evidence of her greater commitment to group-survival, she reaches puberty quicker than the male.

The reduced lateralization and stronger left-hemisphere dominance in the average woman implies better 'earthing', better 'lateral thinking', more common sense, better psychological commitment to the needs of the body; overall, superior mind-body integration. This ensures that she is constitutionally stronger, both physically and psychologically. Whilst she is tougher and more resilient, a man is more vulnerable.

Nature – as if in recognition of this vulnerability – makes a quantified attempt to compensate for the imbalance.[44] There are approximately 120 XY-male conceptions for every 100 XX-female. Due to the greater propensity towards congential flaw in the male foetus, and the greater number of miscarriages of males, the ratio during gestation is reduced to 106:100. Greater male mortality at birth and during infancy and childhood brings the genders into numerical parity at the age of puberty – which, due to Nature's obsession with reproduction, is what one might expect.

During adulthood, the ratio begins to go into reverse. Between the ages of twenty to thirty, a male is more than three times as likely to die (be killed) as the female (despite risks she may have to face in childbirth). This is accounted for not so much by his constitutionally greater vulnerability to disease as by his being more likely to take dangerous risk, the greater likelihood of his being placed in hazardous situations and his greater exposure to stress. In other words, the (traditionally) competing, adventurous and procuring nature of the male's brief renders him more likely to be the victim of accident and strain. Of course, the more that liberated women seek equal rights and opportunities to compete and strive in what used to be called 'a man's world', the more they will expose themselves to similar risk, especially where the stress factor is concerned.

To put the above the other way round, the more pronounced lateralization in the male – i.e., the greater comparative strength of his right hemisphere – makes him more likely to place personal ambition above concern for his own welfare. He is more likely to suppress or ignore his left-side fears of logical consequence and take greater risk with his health and life, i.e. his continuity. He is more motivated by gaining and retaining status than he is with longevity.

Thus, by about the age of fifty-five, men are about twice as likely to die as women, from both external interventions and internal breakdown. By the age of seventy, the original conception ratio has reversed and there are an estimated 120 surviving females to every 100 males. Beyond that, and finally, a woman may expect to live five years longer than a man; hence the considerable preponderance of elderly women over elderly men, probably as many as four to one in developed societies.

Underlying the whole scenario of male striving during life, there is the unrelenting driving power of the testosterone secreted by his testicles, that hormone which twelve weeks after his conception dictated his gender and precipitated his drive for 'maleness', a drive which continues to fire both body and mind right through to old age. (The typically-female hormones cease their compelling effect at menopause, when the woman is only 'half-way' through her present life-expectancy.) That hormone coursing through his bloodstream throughout life promotes the aggression and assertion necessary for him to be able to compete and gain – in sexual and, by extension, in all other arenas of his socio-economic circumstance – right through until almost his dying breath. This drive may have given him reputation as 'the stronger sex' but in many ways it is the cause of his downfall.[45] Its power constantly taxes his constitution; and, as it were, it wears him out. Psychologically, as well as physically, 'castration' means an end to the meaning of 'maleness'.

Some quaint evidence to demonstrate the demand of testosterone comes from unexpected sources. For example, during the time of the Ottoman Empire it was noted that eunuchs tended to live considerably longer than uncastrated servants. It was found also that, in mental institutions in the United States where castration of uncontrollably violent inmates used to be practised, those who had been neutered lived on average some fourteen years longer than those who had been left intact. This is somewhat tenuous evidence but, of course, where humans are concerned, research into the effects of castration is not feasible. Its effect on animals certainly provides corroborating evidence. It is well known that neutered cats live longer than those not neutered. And the degree of stress and aggression shown by numbers of male rats kept in close confinement is much reduced if they are castrated. As a somewhat perverse aside, those militant feminists who advocate the castration of rapists could perhaps, if they had their way, be doing such desperate men an unexpected favour.

Whether or not the demand-effect of testosterone is directly related to the male's shorter life-expectancy, it is certainly responsible for his expending considerable energy in matters sexual. His potency and virility as a young man drive him in pursuit of the female and he will be willing to have intercourse as often as his resources allow. Frequency depends, of course, on degree of opportunity. (If opportunities are insufficient, he may have to relieve build-up of frustration in other ways.) But, given unlimited opportunity, frequency also depends on recuperation time required between emissions. Since the female loses 'nothing of herself' in orgasm and her recuperation time is theoretically minimal, the male's need to pace his advances according to recuperation of his resources has traditionally meant that he should be the one to initiate intercourse.

As suggested earlier, one of the threatening aspects of women's liberation for the male is that the female is now encouraged (by sex therapists, women's magazines, etc.) to take sexual initiative if she so desires. If the male can respond, (perhaps) well and good; if he cannot, his virility comes into question. Nothing is more likely to invite a woman's scorn more than a man's failure to demonstrate his virility. This challenge may or may not present serious problems for the young male. It is perhaps more likely to do so when he reaches mid-life. For at a time when the male is likely to be experiencing longer recuperation times between emissions, and is hence less frequently disposed to have intercourse, the middle-aged female – due to

menopausal hormone-adjustments within herself – is
likely to experience a surge of libido. Significantly, as her
procreative-hormone secretion declines, she experiences a
release of typically-male erotic desire. For a long-term
marital relationship, this shift can obviously have considerable, disruptive repercussions. In this age of liberation, dissatisfied wives are just as likely to seek extra-
marital sex as dissatisfied husbands are.[46] In fact, the latter
are probably more likely to be looking for non-
competitive, sympathetic companionship. At this stage in
heterosexual relationship, it can become all-too-apparent
which is the weaker sex.

Lesser brain-lateralization combined with stronger
left-hemisphere development favours girls in the learning
of language and the ability to put their feelings and
thoughts into words. The stronger and more independent
right-hemisphere in the male can give a boy advantage in
interests requiring visualization. He is likely to be more at
ease with abstract concepts, with spatial relationships and
with the symbolic. He therefore tends to be happier than a
girl with subjects such as mathematics and geometry. But,
on the whole, psychologically, greater polarization of the
two sides of his mind – his greater tendency 'to be in two
minds' – can be socially disadvantageous. He is less likely
to conform with conventional expectations and requirements; and more likely to have difficulty in coming to
terms with the responsibilities befitting sexual conduct.

A fair indicator of this male unease (though now
increasing in the female also) may be seen in the
association by men of drinking alcohol with sociability.
Alcohol affects inter-hemisphere balance, in effect releasing tensions caused by imbalance. Frustrating restriction
and inhibition forced on the right side by left-side conditioning and caution are gradually alleviated, giving greater
right-hand side freedom of self-expression.[47] To a certain
degree, this helps the ability to socialize without worrying
too much about self-image. Beyond that certain degree, the
right side starts to become over-dominant and caution
relatively reduced. Challenge becomes more outspoken.
Sexual desire may be released; but, as the two sides of the
brain lose co-ordination, it is less and less likely to be

pursued and fulfilled. Behaviour becomes less controlled and motor-skills deteriorate. With increasing excess, all sense of balance is lost, both physically and psychologically. At worst, right-side frustrations are released in anger, giving rise to indiscriminately aggressive and violent behaviour.

States of inter-hemisphere balance vary considerably from person to person of either gender. Male stereotypes are typically right-brain dominant and female, left-brain dominant; but the reverse is not uncommon, especially in this age of women's liberation. The states can also vary from time to time, especially from one phase of life to another. It is far from uncommon, for example, to find that men become increasingly left-brain dominant as they grow older whilst women can become increasingly right-brain dominant after menopause. The 'hen-pecked' husband and the 'merry widow' are two images of such reversal. It all depends on balance between the desire for status and power on the one hand and the fear of insecurity and discontinuity on the other.

Although it is difficult to make clear-cut generalizations, there are certain trends which typically apply. The better integration of the female's hemispheres does have general, psychological consequences which demonstrate differences of degree rather than kind. Her lesser dichotomy of mind enables her to be more 'single-minded' in her pursuits. She can make non-intellectual decisions quicker than the male and is more determined in matters which threaten her security and that of her offspring. Fundamentally, it is her superior survival-instinct which makes her the stronger sex.

The measure of how well or how badly the left side is performing is indicated by feelings. In principle, the left side receives messages and is influenced by the feelings generated by those messages. Such feelings may be to do with present physical state, e.g. comfortable or painful. Other, more subtle ones arise as a consequence of interaction with social environment. Overall sense of security and well-being, or lack of it, depends much on success or failure to attract reassuring response from others, through speech and action. Usually, we are disposed to please others by presenting an acceptable – preferably an approved or admired – public image. Feed-back generates the feelings by which we can monitor how well or badly we have performed in the attempt. Because of her left-side bias, the female is likely to attach greater importance to such feelings, and to be guided by them more than the male. He tends to be less sensitive to them or prefers to ignore them.

Meanwhile, right-side motivation – conventionally stronger in the male – desires to compete in order to gain pleasure, status, power, etc, for self. This generates emotions which are essentially out-going messages intended to manipulate or challenge others. In full spate, they are likely to override sensitivity to the feelings of others. Ambition cares little about self-image, disapproval, tact, pleasing others and so on. The male is more likely to give thoughtless and explosive vent to his negative emotions than the female is.

Within the individual, the juxtaposition of conflicting fears and desires can readily cause mental tension and stress. Contradiction between the two sides of the mind can frequently occur when the right wants to pursue something out of self-interest whilst the left simultaneously fears possible consequences. But this is where the female has an advantageous edge. Because her two sides are better integrated, she is better able to 'make up her mind'. With less circumspection and doubt than the male, she will more readily either do what is expected of her or pursue her desires with determination. She is better prepared to abide by her feelings or give controlled expression to her emotions. Meanwhile, the male, in greater confusion, finds himself having to suppress his feelings or fire off his emotions recklessly. Perhaps in no other circumstance is the difference more apparent than in a typical marital confrontation. Faced with the wife's single-mindedness, combined with her better control of emotions and argument, the husband all-too-often finds himself confounded and having to resort to outbursts of anger born of frustration, or having to make a humiliating withdrawal.

Given that the competitive and power-seeking right-side is likely to be more developed in the male, it is understandable why it is he who, through frustration, has gained notoriety as the wilfully aggressive and violent gender. Underlying that display, however, is the fact that he is more aware of the contradictions within himself. His behavioural excesses are often due to his being unable to resolve his inner doubt and guilt. In extreme, in order to mask his sense of desperation, he can seem to have no conscience at all in pursuing fanatical and sometimes highly destructive obsessions. Such arrogance, vanity and bravado as he sometimes exhibits is only a cover-up for a deep sense of inadequacy and uncertainty. Generally speaking, the more inflated the male ego, the greater the lack of inner balance and integrity.

The male's greater awareness of being plagued by the incompatibility of the divided motivations within himself gives rise, for example, to his being a less convincing liar than the female. This underlies the common view that a husband is less able to deceive his wife than *vice versa*. A wife can conceal infidelity far better than a husband partly because she is less aware of the contradiction of loyalties within herself, partly because she has less compunction in getting what she wants, partly because she is better able to persuade herself of the rectitude of her actions . . . and no doubt partly because the husband is so preoccupied with trying to conceal his own infidelity that he does not notice.

Greater lateralization and a more autonomous right-side in the male means that boys are likely to be more disobedient and rebellious than girls during childhood. Their behaviour tends to be more aggressive and they are more competitive, attributes which they are usually encouraged to work out at the physical level in fields of sport rather than anywhere else. Boys are also more prone to epilepsy – which might be described as a kind of mental 'fuse-blowing' in which the two sides of the mind are thrown into confusion and convulsion.

One positive advantage for the male can derive from his greater lateralization. If he has also developed a degree of objectivity and thus perspective, his ability to detach from and witness the two sides of predicament gives him a better sense of humour. In the old alchemical tradition sense of humour means having a balanced view of all constituent elements in a given situation, i.e. a sense of values, of proportion and, often, of the ridiculous. In its modern context, sense of humour means being in a good humour and having the ability to laugh one's way out of contradiction by rising above it. Which is why men make better comedians, clowns, jesters, 'fools', etc. (In its negative aspect, such ability can turn to cynicism and bitter sarcasm.) On the other hand, the female – being less lateralized and thus more likely to be emotionally involved in situations and more seriously committed to a conditioned viewpoint – tends to find relief from the irreconcilable through reducing herself to tears. Which is why women are more distraught than men by tragedy. In other words, whilst men will try to transcend the catastrophic, women will tend to dissolve into it.

Beyond the point where contradictions born of lateralization can be solved or dissolved by laughter or tears, there are conditions where the two sides are so deeply in contention that they simply refuse to co-operate. Such dissociation would give rise to symptoms typical of personality disorders and 'split-mind' conditions, as in forms of schizophrenia.

Schizophrenia is not, of course, confined to males; it is not, for example, uncommon in adolescent females.[48] Case histories of clinical presentation of the disorder can be analysed to show that, in principle, right-side bid for self-expression is being strongly inhibited by over-dominant, left-side conditioning. The right therefore forcefully by-passes and overrules the conditioning of the left, which can give rise to deception, lying, outburst of uncontrolled behaviour and so on. Or it dissociates from the left and withdraws from active participation, which gives rise to a vacuous, near-inert condition in which there is only automatic or habitual response to stimuli. In other circumstances, the former 'by-pass strategy' can be seen represented in the person who adopts 'multiple-personality' or leads a 'double-life'; and the latter may be seen in the elderly person who just sits and stares, showing no sign of taking initiative or interest in anything.

It was suggested earlier that there is likely to be a surge of right-side power – manifesting as desire for self-expression, independence, individuality, etc. – coincident with the upsurge of sexual energy at puberty. Schizophrenic condition in adolescent females may be accounted for by the fact that a girl is likely to be more strongly affected than a boy by social conditioning, especially as conveyed by a dominating parent. When the desire for autonomy comes up against the fear of not conforming to expectation or failing to please, the inner turmoil of contradiction can be difficult to resolve. If the conflict becomes intolerable, 'splitting the mind' may be the only self-defence, self-survival option.

The adolescent male, on the other hand, though not immune from such breakdown, is likely to respond to the right-side surge of desire for autonomy more readily. That side of his mind will usually have been stronger throughout childhood and he will have been more used to rebelling against the authority of conditioning and to acting in self-interest. He is better prepared for taking self-gain initiatives, if necessary challenging or consciously contriving to by-pass parental or social pressures.

The male's difficulty starts to become more apparent during the next phase of life, young adulthood. Whereas, conventionally, the young woman will have little or no difficulty in falling in with social expectation – i.e., getting married, organizing a home, having children – the young man may do. His personal ambitions may align comfortably enough with the expectation that he will earn a living in order to support a family; on the other hand, they may not, and he will then feel reluctant to forego his freedom to pursue them at will. Usually, his love for a particular woman will overwhelm his apprehensions and he will seek to gain wealth and status within the structure of his social responsibilities. Of course, all the above is changing in the wake of women's liberation.

The young man's disciplining of his right-side enterprise in order to align with social expectation may not cause him too much difficulty for some years, though there are likely to be outbursts of frustration in one form or another. It is when he reaches middle-age that past suppression and compromise can seriously begin to erupt into his psyche. He may then begin to feel that he has not succeeded in his career, that it has not been fulfilling, that he was pressured for the wrong reasons, and that he has failed to develop his real talents and interests. The reason for such misgiving is understandable. Formal education is primarily left-brain biased and the young man (or woman), under pressure to follow group-prescribed occupation in established job-markets, is tempted to take the safe, predictable and obvious opportunity which will employ his developed left-brain talents. Coincidentally, right-brain talents are generally not so well-developed and thus to rely on them entirely (e.g. as self-employed) would be riskier, and initially less well rewarded. Bias and pressure is such that he will judge it safer to take up a career in, say, banking than run the riskier course of pursuing his love of, say, music or painting – i.e. anything depending for success on right-side powers of self-expression. Most careers are not, of course, exclusively 'left-black' or 'right-white'; they will involve in greater or lesser degree the use of both sides; but the chances are that the demands of the former will outweigh and eclipse fulfilling development of the latter.

For the middle-aged man, assessment of his career chosen in youth can be the cause of much inter-hemisphere doubt and disquiet. A few may be moved to make an abrupt change of course, abandon their careers and do something totally different in line with their right-side aspirations. The trouble here is that talents may have been denied too long, and they have not been exercised and developed enough for there to be more than marginal scope for application. Most therefore have to content themselves with expressing them in hobbies and pastimes, pressing on meantime with their established occupations for the rest of their working lives. Due to the tendency for the left-brain to become increasingly domi-nant with age, the fires of inspiration are not likely then to burn again with the same compelling urgency as they did in the younger man.

The misgivings underlying the older man's assessment of his working career have deeper ramifications than simply whether the right course was chosen or not. The marital focus on dependent family will by then be losing definition, both husband and wife will be having to adjust to the loss of that common ground, and hence the sense of redundancy will begin to loom in the mental background. And this decline may be exacerbated by awareness that there is not an unlimited future. Horizons are going to be reduced by increasing physical limitations, and possibly by deterioration of mental powers also. There has got to be a living with mistakes irredeemable and ambitions aborted. Needless to say, for the two sides of the mind to come to terms with such anxieties and frustrations is no easy matter. And whereas the female's sense of fulfilment and security may find sound focus in her children and grandchildren, such reassurance is less likely to satisfy the male. For reasons which will be suggested later, the prospect of death seems to haunt the male more than the female.

The more liberated women become, the more they will tend to be affected by the typically-male dilemma, and be afflicted by the kind of stress which accompanies it. There is the possibility that in fact inner conflict will prove even more stressful for her than for him. Whereas paternal commitment requires self-discipline in order to fulfil a supporting role, a woman's bid for status and power in her own right is likely to place such ambition in direct conflict with fulfilment of herself in her instinctive, maternal role. For her, pursuit of ambition will require a degree of self-denial as well as self-discipline.

On the other hand, this may be to underestimate the determination and resilience of the female. Her better hemisphere integration not only gives her better ability to control and change her mind – a facility which is said to be her privilege – but she can compromise without a second thought and better conceal contradiction from herself. This is not to say that such tactics are conscious and deliberate; they are methods of dealing with crises which indicate her better innate capacity for self-defence and self-preservation.

Being more schizoid and less able to convince himself of rectitude – even though through pride he may be forced to put a brave face on a decision once it is made or desperately pursue a course once it has been undertaken – the male is all-too-aware that for him compromise will in the end be self-defeating. He knows full well that in persuading himself he is undermining his own integrity and self-confidence – a penalty for which he may over-compensate with displays of bluff and bluster, or try to escape through some venial indulgence.

Fundamentally, self-confidence is dependent on positive, successful deployment of sexual drive and energy. Physiologically and psychologically, the female's confidence is based on her ability to attract successfully, a more passive disposition related to her success in conceiving. Male confidence is based on his out-going success in competing and penetrating, a more active embassy which is, as it were, open-ended. Biologically, he is programmed to impregnate as many females as he can. As monogamous relationship became the accepted norm in human society, and promiscuity became immoral and less feasible, the male's sexual drive had to be translated into other socially-acceptable pursuits. Success and self-confidence for the male came to be measured in terms of institutional status and acquisition of wealth. But there are now signs that such platforms are not so sure as they used to be – for several reasons, not least among them being increasing male redundancy and female competition. As a consequence, male self-confidence is increasingly under threat, whereas female confidence, moving from its passive base to an active one, steadily strengthens. For him, loss of power equates with sexual impotency. The female may fear failure to attract or being infertile; but not being impotent.

Taking into account all the factors introduced in this chapter, especially the indisputable biological ones, there can be little doubt which is the weaker sex. The 'facts of life' – in the broadest terms but definitely including the sexual – indicate which gender holds the balance of power. 'In some fundamental sense, women, like all female mammals, come first. . . Males are simply modified females tailored to a particular role in the reproductive process.'[49]

In his genesis, the young male is, of course, ignorant of all this preordained, biological bias against him. He enters life, seeks to enjoy the pleasures and avoid the pains of it, and sets out to find adventure, explore possibilities, test authority . . . generally getting involved in the business of learning and surviving. Then the hormones step up their power, urging him to compete and succeed. He becomes aware of gender difference and, as he comes to adolescence, the stimulation of sex focusses his attention on intimate relationship with the female. As he discovers the other gender, he learns also what is expected of his own gender. Unlike the careless games of childhood, the need to prove himself and to win become serious. He begins to understand and sometimes suffer the penalties of failure, and to wrestle with uncomfortable contradictions in his mind. There is no avoiding the demand to make choices and decisions, some of which he realizes will affect the rest of his life.

As a general rule, the adolescent male will make those choices and decisions in deference to rather than in defiance of the conditioning instilled into his left brain. And so he will continue to do so as an adult, especially when he has taken on his assigned role in the reproductive process. No matter what social status and power he may gain en route (even as an 'anti-social' element), he will directly or indirectly still be expending his life-energy in terms dictated by the group in the interests of its survival.

Is there no exception to this rule? Apart from the capacity for technological inventiveness, is there any advantage for the male in having a relatively stronger and more independent right brain? Or is it just an evolutionary anomaly which happens to give him a lot of trouble and thus compounds the weaknesses of his gender?

7   Masculine Right

The accumulation of evidence introduced in previous chapters reads like some kind of fateful judgement on the male: the liberation of women and their retrieval of equal rights, their new-found determination to compete and achieve, their gaining of economic power and independence, the accelerating growth of population and the exhaustion of natural resources, pollution of the environment and growing concern about longer-term repercussions of scientific and technological enterprise, increasing redundancy of the male in his traditional roles, reduction of his prospects to non-creative, unfulfilling occupations . . . and so on. All such factors – and others not mentioned, such as the decline of patriarchal and paternal authority – suggest that the male has lately been somewhat overtaken by the tide of events, and that the unforeseen consequences of his past endeavours are now coming unhappily home to roost.

On the other hand, it may all mean that the male has completed his brief, and is now simply becoming obsolete. If a species comes to the end of its evolutionary potential, there is no further need for genetic mutation and thus no further need for two sexes. As the genders lose the necessity for polarized differentiation of roles and become less and less distinguishable from each other, they cease to be complementary and start to compete with each other for survival. And there can be no doubt which one is likely to lose out. In 'the battle of the sexes', the male is now being forced off the high ground he has clung to for several millennia. As he loses his sense of gender identity, is there any worthwhile and dignified way in which he can justify his continuing existence?

All the considerations introduced so far have been confined to the human being as a sexually-differentiated,

socio-economic creature. Although survival and proliferation have always been man's principal objectives, they are
not, of course, quite the whole story. There are features of
uniquely-human activity which have so far been left out of
account. Space dictates that they can only be brought into
the picture in brief and general terms sufficient for the
purpose of making certain points and drawing conclusions
relevant to this present theme.

The nature of all these areas of activity can be readily
appreciated in one simple respect: they are all interests and
pursuits which do not directly make any contribution to
the chances of the group's existential survival. They are not
primarily intended to improve social security, though in
their effect they can enhance the well-being of the group
and help it to gain status and identity. Fundamentally,
their purpose is to exercise, develop and enrich the mind
and life of the individual.

Although a fair number of such activities could be listed
under this general definition, three principal ones will
here suffice – the creative arts, religion and philosophy/
psychology. All three may be said to have their pure and
fine, their applied and their devalued or decadent aspects.
At their worst, they can be pretentious, deluding and
perverse. At their best, they can be appreciated as man's
'higher aspirations', concerned as they are with desire for
beauty, love and truth or wisdom.

The concepts of beauty, love and wisdom can be learned
about through left-brained education (given an environment which values them); and they can be talked and read
about endlessly in theory. But for them to have real value
and meaning, they have to be experienced in practice by
the individual. Once the individual has an appetite for
them, he or she will be inspired and motivated to explore
and express them personally in whatever ways appeal.
And to do that creatively and rewardingly requires use of
the right hemisphere of the brain.

In the creative arts, for example, appreciation and
expression depend on such right-side faculties as
imagination, visualization, awareness of spatial relationship, appreciation of sound, of light, of colour, of
symbolic meaning, and so on. The right is also the side of

enterprise, exploration and the desire to know and understand the ultimate limits of human experience.

If creative ideas are to be expressed in any form, left-side abilities are required. Without the skills and techniques previously learned, there can be no translating of thoughts, images and sounds into visible, audible or tangible expression. It is only when the aspirant has become fully conversant with a particular medium of artistic expression and has become well-practised in its techniques that it is possible for him or her to exercise individual talents. Left-side abilities on their own only enable the copying, repeating, reproducing of what has already been done before by others. It is only through exercise and development of right-side powers that inspiration will come for creative originality.

We may see here clear correspondence between feminine-left/masculine-right co-operation in the individual's creative act and male/female co-operation in the procreative act – the left being the repository of the means of manifestation and the right being the impregnating inspiration. There is direct analogy between inspiration and 'giving birth' to creative concept at the psychological level and insemination, conception and giving birth at the physical level.

We can only guess as to how man's artistic aspirations first emerged. The earliest humans must have been so committed to procurement, procreation, protection and other survival necessities in a hostile environment that we would assume that they had little time or energy to spare for anything else. And yet, from those earliest times, right-side powers of visualization must undoubtedly have been stirring. Given the incentive to envisage and invent means to enhance their chances of survival, it would be reasonable to surmise that creativity had its beginnings in design. Those first humans will have developed an eye for shaping wood, bone, stone and, later, clay and metal in order to manufacture more and more efficient tools, weapons, utensils, shelters, etc. Such crafts would have been the beginning of applying the talent of visualization to design of product. Perhaps thus was established one of the first principles of beauty – that beauty of form is related to efficiency of function.

At some juncture, however, prehistoric humans took further creative initiatives with far less obvious purpose. For example, they began to draw and carve signs, symbols and images, and make representational objects, of no practical use. Nowadays, we take such activity for granted; but, when one stops to wonder why those first humans began to do such things, the more extraordinary they seem.

Perhaps one of our ancestors was sitting on the ground one day, idly moving a stick through the earth or sand in front of him, and suddenly saw that he had drawn lines which reminded him of the form of some creature he knew well. Or perhaps he came across a piece of wood or stone the shape of which resembled some familiar animal, a recognition which prompted him to carve or sculpt it into even greater likeness. Beyond that, we could assume that he found the pastime pleasing and that he went on doing it for enjoyment, getting better and better at it as his skills and tools improved. Or perhaps the discovery surprised him, even frightened him. Perhaps he thought he had stumbled on some awesome and magical power.

And then, the same kind of accidental process could have happened in his experience of sound and movement, when he found that he could imitate other creatures. Repeating their sounds and movements pleased him, and the magic of it prompted him to devise rituals of song and rhythmic dance. Meanwhile, his ability to relate certain sounds to particular forms and actions gave him the opportunity to create language.

We can only speculate as to what immediate significance these creative and artistic innovations had at the time of their origin. Commentators are generally agreed that these capacities must have become linked in the minds of those ancestors with imagined powers which were invested in such magical images, objects and performances. In particular, they must have felt that they had discovered the means to influence and perhaps control that which threatened them and that which they needed to procure for survival.

Be that as it may, the point is that man was beginning to

exercise his right-hemisphere powers. And he was able to do this because his level of consciousness permitted him to become both self-conscious and objectively conscious. Into his detached 'space of mind', he could consider, contemplate in abstract, imagining and visualizing how he could improve his condition. And as it pleased him to design, experiment, decorate, fashion, sing and dance, he must have felt awe and wonder at the world in which he had become aware of himself. And perhaps from there sprang another principle of beauty – the sheer splendour of the natural world (when non-threatening) and the joy of being witness to it.

Elaboration of vocal sounds allowed increasingly subtle language to evolve, not just to give meaning to a range of objects and actions but to describe feelings and emotions and to convey abstract ideas, thoughts and images. The ability to communicate more and more complicated messages enabled more efficient co-operation, better organization, the passing on of detailed information, and so on. This inevitably helped the group to survive; and it also provided a powerful vehicle for the individual to bid for status and identity as intelligence became as important as muscle-power. But, beyond that, it provided a vehicle for self-expression. Accounts of exploits and experiences could be told; and, with the help of imagination and vision, be retold from one generation to the next as romantic legend. The poetry and drama of the story-teller did not have to confine itself to historical fact; it could relate the whole range of human experience and recount the deepest mysteries of the human condition. And when the means were invented to represent the spoken word by written signs, the wealth of inherited knowledge and wisdom ceased to be dependent on the limits of human memory for its retention through the ages. By the time we come to the beginning of recorded history, self-expression through creative arts and crafts is well-established and has flourished in civilization after civilization ever since, high peaks of refinement often being followed by troughs of decadence.

Although such creativity becomes part of the group's culture and tradition, and is looked upon by the group as a feature of its status and identity – as, of course, many nations hasten to do today – it is as well to bear in mind that all of it originates through the inspiration of a relatively small number of individuals. Also, that all such achievement is projected expression of human psychological experience. It is all man-created and it is of no interest to Nature, which is only concerned with physical survival and proliferation. In other words, it could be said that right-brain aspirations, when directed towards art rather than, say, applied science and technology, are 'unnatural'.

Truly right-brain, creative inspiration in the arts has throughout history seemingly always originated in the male. Which is not to say that the female has not contributed to the artistic activities of the group. But – as in the case of most men involved in the arts – women have participated rather than originated.[50] The vast majority of those involved use skills and techniques learned by the left brain to imitate, repeat and reproduce. Degrees of right-brain talent will be employed in modifications, new interpretations and arrangements, etc. But all such exercise – very important though it is for the development of the individual and the continuity of the culture – tends to stem from the original inspirations of a few. And those few have seemingly always been male.

Feminists have frequently been heard asserting that male dominance in the creative arts is entirely due to women having been denied opportunity to express themselves because of male prejudice against them. It could well be countered that women have had just as much (if not more) time and opportunity as men in many past cultures and civilizations. Besides, in more recent times, women have participated in large numbers in the visual, written and performing arts; yet still the leading composers, dramatists, choreographers, painters, film-makers, poets, etc., are predominantly men. It seems far more likely that until recently women have had neither the inclination nor the inspiration. If they had had, they would have expressed such inspiration, despite any resistance or prejudice. Historical accounts show that creatively-inspired men have frequently had to contend with adverse circumstances, and have often suffered considerable discouragement and hardship in pursuit of their art.

Surely the most convincing explanation for male dominance in artistic and creative fields may be found in the phenomenon of brain-hemisphere differences? As described in earlier chapters, the survival roles which fell to the male were more conducive to development of right-brain powers than were the female's. The male's greater incentive to exercise visualization and imagination inevitably led to his being more receptive to inspiring ideas. He was the one who had to explore ways of putting them into practice. Whilst he had to be creatively enterprising, the female, presumably contentedly, could remain procreative, not experiencing the desire to fulfil herself in any other way. When it came therefore to self-expression in artistic forms, the male was better prepared and more disposed to take initiative.

This explanation also accounts for the difficulties frequently encountered by creatively-inspired men. Given that the group ethos is dominantly left-brain biased – being conditioned in favour of both conforming with convention and directing enterprise to serve the wealth and welfare of the community – the creatively-minded individual can find this bias difficult to cope with. It is as if he cannot readily reconcile both social expectations and creative pursuit. Conceding the former at the expense of the latter causes considerable frustration and stress. Favouring the latter in defiance of the former gives the appearance of being irresponsible and self-indulgent. This is surely why creative geniuses – tending to be more schizoid than others in any case – have so often been notorious for their failure to conduct their personal and social lives conventionally and successfully. The irony can be that if they fail to be recognized, they remain socially ostracized; but, if they succeed (often posthumously), they will be appropriated and acclaimed, all their misdeeds forgiven.

Leading on from this, the feminists' projection of blame onto men for having suppressed women's creativity is seen to be misplaced. The reason has really been in the female's mind, and due to her natural and necessary past commitment to her maternal roles. Her stronger left-brain programming and conditioning has precluded her right-brain development, thus reducing her powers of imagination and visualization. Denied inspiration and creative aspiration, she has thus tended to be confined to decorative, reproductive and repetitive crafts and performing arts. But all that is not to say that she is incapable of becoming and being creative. As suggested earlier, women's liberation can be diagnosed as a surge of enterprise born of accelerating right-brain development. If this is so, one might well expect to witness the emergence of creative talent in individual women. Certainly the number of women now involved in the creative arts is steadily on the increase and a fair number have become outstandingly successful.

What is more, in corroboration of the femine-left/masculine-right hypothesis, it is noticeable that many of the women in the competitive vanguard in various creative fields – especially those of literature, drama and art – exhibit strong, typically-masculine characteristics. And they also seem to have the same difficulty (mentioned above) with coping comfortably with their personal and social lives, a difficulty compounded by their having to compromise or deny their maternal proclivities. Creativity in the male is directly linked with the out-going, questing, competitive, striving power of his sexuality. Creativity in the female, on the other hand, means that right-side powers need to be exercised in defiance of her left-side procreative bias – which means not only suppressing her maternal instincts but also sacrificing aspects of her femininity. The present surge of creativity in the female is mainly concentrated in areas of fashionable and popular entertainment where success is measured in transitory fame and commercial gain. In other words, ambition is focussed on identity, status and power linked with economic security and independence. Whether truly-creative genius willing to sacrifice everything in pursuit of inspiration will emerge out of female embodiment remains to be seen. (And, in case that sounds provocatively sexist, let it be said that relatively few men have ever been in this category. What is more, it seems probable that the more 'feminized' men become, the less likely is the emergence of creative genius in the male.)

If right-brain consciousness, imagination, visualization, etc. were the powers which gave rise to artistic initiatives and aesthetic appreciation in prehistoric times, and if there was also a magical or superstitious element implicit within such genesis, then it may well have been that the development coincided with, or was indistinguishable from, the inception of what we would now call religion.

The word 'superstition' comes from Latin roots meaning 'upon' and 'stand'. Dictionary definitions of the word are such as 'standing over in awe' and 'irrational fear of the unknown'. As the powers of the right brain gave our ancestors experience of self-consciousness and the ability to contemplate objectively, they must certainly have stood in awe of the vast creation around them and felt themselves vulnerable in the face of so much that was unknown and not understood.

Given 'space of mind' for contemplation, there is clearly great significance in the experience of superstition (whether or not it may be properly described as 'irrational'). Those ancestors would have been justifiably apprehensive that at any moment some disastrous event might overwhelm them. There could have been no more effective a spur than fear of such calamity to prompt the exercise of their right-brain faculties. And, in due course, those faculties brought about the invention of limited means to assuage their fears – limited, that is to say, to their physical strength. But they will have been aware that their best physical endeavours were no match for the larger-scale natural hazards, hazards which they could not hope to contend with or continually avoid. Thus, they must have quickly realized that their fate was in considerable measure dictated by forces over which they had no control. So it would then be reasonable to suppose that at some point in their history one of those ancestors conceived the notion that, if such external forces could not be eliminated, then at least it might be possible to influence them favourably.

As a brief aside, an idea dropping into the mind is analogous to insemination in the womb. If mental 'fertilization' takes place, notions are conceived and bear the offspring of expression or action. Some ideas, however, are conceived in the mind but become aborted through lack of desire to, or fear of, carrying them out (mis-carried).

In those early times, our predecessors would understandably have assumed that the forces at large in the world had intelligence and that therefore it should be possible to communicate with them. From such simple deduction born of imagination, there would have arisen concepts of invisible super-powers which could be solicited, placated, worshipped, deferred to, obeyed, and so on. Such mind-projected strategy to cope with the experience of superstition gained such authority and respectability that it became an integral part of the group's 'collective psyche' – becoming known later, especially when the super-powers were anthropomorphized, as the religious factor. Such basic strategy of projection to alleviate irrational fear of the unknown is, in various sophisticated forms, still very much with us today – though we are more likely to look to the scientist rather than some unreliable deity to help us out.

Although those early superstitious initiatives seem very remote – and though the intellectually arrogant may regard them as merely 'primitive' – we have not, when one really penetrates the superficial confidence and the sophistication of complex belief-systems, advanced that far over the millennia. Each one of us, after our mysterious birth into existence, has to contend with the challenge of being here – a task which each individual has to undertake for himself or herself alone, no matter how many others accompany us from time to time. Each needs to try to work out how best to survive and make sense of the life he or she is having to live, no matter how 'awe-ful' it may seem.

As we progress, we find that the ancient parts of the brain influence us – and in large measure govern us – just as powerfully as they did our prehistoric forbears. We may have inherited relatively longlasting traditions, well-tried belief-systems and social institutions, all devised to support us and give us structures to abide by and rely on; and we may have contrived numerous doctrines of explanation and self-aggrandisement; but really, underneath all this fabrication, the bottom line has to be whether we happily trust it or not.

Further, we have developed with great ingenuity numerous technologies which have advanced the survival and proliferation of the human race and, in many societies, improved the average lifespan of the individual. Along the way, we have accumulated massive libraries of information about the nature of ourselves and the world we live in. But being well-informed, begetting offspring and living into old age do not guarantee becoming wiser. *En masse*, humanity at large is still at a loss to know for certain why we are here, other than to reproduce. We are aware of ourselves and of our success as a species, but do not know why we have been made so aware. Beneath our sophisticated facade, we are still, when shaken out of our complacency, superstitious and fearful; and many, especially in times of disaster, rely on the belief or persuasion that there is indeed a supra-human intelligence governing our fate to useful purpose.

Our ancestors will surely have stood in awe of such mysteries as the sun, moon and stars, the sea and sky, the wind and rain, the mountains, forests and deserts – an awe which we have lost since we think we know all about them and take them for granted. And they will have been fearful of thunder, lightning, storm, hurricane, drought, flood, volcanic eruption, earthquake. No wonder they saw fit to credit such influences upon them with spirit and will of their own. To what extent such powers were personified and given gender in the earliest times we do not know; but we do know that that is what eventually happened.

Out of the multitude of powers influencing their lives, it will have become evident that, of those most continually and pressingly important, the ones influencing fecundity were of the highest priority. Not only did day-to-day survival depend on the reproduction of animals, birds, fish and plants, but longer-term survival of the group depended on its own reproduction. Since the female gave birth, it was inevitable that the powers governing fertility and growth should have been personified as female; and that eventually they would be envisaged as goddesses.

From then onwards, the governing power in human

society, continually endorsed by the doctrines and rituals of its religious factor, was well and truly established as matriarchal. And so it has remained ever since, even though male initiatives later introduced or superimposed in different parts of the world the concept of an equally-powerful or almighty male divinity in the interests of establishing patriarchal parity or supremacy.

However much feminists decry what they judge to be the bias in Western societies in favour of patriarchal authority (based on the supposed omnipotence of a male god), they do not seem to realize just how tenuous, superficial and illusory that assertion of authority is. Much as the strong influence of the ancient, instinctive parts of the brain underlie the intellectual performances of the superimposed forebrain, so the ritualistic performances of orthodox patriarchal religion are upheld and sustained by the ancient priorities of matriarchy. Apart from the fact that the idea of devotion to an idealized father- (and, in the Christian case, son-) image is not unattractive to the female worshipper, patriarchal religion gives the highest priority to matriarchal imperatives – birth, marriage, procreation, motherhood, family, social responsibilities, and so on.

For example, in the case of Judaism, for all the presence of male officiants in the synogogue expounding the doctrines and laws of the tradition, considerable emphasis is placed on the home, the family and regeneration of 'the chosen race'. The Jewish son's conditioning places stress on loyalty to the mother-figure and the responsibility to succeed in the world in order to provide for wife and children. Likewise to a large extent in the Christian tradition, though here the stress could be said to be less on the mother-figure as authority, more on respect due to her as the maternal principle. In the Roman Catholic tradition, for instance, the Virgin Mary, the Holy Mother, remains a central focus for devotion and worship.

And yet, even though the emphasis on the imperatives of matriarchy has persisted and tended to dominate in the orthodox establishments of patriarchal religion, was that the intent of the male originators? Were those founders perhaps taking initiatives in order to shift the emphasis – not necessarily in order to gain authority over the female but to introduce an element of higher aspiration into the religious ethos?

For instance, from a small amount of historical record and a few memoirs written by contemporaries some years after his death, we gather that Jesus of Nazareth, himself a Jew, set out to expound teachings which were alien to the existing Jewish orthodoxy of the time. It could be said that, in several respects, his adult life was a deliberate demonstration of 'male liberation', of the need to acknowledge that there are important responsibilities in life beyond those promoted by matriarchy. Among other things, he on one occasion publicly rejected his mother, was totally committed to paternal authority, preferred the close company of other males (his disciples), persuaded several of them that following his initiatives was more important than their roles in society, apparently had no sexual relationship with a woman, did not marry, had no children, generally allowed women to play only secondary roles in his life and ministry, and so on. Clearly he did not suggest that all men should follow his example. But, when speaking of love, it was always in a sense transcending sexual or marital relationship, in terms of compassion rather than passion, of the spiritual dimension rather than the incarnate. And in the end he chose to invite his own death rather than compromise his teaching that individual salvation depended less on the desire to perpetuate life, more on willingness to surrender it consciously.

The above reflections indicate a psychological shift from feminine-left to masculine-right. It may even be that such male initiatives in the relgious domain – going back to such figures as Moses and Zoroaster – indicate that right-brain power in the male had become sufficiently strong some four or five thousand years ago to challenge the dominance of matriarchy. And at the heart of such initiative there was endeavour to come to terms with death. Whereas matriarchy was primarily concerned with the continuation of the group through succeeding genera-tions, patriarchy focussed on death of the individual and the possibility of immortality in some after-life dimension.

So far as we know, the human being is the only creature on the planet aware during life of the inevitability of death in the future. Such awareness must once again have something to do with forebrain development, and in particular with hemisphere differentiation. Left-brain memory combined with right-brain visualization leads to the ability to contemplate in abstract eventual discontinuation of present existence. The challenge of such realization must have begun to exercise the power of speculation since the dawn of *homo sapiens* – a challenge which dawns in the mind of each individual now, at some point in childhood after self-consciousness has awakened.

As an intervention into the security of left-brain conditioning with its assumption of indefinite continuity, the sudden right-brain realization that one's own continuity is neither indefinite nor secure comes as a considerable shock. What is more, the mystery of death seems to remain as impenetrable as it always has been. However much religion, as one of the planks of its authority, has sought to dispel fear and uncertainty about death, it has as yet failed to produce any solid guarantees. The possibility of individual continuity after death, as far as religious orthodoxy promotes it, remains a matter of belief and faith. No other institutionalized authority in society attempts to offer assurance or guidance in the matter. Even in this age of prodigious factual information, we are no nearer proving the existence of an after-life. Even science is at a loss in this respect, having to content itself instead with attempts to prolong existence.

Psychologically, the prospect of death appears to affect male and female in different degree, the latter being generally less affected. A German feminist (in conversation with me) asserted that the female is much better adjusted to the prospect than the male: 'I'm sure that women – being closer to death because of their biology – are more accepting of it.' On being asked to explain, she pointed out that women have always had to face the threat of death in giving birth. Whilst conceding that childbirth had certainly been a considerable hazard for women in the past, I suggested that it had been a relatively 'passive' one compared with the hazards continually confronted by men in 'active' pursuit of their procuring and defence/attack roles. It seemed to me that on the whole men have had to risk their lives deliberately more frequently than women and that, on the basis of her argument, it should be men who would be more accepting of it.

Another feminist states, 'It is hard to believe that men have spirits or souls at all given their love of death.'[51] To suggest that men love death sounds gratuitously melodramatic. That they are more fascinated by death, most probably; that they are more accustomed to having to kill, certainly. The latter is, of course, rooted in the fact that the male has been conditioned to fight in the interests of group and female survival, a fact which feminists prefer to ignore. But they surely do have justifiable grounds for concern and complaint when they accuse men of going to war and killing other human beings (women and children included) in the interests of propagating some abstract ideology. And of all wars perpetrated in pursuit of a cause, those undertaken in the name of religion have been (and are) surely the least comprehensible and defensible. The only explanation must be that there is a factor in the male psyche especially which causes him to perceive that continuation of life for its own sake is not in itself the be-all and end-all of human existence and purpose. His willingness to espouse a crusade or a cause, and to kill or die in the upholding or propagating of it, denotes the presence in his make-up of aspirations he regards as transcending those of existential survival for its own sake.

When surveying the traditional practices of different societies over the ages, the officials attending the ceremonial rites of death have tended to be male whilst those attending the rites of birth have been female. (In modern Western societies, the latter has tended to become the exception rather than the rule, a fact which gives rise to further, understandable, feminist complaint.) This division of responsibility aligns with the right-side disposition of the male and the left-side proclivity of the female. Whilst she generally prefers to put her mind to the continuity and regeneration of human life on earth (hoping for the best where possible life-after-death is concerned), he is more given to pondering the mystery of his own discontinuation. Or, to put it glibly, she prefers to think about 'the way in' whilst he wonders about 'the way out'.

It seems possible therefore that the reason for difference between the genders in attitude towards death lies in typical inter-hemisphere biases. Left-side bias in the female inclines her to concentrate on continuity and security in this life. Right-brain advance in the male, combined with his risk-taking roles, compels him to ponder the imminence of death and to try to penetrate its mystery. Whilst a woman will be moved to tears by bereavement, her lament is likely to be due to her having lost someone who held a place in her sense of stability and security. The loss knocks a hole, as it were, in the familiar fabric of her surroundings. A man, on the other hand, will grieve the loss of a close companion but he will be more inclined to wonder what has happened to the person who no longer exists in his world.

Back in the superstitious beginnings of religious aspiration, when the human mind had envisaged a constellation of divine powers, the chances are that any gender identity given to a particular power was of little significance. And, if it was imagined that these powers were at times in competition or conflict with each other, then such contention would most likely have been thought of as being due to differences of nature rather than gender incompatibility. (When we come to the Greeks, it becomes difficult to tell from the machinations of their gods and goddesses whether gender difference mattered at all, so ruthlessly did they all behave towards each other.) Eventually, however, as mentioned earlier, a distinctly female power took precedence because procreation via the female was recognized as being crucial to the strength and continuation of the group.

Archaeologists have discovered clay figurines dating back to the Palaeolithic period and have suggested that female power vested in the 'Great Mother' concept dominated the conduct of human society at least ten thousand years ago. There is some disagreement amongst the experts as to whether the mother-figure was regarded primarily as provider of food or as giver of birth but, either way, fertility is the prerequisite. What does seem beyond dispute is that the goddess-regime served survival of the group well enough during those times. Evidence unearthed in Anatolia, for example, indicates that a goddess-worshipping society prospered there peacefully for at least a thousand years. Excavations revealed no evidence of violence, sacrifice or the eating of meat. The implication must be that, at that time, men behaved themselves. Their competitiveness, aggression and sexual appetite, etc., must have been kept well under control by the governing regime of women, ruling under the auspices of the goddess. Presumably, any right-brain initiatives envisaged by the male would have been turned to collective benefit, being too weak to countenance dissent or rebellion.

Several thousand years later, such rebellion did evidently begin to succeed. But, if the previous, female-dominated systems had been so successful, why should the male have seen fit to demote and displace them?

For one thing, the goddess, for all her benevolence, was evidently not always benign in her dealings with mortals. Presumably because things did from time to time go wrong, and societies suffered accordingly, it had to be conceded that the goddess could be fickle and unpredictable, sometimes cruel and destructive. 'The Great Mother provokes profound ambivalence; her cruelty is no less salient than her benevolence.'[52]

The same commentator goes on to suggest that, 'Perhaps it is the greatest gift of the goddess to teach us that good and evil, life and death, are inextricably intertwined.' Whether one considers such teaching a blessing must be a matter of opinion. For those struggling in times past to survive under her jurisdiction, such revelation will not have made their living any easier. It is then not surprising that the goddess' ambivalence eventually provoked the male beyond endurance. Increasing frustration in the right-side of his mind gave him the power to rebel, and to envisage a male god who would deal with mortals justly and straightforwardly. Disenchanted with the wilfulness, cruelties and vagaries of the goddess – and perhaps exasperated with women and their relentless commitment to nurturance and having babies – the male found himself inspired by the prospect of a totally different order with far more exciting prospects. Amongst other things, his god would ideally have the power to eliminate evil and shed some light on the mystery of death. And perhaps reveal to man a grander role in the scheme of things.

However the initiative may be explained, the fact remains that, at some point in the human story, male aspiration challenged the domination of matriarchal convention. Psychologically, the same process takes place in the minds of all of us at a certain stage in our development – when right-side quest and ambition challenge the authority and limitations of left-side conditioning. For the male especially, such revolution means the need for him to break free of maternal influence and ties if he is to prove himself as an independent male. In the first phase of life, both mother and conditioning represent protection, just as the egg-shell provides protection for the growing chick. But, just as the chick must at a certain point in development break out of the shell if it is not to be suffocated, so the individual must liberate himself or herself from the restrictions of conditioning if he or she is to develop understanding of individuality and become truly independent in his or her own right.

In this revolutionary sense, the bid to institute the omnipotence of a male god would suggest a 'men's liberation movement' and we may suppose that it did not altogether meet with women's approval. Not only would they have been reluctant to relinquish power and would therefore have attempted to resist it, but they would have seen it as both a threat and a rejection – a threat to stability and security, and a rejection of matriarchal authority. It would not be unreasonable to suspect that this male initiative some five millennia ago marked the beginning of 'the battle of the sexes'. Whereas previously the genders had worked together as harmonious complements, they were now competing for authority. As described in a previous chapter, the masculine needs to make a bid for development if it is to overcome predisposition to remain feminine. So, psychologically, that historical event probably also marked the beginning of increased polarization of the brain hemispheres in the male and the beginning of his bid to gain independent status and power for himself and his gender.[53] The female, however, though she may have lost that particular battle at that time, had certainly not lost the war. Five thousand years later, the tables are once again turning and it is women who are on the advance and men who are in retreat.

The origins of that inter-deity, inter-gender and inter-hemisphere 'split' are most strikingly and appropriately depicted in the Babylonian legend of the young god Marduk's overthrow of Tiamat, female monster of the sea. The story represents a total revolution, a complete reversal of the cosmogeny of the Sumerians who had held power in Mesopotamia before being overcome by the might of the Babylonians. The Sumerians had revered the sea-goddess as the almighty creatrix of the world but 'suddenly' she was re-cast by the Babylonians as the begetter of chaos and all-destroying conflict. Young Marduk triumphs over her, heralding an era of patriarchal challenge to matriarchal domination. It is not difficult to see in this myth genesis of the dualistic view the male holds of the female – that she is both life-giving 'goddess' and all-consuming 'monster'.

Whether the origins of the 'split' pre-date the Babylonians or not, from then onwards history records its persistence through civilization after civilization to the present day, especially in the West. The patriarchal monotheism of Judaism passed into the ethos of Christianity and then into that of Islam. Zoroaster, the Hebrew prophets, Jesus, Mohammed and others – all reinforced implicitly or explicitly in their teachings the importance of male autonomy under the guidance of the father-principle, independent of the mother-principle. Such initiatives meant that the male had to take overall authority in society; and it meant that the hierarchy of power-holding in the religious establishment itself had to be male – a privilege which did much to enhance the male's sense of status and power.

It seems that there was no serious question of equal power-sharing.[54] It must have been realized that a kind of 'duo-theism' of father-god 'married' to mother-goddess would not work. Neither, it seems, was some kind of androgynous blend of the two acceptable. At the same time, there could be no question of patriarchy eliminating matriarchy; the group's strength still depended on maximum reproduction via the female (and the priesthood needed to be replenished from one generation to the next). Whilst it was still important therefore to retain and revere the divine mother-goddess, it was also important that she was kept under control and obedient to the father-god; otherwise her monstrous, all-devouring aspect could re-emerge at will. The priesthood will have been well aware from past experience that the female, like Nature herself, has two sides to her nature – the one sacred, beautiful and beneficent, the other cruel, ruthless and devouring. (Which is not to imply by omission that the male does not have such dual aspect to his nature also.) Inevitably, this patriarchal strategy had the longstanding psychological effect of making the female feel herself relegated to inferior status.

Through attempting to keep the female under control and dedicated to her maternal roles, patriarchy would have been seeking in particular to curb what it saw as the seductive aspect of female sexual power. Such power could tempt the male away from giving proper attention to his higher, especially spiritual, aspirations. Religious doctrines warned the male against succumbing to such temptations and threatened dire penalties for breaking the rules of relationship and conduct laid down. So seriously were such dangers regarded in some traditions that men aspiring to lead a religious life were required to take vows of celibacy; in extreme, even to shun association with women altogether and adopt a monastic life. In principle, advocacy of such drastic measures reflected the effect of increasing 'mind-split' in the male – that it was not possible to devote oneself to the 'earth-mother' and the 'heavenly-father' at the same time; it had to be one or the other. Or, in other words, worldly involvement and spiritual aspiration were seen as incompatible.

Although in effect this view does seem like some kind of reactionary, chauvinistic fantasy on the part of the male, it does represent, psychologically, an aspect of right-mind experience familiar to anyone who knows what it is like to pursue some creative enterprise. Such aspirations frequently require a degree of dedication which will fend off diversionary temptations and which will, if necessary override social expectations, even responsibilities on occasion. Any individual in quest of self-development knows what it is like to come up against pressure to conform with group-approved criteria. Right-side enterprise can often find itself in frustrating contention with left-side conditioning: 'I want to do this but I ought to do that. . .'

In this juxtaposition of individual aspiration and social commitment, we may see the link between endeavour in the creative arts and the religious context. Both are essentially concerned – in their refined and 'higher' sense – with individual self-fulfilment in terms which transcend the mundane business of everyday survival, both depending for such elevation on inspiration. Both are subject to the 'downward' pull of social expectations and temptations, becoming relegated to group-serving occupations. The arts can be reduced to popular, commercial entertainments; the religious establishment to simply a social service.

That relegation, however is not the worst that can happen. The arts can become decadent and subversive; and religious power can become insensitive and autocratic. For whilst the right-side is capable of the noblest aspirations, it is also the seat of ambition in all respects. Whilst the feminine-left is procreative, the masculine-right can either be creative or destructive. No doubt the initiators of patriarchal religious endeavour, and many of their reforming successors, were truly inspired. But later inheritors of high office all-too-often abandoned spiritual aspiration in favour of secular ambition. They were tempted to gain political and economic power, which led them into absurd theological contradictions. Even worse, their ambitions led them into 'holy wars' against rivals, and to persecute without mercy those who disagreed with them. Destruction of the upholders of other faiths (even if their allegiance was to the same god) became justified.

It is now well over a thousand years since the last founding of a patriarchal 'world religion' and it is perhaps surprising that the principal faiths have maintained their power and influence over so many centuries, given that their doctrines and rituals were formulated so long ago. However, though the faith-religions are still very powerful in less developed countries, their credibility has been, for some while, much tested in more advanced societies. Scientific knowledge combined with the powers of logic and reason have had their undermining impact on faith and belief. Materialistic ideologies have sought to discredit the bases of religious power and in some parts of the world have tried to eliminate them. And, perhaps ironically, the more liberal and accommodating some religious establishments have become in order to stem the tide of disaffection,[55] the more they have had to compromise doctrinal principles, thus further undermining their credibility. Only the more autocratic and fanatical elements of patriarchal religion in less well-educated societies have managed to withstand erosion of their power, and then only by intense indoctrination and propaganda, combined with threat of fearful retribution for disobedience.

To such siege of patriarchy, there may now be added the assault of the liberated woman. The women's movement in several ways and on a broad front challenges patriarchal religious authority. Apart from a general questioning and defying – and in the feminists' case, a denouncing – of male attitudes born of the patriarchal ethos, some women seek with determination to gain access into the presently exclusively-male higher reaches of hierarchical power (only, as yet, in the non-Catholic sects of Christianity). Some simply want equal right to gain higher status; a few of the more militant want no less than a reformation of the entire doctrine and liturgy – in effect, a re-write of the scriptures to expunge the slightest nuance of prejudice against or seconding of the female. Yet others see no point in making a takeover bid; they want no less than restitution of the goddess and matriarchal authority. (Shades here of the fact that the male embryo, if emasculated, reverts to becoming female?)

Understandably, male resistance to women's current initiatives is more evident in the ecclesiastical hierarchy than anywhere else. To surrender an inch would be tantamount to giving a mile. One false move, even at the lowest level, could lead to collapse of the whole structure. After all, the whole edifice is founded on male authority

over the female (as described earlier) and the direct
communion of 'heavenly father' with 'incarnate son'.

Whether the religious basis of patriarchal power
eventually collapses or not, there can be little doubt that to
the roll of increasing male redundancy there will have to be
added that of the priestly role. He may continue to be
turned to by some in trouble; and he may continue to be
employed to add solemnity to the rites of marriage and
death (the left-side, pastoral aspect of his role); but how
much longer will he retain influence as adviser, confessor
and teacher (his right-side aspect)? It may be that just as
science – religion's arch rival – has perhaps reached
penultimate limits of relevance in improving the human
condition, so perhaps religion also is bordering on such
limits as it presses on under the residual momentum of
past prestige.

If the era of patriarchal religious authority is drawing to a
close, what, in the higher aspirational sense, may replace
it? Reinstatment of the omnipotent goddess and a
matriarchal hierarchy would hardly be an evolutionary
initiative; rather, a barren step backwards – and not at all
appropriate if fertility were reinstated as being of
paramount importance. Nor one imagines would the
reintroduction of some kind of polytheism or the concept
of some androgynous deity be likely to appeal. Human
consciousness and intelligence have surely evolved now to
the point where it is no longer appropriate to invite
superstitious belief in mind-projected super-powers?

That is not to suggest that universal adoption of some
materialistic, atheistic ideology will now suffice; not at all.
On the contrary, that would be a fatal renunciation of
spiritual aspiration. It is to say that mind-projected,
externalized deities served well in the past but that
strategy for dealing with superstition now presents
problems which have become intractable, especially those
concerning the deity's gender. The emerging strength of
masculine-right visualization proposed the strategy and
the feminine-left side adopted it as a matter of faith and
belief. But now that right-side powers have developed
further and become more mature, the strategy has become
outgrown. The mind is more capable of working with

abstract principles. Through contemplation, it can internalize and reflect upon its own nature. Thus, instead of projecting concepts and images of invisible super-powers, it becomes possible for the individual to discover and realize that the formless, gender-less, divine and immortal principal or 'spirit' resides in his or her own mind.

This is not a new proposition. Both Eastern and Western esoteric traditions have understood and taught such process of inner revelation for a long time – probably as long as the exoteric faith-religions have themselves existed. But throughout history it seems that only small minorities in different cultures were drawn to such teachings and prepared to undertake such introspective quest. Over the past few decades there has clearly been a resurgence of interest in ancient, esoteric teachings and their modern extrapolations in schools of self-development. It is probably too early to say how well they will prosper and impossible to predict in what forms they will develop. But given the decline of orthodox religion in developed countries, and their current preoccupation with materialism, the time and the climate must promise well for a renaissance to fill the spiritual vacuum. If so, it will be a sign that human psychological evolution is entering a new phase, perhaps one of 'spiritual individuation' i.e., one based on (right side) self-realization and not on (left side) group-indocrination.

It is one of the principal features of esoteric, spiritual teachings that they are not presented as ready-formulated belief-systems which the aspirant is asked to adopt unquestioningly as a matter of faith. They are more by nature propositions and commentaries based on the observations, experiences and understanding of individuals who have discovered self-evident answers to their deepest, inner questions. Unlike doctrines of belief, the fruits of these individual testaments of quest and contemplation cannot be transferred directly to another. For no matter how accurately the understanding of experience may be expressed by one, it must remain hearsay for another – unless or until the latter clearly cognizes it in his or her own way through his or her own experience. This is simply because, whereas doctrines of belief can be learned by the left brain, understanding of experience requires perception, cognition, intuition, etc, which are right-brain powers. Understanding the meaning of experience therefore requires exercise and development of the right mind. Whereas beliefs can be quickly adopted and remain more or less fixed, understanding of experience changes and getting to the deepest truths of what experience is revealing can be a lifelong aspiration. Which is why, as suggested earlier, the most learned and well-informed are not necessarily wise.

In case the above sounds remote and hypothetical, the following beautiful expression of personal revelation appears in the writings of C.G. Jung:

'From a low hill in the Athi plains of East Africa, I once watched the vast herds of wild animals grazing in soundless stillness, as they had done from time immemorial, touched only by the breath of a primeval world. I felt then as if I were the first man, the first creature to know that all this *is*. The entire world round me was still in its primeval state; it did not know that it *was*. And then, in that one moment in which I came to know, the world sprang into being; without that moment it would never have been. All Nature seeks this goal and finds it fulfilled in man, but only in the most highly developed and most fully conscious man. Every advance, even the smallest, along this path of conscious realization adds that much to the world.'[56]

In that witnessing, born of a quiet and contemplative state of mind, there was revelation of spontaneous, self-evident truth about human experience. No doubt it had deep and lasting effect on Jung and no doubt he regarded it as a profoundly spiritual experience, which had nothing to do with belief. His written account of it may be inspirational to one; to another it may sound utter nonsense.

The significance of such revelatory experience is that it goes to the heart of things, answering the deepest inner questioning. After the dawning of objective consciousness, such questions as 'Who am I?' and 'What am I here for?' arise in abstract into the space of mind created by contemplation. In youth, such enquiry is likely to find stock left-brain answers: 'You are ... (your name) ... (either male or female) ... (nationality) ... (creed) ...' and 'You are here to ... work ... earn a living ... have children ... support a family ... help others. ..' Such socially-prescribed labels and functions will satisfy most group-members most of the time; but they do not penetrate deeply enough for others. They do not satisfy the right-brain's quest for the truth concerning man's real identity and status.[57] From such dissatisfaction there arises higher aspiration to discover the truth for oneself – which is the essential and real meaning of spirituality.

The individual's quest to discover the truth concerning identity and status, and the meaning and purpose of human life, brings us to the higher aspirations of philosophy/psychology. Philosophy means love of wisdom and, given that wisdom has less to do with assimilation of facts and more to do with understanding experience, it is inextricably linked with psychology which means knowledge of the mind. In what follows, the word philosophy is used as a correlate of psychology in that wisdom is a product of understanding mental experience.

In previous centuries, before the scientific age, the creative arts, religion and philosophy/psychology were not departmentalized as they have now become. They were three aspects of a singular quest – to understand the nature of man, the divine and the universe, and how all three are related. Once science had begun to undermine religious authority, artists, priests and philosophers began to go their separate ways. As a result, the academic world, for example, started to treat the three disciplines as separate and distinct fields of intellectual interest, each becoming hedged about with barriers of exclusivity and elitism.

There can be no higher aspiration for the human mind than to seek to understand and express the truth about the human condition. That is to say, to discover for oneself the undeniable truth about life and death rather than to rely on the changing beliefs and opinions held by the consensus. There is surely no point in our being more conscious than, say, the giraffe or the rat, unless that gift allows us at least some deeper insight into the meaning of our lives? It cannot just be to enable us to survive and proliferate more successfully than other creatures.

Testaments of revelation passed on to us down through the ages persistently point to the importance of contemplation for the realization of self-evident truth. Contrary to popular assumption in this age of science, the gaining of wisdom is not dependent on the amassing of information but on the dispelling of self-delusion. Thus, true philosophy is not only the debating of speculative hypotheses but also the resolving of contradictions and confusions encountered in personal experience. Wisdom is gained, as it were, through realization that the conflicts of duality can never be properly resolved by championing one aspect at the expense of its opposite. It is that understanding (standing-under) of principles which reconciles the incompatibility of opposites by transcending them.

The creative arts seek to express that which is beautiful; but they cannot ignore that which is ugly. Religion may champion the virtues of love and goodness; but it cannot eliminate hatred and evil. Philosophy, however, seeks to understand the meaning of both beauty and ugliness, of both love and hatred, of both good and evil. It demonstrates that the positive aspect cannot be revealed without the presence of its negative counterpart and that, therefore, from a transcendent viewpoint, both are essential to understanding the truth. Thus it becomes evident that consciousness and mental dichotomy give the human being unique potential – to realize a spiritual realm of transcendent understanding and reality denied to all other creatures.

The creative arts, as well as being enriching and uplifting, can also be decadent and dispiriting. Religion can be supportive and comforting; it can also be dogmatic and tedious. Philosophy can be challenging and inspiring; it can also be dull and irrelevant. However, whereas a person can go through life doing without the arts and religion, he or she cannot do so without philosophy. Whether they would think of themselves as such or not, all people – unless totally dependent on others due to some mental defect – are in some degree philosophers. Otherwise, they would have no basis on which to make the simplest decision in their day-to-day lives. Personal philosophy begins at the level of the most mundane everyday conduct and operates right through to life's most important decisions and realizations.

If a person gains any wisdom from experience, their philosophy of life must in some measure develop. Such philosophies are born of ambition and they are moulded by success and failure. They are not then looked upon as being much more than tactics of expediency in the worldly business of surviving and procuring. Thus, not all people raise their philosophical sights from self-survival to self-understanding, not realizing that the quality of their lives is far more dependent on psychological development than on social and material gain. Often, they only wake up to the state and limitations of their philosophy when they are faced with catastrophe, especially death. Their philosophical aspirations have not reached out to the ultimate duality – that of life and death.

Most people nowadays have unfortunately been led into the assumption that philosophy is just a form of abstruse intellectual occupation, mainly because, in academic institutions, that is what it has largely become. Such philosophy is commonly reduced to comparing what one philosopher has thought and said with what another has thought and said. Such predominantly left-brain exercise engaged in by an erudite minority is a far cry from right-brain aspiration to understand oneself and the meaning and purpose of one's life. It is perhaps because philosophy lost its creative and inspirational edge in that respect that it has been overtaken by its younger off-shoot, psychology, and is being increasingly abandoned in institutions of higher education. Since all notable philosophers in the past have been male, to the list of male redundancy we will, alas, have to add that of the philosopher or sage.

For wisdom to have any meaning and significance in human society, it can only be manifest through the conduct of individuals who have taken initiative to understand themselves and have hence taken responsibility for themselves. Unfortunately, social conditioning tends to be biased against introspection, usually seeing it as an unhealthy self-indulgence. And yet, having arrived at a situation today where conflict and confusion are as rife as they have ever been in human history, how much longer can people be expected to have confidence in the persuasions of consensus based on belief-systems which have consistently failed to fulfil their promises? Subjective self-interest may indeed by anti-social and not at all helpful for the individual indulging in it; but what hope can there be if individuals are not encouraged through objective self-observation to understand consciously the meaning of self-responsibility? Without self-integrity, a group-member becomes vulnerable to any and every fashionable belief and then has no power to control the consequences of having made that commitment.

For example, in technologically-developed, modern societies today, there is continuing concern at the number of people without employment. This is considered to be a bad thing on several counts: that the full potential for group-wealth is being denied and welfare suffers accordingly; that the unemployed person becomes demoralized and loses self-respect, and may turn to breaking the law in desperation; and so on. It is thus believed, by right- and left-wing politics alike, that jobs must be created and that it is the government's responsibility to create them. If there is a lack of demand, then engineer it. Fair enough, at one level of analysis. But such belief under-estimates human aspiration. The underlying fallacy is the assumption that if the whole group is employed and earning money, all should be well. And if the jobs created offer opportunity to earn more and more money, even better. But what about self-fulfilment in the jobs on offer? Sure enough, if the only criterion for doing a job is the making of money, then all will not be well and good. Government may argue that self-fulfilment is not their responsibility; in which case it has to be a self-responsibility. In the final analysis, the only person responsible for self-fulfilment is oneself.

Whatever the diagnosis of the present human state and its prognosis in the future, it is difficult to see the old criteria for self-fulfilment – maximum procreation, maximum wealth, etc. – being maintained indefinitely. Even if there were unlimited wealth to be shared fairly amongst an expanding population, that would hardly be an evolutionary achievement. As suggested at the beginning of this chapter, higher aspirations in their purest form have nothing directly to do with continued socio-economic survival. The quest for fulfilment must be in individual spiritual terms, not in the group's existential terms.

The human spirit in its most noble aspect has long and strenuously sought to uphold and express the highest ideals of beauty, love and truth. Such aspiration is thus 'spirit-ually' motivated. Because in recent centuries all such endeavour tended to be promoted and pursued under the patronage and influence of religion, the word 'spirituality' became virtually synonymous with religiosity. Being religious may include being spiritual but being spiritual does not necessarily mean being religious (in the conventional sense). Religion does not have a monopoly on spirituality, if the latter is taken to mean the moving of the human spirit to aspire to a transcendent realm of reality beyond mortal confines.

In whatever way the spirit within each person moves them to discover the virtues of beauty, love and wisdom, that way is a spiritual quest. And it cannot be generated anywhere other than in the mind of the individual. A group can be religious in that its members may share common beliefs and feel themselves bound by the same moral laws; but only the individual can be spiritually motivated. Beauty, love and truth do not exist as common property; they can only be realized in the eye, heart and mind of the individual witness.

The belief-systems of religious and secular authority for obvious reasons discourage selfishness. Altruism is more conducive to social cohesion and welfare. There is nothing in principle wrong with such conditioning; but where it can go astray is when it so ignores and overrides individual aspiration and questioning that it obliterates self-confidence. Indoctrination can render impotent the desire for self-understanding and self-expression. The individual needs to be selfish, needs to be self-interested, if he or she is ever to discover the true meaning of self-responsibility on which genuine altruism depends. Hence one finds a spiritual teacher such as Jesus saying,

'Thou shalt love thy neighbour as thyself'; or a teacher in Islamic tradition saying, 'He who does not love himself cannot love another. He who hates another, hates himself.'

Once the feminine-left-brain programme in every person has become established through childhood education, there are three principal possibilities for emerging masculine-right-brain ambitions and aspirations. First, they may be overwhelmed by externally-imposed social conditioning; pressure to conform and serve is such that they remain underdeveloped and the person remains in effect an obedient 'public servant'. Second, they may be directed into the gaining of identity, status and power in worldly terms, with or without the group's approval. Such a person succeeds or fails in terms prescribed by the group and the world at large. Third, they may be directed into the higher aspirations of self-understanding and self-expression. Such a person looks for self-fulfilment in self-generated terms, i.e. looks for status and identity through the understanding of personal experience. The three options may be likened to being employed, being an employer and being self-employed.

At best, the group at large tolerates the third option, encouraging it only if it proves to be beneficial to the wealth and welfare of the group. At worst, the group can actively discourage or persecute such independent initiative (as happens, for example, in the suppression of self-expression or 'freedom of speech' under totalitarian regimes). Such attitude tends to be taken because right-brain intiatives are likely to question the *status quo*, challenge orthodoxy, rebel against convention, disrupt continuity, threaten authority, and so on. Consensus sees attempt to change as threat and therefore resists revolutionary ideas, not being able to tell whether they are evolutionary or not. It prefers not to take the risk.[58] Resistance to innovation is particularly strong in the religious context where any proposed departure from established doctrine is instantly rejected as heresy.

The questioning and renunciation of popularly-held belief – akin to the growing adolescent's breaking free from parental influence and support – is related to what used to be described, in the spiritual aspect of religious aspiration, as renouncing the world and its ways. In the Christian case, for example, Jesus on several occasions taught the necessity to do this in forthright manner: 'Ye cannot serve God and mammon' or 'Follow me; and let the dead bury their dead.'[59] It is amazing, when you come to think of it, how subsequent orthodoxy has managed to live with such uncompromising statements.

In philosophical traditions, it has not usually been seen as necessary to take renunciation so literally, even though philosophers have often lived remote and secluded lives. But such traditions do encourage penetrative questioning, as a result of which there is bound to be some disillusionment with popular belief and convention. Such enquiry may well reach the point of realization that social conditioning only provides for a person's survival as a member of the group and does nothing to guarantee an individual's fulfilment in terms exclusive to his or her right-brain powers and talents. To put it bluntly, the group at large is not interested in whether a person is being true to himself or herself or not; it is only interested in whether that person's behaviour as a group-member is acceptable or otherwise.

Inevitably, the group's criteria for judging the development and expression of right-brain powers and talents in the individual have always been directly related to the group's survival and success. For the male, that responsibility has been focussed on procurement, reproductive support, defence/attack, technological development, etc. But we are now witnessing a strange juncture in the state of human affairs in which male right-brain participation in all these roles is becoming increasingly dispensable. Paradoxically, it could now be said that the aspiring male does not have to renounce the world and its ways because they are renouncing him.

It is as if in this present age the masculine-right in the male is being 'liberated' from its traditional responsibilities (i.e., from the second option mentioned above); partly due to technological advance and partly due to the masculine-right initiatives of the female relieving him of them. The male is thus increasingly left with only the two other options – the first, a serving or servicing contribution; and the third, higher aspiration in the realms of creative art, spiritual fulfilment and philosophical or psychological understanding.

Either option requires a kind of psychological revolution in the male – one commensurate with that taking place in the liberated female. The first option would require a down-gearing, or even renunciation of his traditional, patriarchal authority and all his exploitive ambitions. The third option could be an evolutionary opportunity; a reformed-masculine initiative which could lead to an ethos the like of which humanity has not experienced before. It could be a fully-mature flowering on universal scale of that renaissance which so bravely emerged in Europe five to seven centuries ago, with its emphasis on the potential of the individual.

Such a renaissance would, of course, take some while to evolve and be recognized. But it could be said that the male needs to take initiatives in that direction very soon if he is to restore his self-respect and restore the female's respect for him.

What is the difference between, or the connection between, the image of a religious woman worshipping an effigy of a near-naked, bleeding man impaled in agony on a cross and the image of a male voyeur looking lustfully at a pornographic photograph of a nude and bound woman being whipped?

Why is one 'respect-able' and the other not? Why is one classified as sadistic and the other not? If either image appeals or repulses, what does such reaction reveal? What dictates the difference between the passionate, the compassionate and the dispassionate?

To understand the generation of the two images and the connection between them would be to understand a good deal about the natures of the two sides of the mind. Also about the difficulties likely to be encountered in the restitution of mutually-fulfilling, long-term relationship between the genders.

8 Marriage On The Rocks

Women's liberation has challenged and has already undermined many of the traditional concepts on which long-term relationship between the genders has been organized for millennia. The popular image of marriage is changing as the old, religiously-endorsed, socio-economic arrangements based on clear-cut role-differentiation begin to lose their relevance. It seems improbable that the current trend towards abandonment of such long-established patterns could ever now be fully reversed, especially in developed societies.

Is there then any validity in persisting with the practice of lifelong marital contract? Is it just an outworn habit born of long conditioning or is it for some reason psychologically indispensable to both genders?

Before considering what virtue may remain in the custom of one man and one woman committing themselves to each other for the rest of their lives, it would be as well to reiterate briefly some of the factors which led to establishment of the practice in the first place.

Anthropological evidence leads to the assumption that during the early days of the human race our predecessors must soon have realized that prospects for survival were much improved by living in mixed-gender groups. Given the generally-hostile circumstances of the time, a group of families stood a better chance of surviving and prospering than an individual or a single family alone. One of the first consequences of this strategy must have been that numbers of males had to learn to co-operate with each other rather than following their instinct to compete and eliminate each other. A group of males offered greater effectiveness for defence against threat and for the procurement of food. But it must also have detracted to a degree from the survival-of-the-fittest principle; some weaker males will have been able to survive and pass on their genes to following generations.

Our forbears will also have realized that the group's strength depended on optimum reproduction. It was crucial that all females should be continually engaged from puberty to menopause in the begetting and nurturing of children. Whatever rules and customs a group may have adopted for individual male participation in this endeavour, maximum reproduction along with group stability will have been the guiding concerns.

Evidence from different parts of the world suggest that there was a tendency for groups to gain a preponderance of females. The reasons for this imbalance are probably various. Most likely it was due to a combination of factors – more males than females being killed in their role assignments, females being protected and constitutionally stronger, possibly a higher male miscarriage and infant mortality rate, and so on. Whatever the explanation, polygamy became more common than monogamy – not as a reflection of the male's insatiable appetite for sex but because maximum reproduction required that no female should be left uncatered for.

Gradually, as groups became less nomadic and more committed to agricultural settlement, the male's procuring roles and his technological expertise led to his gaining and holding the economic power within the group. Presumably, alongside the establishment of more stable communities with more secure prospects, possessions and property accumulated; and the need to devise more formal marital arrangements arose also. As competition between males for status and power translated from sexual rivalry to the gaining of wealth so less emphasis was placed on the male's virility and more on his ability to support a family. No doubt the economic-support factor encouraged the trend towards monogamy and, as a consequence, the greater likelihood of females remaining single. (Perhaps here also were the origins of the 'oldest profession'.)

Important factors in the formalization of the marriage contract would have been both the female's desire to secure continuing economic support for herself and her children and the male's desire to ensure that his wealth would be used to support his own offspring and be passed on to his own offspring, especially his sons. From the latter arose the stress in marital contract on the wife's fidelity. Quite apart from damage to his sexual pride, no husband would want to invest his energy and wealth in providing for a woman who was not contractually bound to him and who might deceive him into supporting children of whom he was not the father.

The overlaying of increasingly important economic constraints onto the basic need to procreate could be seen as one of the principal reasons for patriarchy imposing itself on matriarchy. In modern parlance, that would be for a husband to say to his wife, 'You can't have another baby because I can't afford it.' Finally, all these factors governing one-to-one heterosexual relationship came to be endorsed by the doctrines of patriarchal religion, one of the principal tenets of which was that the wife should obey the decisions of the husband.

As societies developed technologically, the economic factor became even more important. It was not then simply a case of affording to house and feed children for a few years. As survival through muscle-power gave way to development of brain-power, the education of children took longer and the commitment to support them extended accordingly. In other words, the period before they became 'economically viable' was increasingly prolonged. In some parts of the world, even today, where the economy is still based on relatively primitive agriculture and where education is minimal, children are expected to work as soon as they are strong enough. (I vividly recall watching a ten-year-old girl in Colombia as she slaughtered and dismembered a sheep in the forecourt of her family's farmstead.) In contrast, a girl or boy in a technologically-developed society may well go right through adolescence into young adulthood before being expected to earn a living.

If the economic factor was instrumental in consolidating the practice of contracted, monogamous marriage – i.e., it was not so much that a man might prefer to have only one wife as the fact that he could not usually expect to be able to support more than one family – then, paradoxically, it is now the economic factor (in conjunction with others) which is undermining its continuation . . . for at least two particular reasons.

The first reason – linked with the expense now of raising offspring in an advanced, modern society – is a total change in the parents' expectations. In the not-too-distant past (and, as above, still today in poorer parts of the world), the economic viability of a family was partly based on the fact that a child was looked upon as an asset. Not only were sons expected to help support the family as soon as they were able to do so but, even when grown up and married, they did not in the main leave the family ethos. They would, for example, be expected to 'follow in their father's footsteps', to help expand 'the family business', to have sons themselves so that 'the family inheritance' could be passed down from one generation of the family to the next, and so forth. Daughters were looked upon as an asset in that as girls they could be expected to help their mothers in the home and, if possible, also make a contribution to the family livelihood. And when it came to their marrying and moving as an asset into the ethos of another family, the parents could expect to receive a price for releasing her. Such expectations are now almost-totally reversed. A child of either gender now represents an investment in which there is no promise of economic return to the family. Both are likely to be only a liability. When both have been supported through the lengthy educational process, they are only expected to become economically independent, i.e. no longer a liability.

The second reason, closely linked with the first, is the gaining by women of a share of economic power. Several factors would account for this – technological progress reducing emphasis on muscle-power, shift of emphasis away from the need for maximum reproduction, opportunity for the release of right-brain enterprise in women, and so on. All such factors combined began to remove the necessity for differentiated role-assignment. As segregated conditioning became less important, there was no reason why both boys and girls should not go through the same educational process, increasingly prolonged though it had become. As a consequence, girls were able to see themselves as participants in the procuring role, rather than being confined to their traditional, home-based roles.

Alongside this development – and perhaps helping to bring it about – was the fact that daughters had become less and less of an economic asset to the family. A quaint indicator of this transition may be seen in the custom of dowry. Oddly enough, dictionary definition of the word gives both 'present given by a man to or for his bride' and 'the portion given with the wife'. In other words, and to put it more explicitly, we have the old practice where it was customary for a price to be paid to the parental family for releasing an asset reversed into the more recent custom where, in effect, a price is paid by the parental family for being relieved of a liability.

Be that a valid comment or not, the present-day women's liberation movement has been made possible by a non-discriminating educational climate which can enable a daughter to become economically self-sufficient in her own right. She (like her brother) may still be a parental liability whilst growing up but, if and when it comes to marriage, her worth lies in her own estimation and there is no question of her being bartered. From the feminists' point of view, this development allows women to escape from an oppressive patriarchal ethos which has always tended to treat women as possessions to be negotiated over. On the evidence of many cases throughout history, the justification for such charge cannot be denied; but the moral tone of the feminists' indignation suggests lack of appreciation of the fact that in the past the stark realities of group-survival demanded that all members had to be accounted in terms of their economic worth. Nevertheless, now that we in wealthier societies can afford to be more liberal, no one could sensibly argue against the right of any person, male or female, to strive to become economically independent.

All the group-survival factors which led to the formalization of marriage have become increasingly irrelevant. From a man's point of view, a woman is not likely to look to his muscle-power to defend and protect her. She may or may not want a husband to father her children; and, if so, usually only once or twice. And, more than likely, she will hope not to be entirely dependent on his providing for her. All the exhortations of the once-influential religious establishments fall on increasingly deaf ears. They sound old-fashioned and almost out of touch with the way modern generations see the challenges of their lives and their relationships. They do not see why they should be contractually bound 'for better or worse' to one other person 'until death doth them part'. Young couples in love are naturally optimistic about their future together; but, at the same time, they are all-too-aware of the mounting difficulties that future may hold for them. As the female becomes increasingly less dependent on the male and the male becomes increasingly dispensable, there is less and less convincing reason for a woman to feel confident in totally committing herself for the rest of her life. As far as her survival and aspirations are concerned, she sees herself as having less and less to gain from such commitment. A man, meanwhile, may well begin to feel that he has less and less to offer.

In addition to the above changes of circumstance, there are further modern factors which compound the view that the institution of marriage needs to be radically over-hauled if it is to be continued as a mutually-agreeable and -fulfilling *modus vivendi*; that is to say, as far as the attitudes and expectations of those entering it are concerned, and as far as the rules governing its conduct are concerned.

One of the modern factors is that of duration. Within the relatively-recent past – at most, say, over the past century or so – life expectancy in developed countries has steadily increased. At the time when the religiously-endorsed, economically-expedient marriage arrangement was established as a lifelong commitment, prospects for the duration of that relationship were considerably less than they are today.

Death through disease, war, childbirth, starvation, deprivation and sheer wearing-out through labouring to survive meant that a vow to live with a chosen partner until death was commonly far less of a long-term commitment. Even though marriages tended to be contracted at a much earlier age, nearer to the age of puberty, the chances were that the dedication would be, at best, for a period of, say, three decades. Gradually, the prospect has extended until, these days, the likely duration has risen to, say, five decades (even though young people with careers are tending to marry later[60]). What is more, of the possible fifty years or so together, only for something like half of that period will the couple be jointly and actively engaged in raising and supporting a family. In other words, for perhaps half of their married life, they will not have the binding influence of their most important, shared responsibility. Furthermore, there is the presently-increasing likelihood – due to earlier retirement, redundancy, etc. – that the husband will not be engaged in earning a living away from the home for most of that post-family period.

Linked with the extended-duration factor, there are what may be termed the 'intensity' and 'frequency' factors which have been brought about by technological advances – long range communication and fast travel. Partners in a marriage (or any other established relationship) now tend to be more immediately, closely and frequently in touch than in the past. The availability of fast, long-range communication increases the pressure to keep in touch and that means being far less out of touch; hence the intensity factor. In the past, slower travel meant that for many reasons husbands and wives were separated for longer periods – days or weeks, sometimes months or years. Fast travel has much reduced such periods of separation and hence increased frequency of contact. If there was a validity in old adages such as 'absence makes the heart grow fonder' and 'distance lends enchantment', then it has now been largely eroded.

It might at first be thought that increased intensity and frequency of contact would help cement relationship. Being less out of touch may provide for reassurance and hence some alleviation of worry; but it can also increase pressure of demand. The fact is that quantity of contact is no substitute for quality of contact. If anything, overload of the former is likely to undermine the latter.

Psychologically, the above effects are closely connected with the potentially-conflicting split-motivations of the mind. On the one hand, frequency of being in touch will help allay left-side fears of insecurity and discontinuity, i.e. awareness that during a period of separation the relationship may be threatened or broken by some unwelcome intervention. But, on the other hand, excessive intensity of 'being in each other's pockets' can put frustrating pressure on right-side desires for freedom, independence, autonomy, etc. That side of the psyche, being interested in the quest for self-development, self-integrity and individuality, values privacy, being alone, 'having one's own space', exploring new opportunities, 'doing one's own thing', and so on. Both self-sanity and good relationship require a sensitive balance between being allowed to be oneself and being a responsible half of a partnership. So many of the problems in the marriage commitment nowadays – arising from the duration, intensity and frequency factors – are to do with difficulties in balancing the expectations and requirements of maintaining a relationship with individual ambitions and aspirations. In the past, this has been a typically-male problem in his role as husband. Now, in the wake of women's liberation, it has increasingly also become a problem for the ambitious and aspiring female vis-à-vis her conventional roles as both wife and mother. It could be said that this development has more than doubled the difficulties likely to be encountered in establishing a mutually-fulfilling marriage.

A further modern factor which ought to be brought into the picture is that of family dispersal. Technological advance has given rise to increased specialization in the later stages of education. Specific qualifications designed for application in particular occupations has meant people having to live where appropriate work can be found. Advancement within a chosen career can then mean taking opportunities which require moving from one location to another. Greater mobility of the population has as a result reduced the past tendency for different generations and relatives of a family to be within close reach of each other. One effect of this – apropos the extended post-parental phase of marriage – is a decline in the value and usefulness of couples in grandparental roles. Despite long-distance communication and faster means of travel, these are no real substitute for being 'just down the road'. This can only add to an older couple's sense of redundancy and isolation when their children have moved away, a situation which can only increase the intensity and inter-dependence of their own relationship. At a time when they no longer have the shared focus of raising their offspring and are having to adjust to being on their own again, the marriage can come under considerable, unexpected strain.

If all the foregoing factors are added together, one may well begin to wonder how much longer the custom of lifelong commitment to one partner can sensibly be promoted and justified. Even if the view still persists that a marriage contract is the most secure and beneficial context in which to beget and raise children, what then of the third third of each partner's life and the second half of their relationship? Long-established habits and rituals? Mutually-agreeable pleasure-seeking? A shared home and possessions? Are fear of loneliness, decline in vision and gradual reduction of horizons positive enough grounds for continuing a taken-for-granted companionship which may be soured by undercurrents of long-suppressed frustrations and resentments? Of course, for some, it may not seem like that. But, for others to whom it does, the answer can only lie in individual pursuit of self-fulfilling, higher aspirations – if necessary, independently of the partner.

As far as promotion of traditional marriage is concerned, religion has been, and to some extent still is, highly influential. If all else in the conduct of a marriage has fallen into confusion and disarray, there may still be the binding power of the original dedication to abide by the vows exchanged in public under the jurisdiction of divine authority. Nowadays, it is far less likely that a young couple will believe that some remote and almighty deity will have the slightest interest in what two fallible mortals may attempt to promise each other. But some will still prefer the religious ceremony, partly because it provides a special sense of occasion and because the vows exchanged seem more profound than an exchange of contract under civil law where the commitment has more to do with legality than morality; but partly also because, in dedicating themselves to each other, they want to raise the status of their relationship to one which will transcend the ordinary business of everyday survival and ambition. They wish to see themselves joined together to support each other in developing and fulfilling their highest aspirations (whether or not those aspirations are clearly understood at the time, or if they are ever subsequently developed).

One of the principal features of an official marriage ceremony, religious or secular, is that the couple welcome the opportunity to announce their commitment publicly. Nowadays, this act is psychologically important. They will privately have sworn their dedication to each other; they will most likely have been sexually intimate; they may well have lived together for a while; they may even have a child. To all ordinary intents and purposes, they are already 'married'. But they have not publicly put themselves under obligation to each other. The public making of promise is, of course, a genuine and sincere gesture intended to assure the partner; but it is also – especially when the superstitious element of the religious dimension is added – an accepting of certain standards and rules of self-discipline which may invite public accountability if broken. The binding effect of this formality is one of self-obligation – giving oneself the challenge of keeping one's word. The breaking of one's word may not now be regarded as reprehensible; but, psychologically, to the person concerned, it has self-imposed penalty. It represents a failure of authority over oneself. Losing the respect of others may be of little significance; in the modern world, a man's or woman's word is far less likely to be taken as his or her bond. But the losing of self-respect through having proved oneself incapable of truly meaning what one has publicly announced is something quite other, something one will have to come to terms with within oneself. If you cannot trust yourself (and you do not have a deity to forgive you), who else will you ever trust?

Whatever the actual intents and purposes of the likes of Moses, Jesus and Mohammed – heroes all, in their own time – they can surely not have imagined that their utterances (or subsequent interpretations of them) would still be affecting millions of relationships hundreds of years after their passing. That their pronouncements should still be providing the moral background upon which the commonly-accepted tenets of modern social institutions still depend betokens their deep understanding of human predicament. Nevertheless, in modern Western society, that influence is being seriously eroded, especially where dictation as to the proper conduct of man and women in marital relationship is concerned. In no small measure, this erosion is due to the assault of the feminists who (understandably) pour scorn on the archaic assumptions of the patriarchally-instituted concepts of 'holy matrimony'. They wish to see exorcised from the social ethos all such notions as the undefiled Virgin being handed over by the autocratic Father to a virile Hero who has proved himself entitled to possess her and expect obedience from her for the rest of her life.

Although such a scenario does in fact symbolize biologically-based, psychological principles in the relationship of the feminine to the masculine sides of the psyche, there is no denying that it is quite out of touch with the social realities of the modern world in general and the outlook of the liberated female in particular. As a bride, probably well into her twenties, she is most unlikely to be a virgin, her father is very unlikely to claim any dispensing authority over her wish to marry and the groom is unlikely to expect to command her obedience. In other words, the conventional marriage ceremony has been reduced to little more than a ritualistic performance. In view of the feminists' charge of patriarchal exploitation, it perhaps seems paradoxical that women are still generally keener to retain the ritual than men are. This may be due to the female's stronger left-brain − i.e., inclination towards continuity, conformity, repetitive performance, identification with the body, simulation of the mother, etc. But it may also be due to a deeply emotional factor within her psychological make-up which urges her to sacrifice herself (on the altar). Oddly enough, the feminine side of her psyche does wish to surrender to the ideal masculine. Although in the Anglican ceremony the word 'obey' has been dropped from the bride's vows to her husband, in principle, deep within herself, that is precisely what she wishes to do (given her confidence in his being able and willing to provide for all her needs).

Due to the relative ease with which divorce may now be obtained (at least, in Western society), the marriage vows, though they will initially have been sincerely made, are not likely to exert much influence if the going gets rough in later years. The fears aroused by the prospect of marriage breakdown are more likely to be of insecurity than of breaking one's word. The latter is not nowadays thought of as a failure of self-authority; nor does it attract public disrespect – especially in a world where sticking to one's word is all-too-commonly regarded as being obstinate or arrogant.

Whatever the private consequences of breaking one's marital vows, the fact remains that the social expectations which originally governed the form of 'divinely-ordained' marriage contract have changed considerably. The under-lying matriarchal imperative to procreate has lost much of its momentum. Due to population pressure, the expense of raising children, the availability of contraception and the legalization of abortion, the matriarchal-cum-patriarchal exhortation to regard sexual intercourse as primarily, if not exclusively, an act of reproduction is increasingly ignored in favour of its attraction as a source of pleasure only. In the first phase of marriage, this change of emphasis may not in itself cause problems. But, as mentioned earlier, it obviously can do later if the appetites of husband and wife do not continue to match. As a consequence, we have now reached a situation where extra-marital affairs are com-monplace and fidelity is exceptional (even abnormal).[61] Needless to say, none of this augurs well for happy and enduring marriage.

Further erosion of the foundations of marital contract comes with the emancipated female's gaining economic power. It is all very well in theory and in the first flush of commitment to agree 'to share all worldly goods'; but in practice, if there is any factor in marriage more difficult to balance than sexual appetite, then it has to be negotiating equable sharing of expenses and agreeing joint-ownership of possessions. In times past, it was usual for the husband to hold the economic power. In return for his promising to support his wife and their children, she promised to abide by his decisions.

The likelihood that both partners in a modern marriage will be contributing financially towards upkeep of their domestic arrangement not only means a radical shift in the dynamics of the relationship but also introduces a wide area of potential conflict. And, as is well known, if the marriage does founder and divorce takes place, a great deal of bitterness and wrangling is likely to ensue over claims of entitlement to assets and possessions. What began as an unconditional covenant to share ends up as claim and counter-claim over rights of ownership. It then becomes all-too-evident that willingness to share did not mean surrender of ownership.

The kind of potential conflict created by shared economic power within marriage is not difficult to anticipate. There is danger of dispute over who pays for what, of either partner considering that the other is not pulling his or her weight, of one accusing the other of incurring unnecessary expenses or making indulgent purchases, or spending to much or not saving enough, of disagreement over priorities, and so on.

And, because both partners are actively engaged in earning, there may well be difficulty in agreeing on how to share fairly the responsibilities and tasks of running the home, especially if the demands of parenthood are also involved. In other words, problems of role-playing. The difficulties of role-assignment can be further compounded by changing circumstances in the working career of either partner. For example, the husband's promotion may require him to change the location of their home, a move which may well not suit the wife in pursuing her career. Or the wife may begin to succeed in her career far better than the husband in his, improving both her status and income beyond his capacity. This the husband may find difficult to accomodate, not only because of its effect on his self-esteem but also because he may find himself under pressure to defer to her ambitions and to compromise his own in order to take on domestic responsibilities with which she is increasingly unable or unwilling to cope. These are but two examples of the kind of issue which can arise out of women gaining occupational rights and opportunities. They, and others like them, can only make the married state more and more difficult to sustain harmoniously.

Quite apart from the marital stresses caused by the sex-for-pleasure factor, by the problems of a shared economy and by the confusions of role-sharing, each partner will more than likely be having to cope with mental tensions caused by conflicts between the two sides of their own minds. Any conflict between the partners will be a direct reflection or projection of conflicts going on in the heads of both.

For example, the masculine side of the ego in the husband will be endeavouring to compete and succeed in the world at large; but, in addition, in this modern state of matrimony, he will also be having to see himself as competing and succeeding in relation to his wife, no matter how sincerely the couple may see themselves as both working for the same goals. This is something which, in the old dispensation, he did not usually have to consider. His wife was his complement, not his competitor. Meanwhile, the feminine side of his ego will be fearful of failing, tending increasingly to be on the defensive for fear of becoming dominated and impotent. Needless to say, this is not a situation conducive to easy companionship and compatibility.

Simultaneously, the masculine aspect of the ego in the liberated wife, fired by opportunities for self-advancement, will not only also be competing in the world at large but will be sensitive to any objection, resistance or diverting demand from her husband (real or imagined). In anticipation of same, she will probably have been encouraged by women's liberation propaganda advocating her right to assert herself. (Fair enough; but assertion is a very close neighbour of aggression.) Meanwhile, the feminine side of her ego will also be haunted by fears of failure, not only in relation to her career but possibly also in relation to denial of or being less than adequate in her maternal commitment.

Related to the latter anxiety, research studies have shown that pre-menstrual disturbance tends to be more aggravated in women involved in competitive work situations. Beyond that, it would not be at all surprising if it were found that occupational stress incurred by women who work whilst they are pregnant (and just take a month off to give birth) did not have some significant, deleterious effect on the physical and mental constitution of her offspring (cf. p. 101). As a well-publicised American feminist[62] complained – having placed, it should be explained, all the blame for the problem on oppressive male prejudice – 'The guilts of less-than-perfect mother-hood and less-than-perfect professional career perform-ance are real because it is not possible "to have it all" when jobs are still structured for men . . . and homes are still structured for women.'

Perhaps in due course the work and domestic structures will be reorganized and a way will be found for women to be able 'to have it all'. But complaining about oppressive, patriarchal systems – which have in the main served conventional matriarchal priorities well enough in the past – is surely not helpful, being de-structive rather than con-structive? Would not the energy spent in complaining be better spent in trying to come up with some sensible solutions?

Increasing mental preoccupation and stress induced in both men and women owing to their both trying to meet the demands of both workplace and home does not bode well for either being able to relax, recuperate and share pleasure in the others' company. The growing tendency for both husband and wife must be for neither to have sufficient energy to spare to support, comfort, sympathize with and encourage the other – let alone their children. In other words, the security, stability and sense of 'home' is bound to suffer as both become constantly engaged in meeting the pressure of demand upon them, whether that demand comes from their external commitments or from within their own relationship. Not only will all such tensions have an unsettling and 'centrifugal' effect on children living in its climate but they will gradually undermine the whole point of having a shared home.

Taking into account all the factors mentioned in this chapter – and there are doubtless others – the liberation of women does not promise well for the continuation of traditional marriage as a contract and commitment for life. The arrangement is clearly already becoming difficult to sustain, as divorce statistics, the number of unmarried couples living together, the number of single-parent families, the number of people living alone, and the number of homosexuals amply testify.

At the present rate of increase (in the United Kingdom), it will not be too long before one in every two marriages will end in divorce.[63] (The figures would undoubtedly show a good deal more than fifty percent if there were added in all those couples whose marraiges are really defunct but who for one reason or another prefer not to go formally and legally through the procedures of separation.) Many divorces occur in marriages of less than seven years duration; the majority take place in less than fifteen years. And more than half of the couples involved are less than forty years old (from which it may be inferred that survival of the marriage concept has more to do with the conditioning influence of pre-war generations still maintaining it than with recognition by post-war generations of its validity for its own sake). Statistics for unmarried cohabitation are difficult to obtain, for obvious reasons. But the number of single-parent familes – the vast majority maintained by women – has risen rapidly and dramatically over the past twenty years or so.[64] Statistics do not reveal reasons; but there can be no avoiding the deduction that traditional marriage is not the central and stabilizing feature of society that it used to be – regardless of whether it has ever been the desirable institution it has always been promoted as being.

It is said, and truly said, that 'hope springs eternal'; so, doubtless, does the desire to love and be loved. A young couple romantically in love and pledging to share the rest of their lives together touches the deepest yearnings of the heart. There could be no more poignant a representation of the perennial hope in each person that he or she will find the key to complete happiness and fulfilment through love.

Psychologically, the commitment to marry another person represents the desire to join together and bring into proper relationship the two sides of the mind. In other words through the selfless loving of another, it is possible to come to terms with oneself and to resolve the contradictions within oneself (and, let it be said, that will not necessarily in the longer run be as easy as the first flush of enchantment might suggest). Whilst the masculine right-side, represented by the groom, promises to serve and support the feminine left-side, represented by the bride, the latter promises to obey (meaning 'being willing to listen to') the aspirations and authority of the former. The 'marrying' of the two sides of the mind depends entirely on the disposition of the 'heart' – whether the person concerned is 'free of impediment'.

The feminine, 'conceiving' side of the mind in both genders is primarily concerned with their mutual responsibility to beget and care for their shared offspring – hence the term 'matrimony' which comes from Latin roots meaning 'mother' and 'formed'. The masculine, 'governing' side of the mind in both genders is concerned with their joint desire to fulfil themselves through higher aspiration. In principle therefore, the marriage contract between two people ideally serves two purposes. It is intended to provide for their comfort, security and procreative fulfilment; and it is also intended to provide for mutual support in their higher, spiritual aspirations as individuals. That such principles should be lost sight of in an ethos devoted to the pursuit of pleasure and material gain is hardly surprising.

In societies where parental authority is strong and the culture focuses primarily on the economic power and cohesion of family, the marriages of offspring are more likely to be arranged by the parents. In other societies – particularly in the West where there is greater emphasis on the autonomy of the individual – choice of partner is usually left to the offspring themselves. Even so, parental influence can still be important; and an economically-dictated stratification of society usually means choice of a partner from similar background. However, the alchemy of attraction often ignores all such considerations and remains a mysterious and largely unpredictable process. The power of a right-side marriage of romance is likely to be far more persuasive than a left-side marriage of convenience – even though the former may be a more hazardous enterprise. If there are no serious impediments, externally imposed or internally invoked, then the heart will have its way. Each gives, devotes, sacrifices and worships; and each gains sense of status and self-worth.

Naturally, each looks upon the other as being the cause of release from all uncertainties and fears. The other becomes the one through whom and in whom all desires may be fulfilled. In the full spate of intoxicating enchantment, sense of well-being and confidence is such that each experiences willingness to surrender all self-will in order to please the other. The heart experiences passionate longing to be totally at one with the other, both physically and mentally. It could be said that the state of being in love is transformative and blessed with intimations of the full measure of spiritual aspiration for self-immolation. It is as if the blissfulness of the state opens the way to some transcendent and magical dimension of the mind.

The desire to marry which distils out of romantic engagement represents the desire to unify a duality, to merge together two 'halves' which on their own seem separate and incomplete. As suggested above, such yearning reflects the longing to reconcile the seemingly-irreconcilable split-motivations of the mind. The longing is to bring about a steady, inner state of peace and harmony in which all fears will be resolved and all desires fulfilled. The feminine left-side of the mind yearns for the inspirational guidance of the right side (the ideal husband) whose authority is founded in wisdom. The masculine right-side seeks a devoted and obedient left side (the perfect wife) whose virtue manifests as beauty. The marrying or joining together of the two in harmonious intercourse gives rise to their offspring, unconditional love – just as the sexual intercourse of the married couple ideally begets their perfect child.

Such high-flying, 'metaphysical' principles apart, psychologists have devoted a considerable amount of thought to the 'mechanics' of inter-gender attraction and rejection. Their models are often prosaic, logical and akin to the precise laws governing the interaction of physical phenomena. For example, it is suggested that mutual compensation plays a major part in reciprocal attraction; that it is due, as it were, to the neat balancing of an equation. Imbalances in one will look for compensating imbalances in the other. Or, in other words, weaknesses in one will be attracted by compensating strengths in the other.

There is thus a tendency as the relationship develops for each to transfer to the other unwanted responsibilities, a tactic which relieves each partner of the anxiety of having to fulfil them himself or herself. 'If you do what I don't want to do, I'll do what you don't want to do.' The compensation idea can be described in other terms, as in the following by a Jungian analyst:[65] 'The tragedy of marriage based on romance is that peers rarely marry. All too often, the daughter marries a substitute father (protection and authority) and the son marries a substitute mother (comfort and attention).' Although compensations are attractive in the phase of romantic engagement, they tend to develop later into dependencies and demands which can all-too-easily lead, if not met by the partner, to frustration and resentment.

Another commentator[66] states: 'Often, the entire basis for the relationship is a balancing act, each person compensating for the deficiences of the other. . . (As either one begins to change), the very foundations of their relationship may begin to disappear because they have nothing else in common to hold them together. Any change in one person, therefore, becomes a threat to the other and will be met with resistance.'

Although compensation may well play a part in logical explanations for people being attracted to each other, such explanations surely cannot be the whole story? There must also be a spiritual element, a dimension transcending the mundane, in that overwhelming magic of falling in love and being in love. If there is not so, then human aspirations are but fanciful illusions and the human condition is reduced to the level of pathetic machination. Alas, however, it has to be admitted that the magic of romance is somewhat ephemeral. It is apt to vanish as rapidly as it first took hold as both partners, drawn into the practical business of living together, become vulnerable to all manner of persistent demands and pressures. As disillusionment insidiously invades the ethos of the relationship, the original unconditional love is compromised by conditions. Fears that the love is being lost invite demand that it must be proved: 'If you love me, you will do . . . (this or that for me) . . .' Evidence is continually required and, if it is not forthcoming, the worst is feared. What began as the desire to give becomes desire to possess: 'You will not do (this or that) . . . if you love me.' Possessiveness breeds resentment which turns to anger and hatred. Blame for failure is projected onto the other. The gravitational pull of the mundane brings the aspiring relationship down to earth and the original enchantment vanishes as if it had only been some hallucination or hypnotic trance.

'Once locked into a relationship, the balance between the two people may be so sensitively tuned that the slightest change in either one sets off a cataclysm. The more extreme the polarization and, therefore, the more "romantic" the couple, the more rigidly balanced they are and the less play or tolerance for change there is. Thus the high-intensity romance transforms itself into stagnant boredom. It is as if one partner or both were hanging on for dear life.'[67]

Part of the inevitability of the process of disenchantment is due to the fact that in these modern times of high expectation neither partner is likely to allow the other much credit. Pressures are greater and fuses are shorter. Rights have become more fashionable than responsibilities. Being quick to demand and quick to blame eclipse the old-fashioned virtues of patience and forgiveness. With the emergence of women's rights and the strengthening of the assertive aspect of their egos, the 'centrifugal' tendency accelerates. All the conventional balances and dispositions designed to allow a man and a woman in married relationship to complement each other are increasingly abandoned. In particular, as already mentioned, there is dismissal of the traditional prerequisite in entering the marriage contract that the woman should promise to obey the man. It is worth taking this matter a little further because, on analysis, it may be seen as the key factor determining whether there is any real sense in trying to maintain the institution of marriage.

Of course, in this day and age and in Western society, it is now out of the question that any woman – or the majority of men for that matter – would expect such a commitment as a requirement that a wife should agree to obey all her husband's instructions to be reinstated. (Neither is it likely that the reverse could be instituted, i.e. that the husband should agree to obey the wife.) The trouble is that the word 'obey' has subtly changed in meaning. Fundamentally, as mentioned earlier, it means simply 'willingness to listen to'. It would be reasonable to suppose that, originally, when the male in his traditional roles was responsible for coming up with all survival initiatives, the female in her own interest was well-advised to follow her partner's lead. It would also be reasonable to imagine that this mutually-beneficial expedient sooner or later tended to drift towards the idea that a husband had the right to expect his wife to comply with all his instructions. Hard on the heels of that shift there will have followed all the negative connotations of imposition, exploitation, subordination, domination, etc. Women's liberation understandably demands that all such imposition should be removed. The question then arises as to who is going to be willing to listen to whom if both are keen to have their way?

The subtle yet profound effect of neither partner in a relationship now necessarily expecting to obey the other (in the sense of accepting instruction) inevitably leads to conflict, especially where deciding priorities is concerned. It might at first be optimistically thought that two intelligent people would be sensible enough to discuss problems and work out mutually-agreeable solutions. That may be so some of the time, especially during the early phases of a marriage when both are keen to prove the success of their relationship; but it is most unlikely to be so all the time. Emotions and feelings are not easily governed by reason. Occasional flares of frustration and resentment suppressed tend to ignite a smouldering fire beneath the surface. Inner dissatisfaction begins to cloud and poison disposition. One or both may begin to see married life as a series of concessions, compromises and frustrations borne under the shadow of unspoken and unresolved issues which insistently keep recurring. Human nature being as it is – much influenced by subconscious fear and uncertainty – either partner may begin to feel exploited and dominated by the other. 'In order to please you and allow you to do and have what you want, I am always giving seventy-five percent and only getting twenty-five percent in return.' Self-defence barriers are erected; no-go areas established; rows erupt or skirmishes of attrition become frequent. If neither has authority respected by the other, neither will obey the other (in the sense of being willing to listen). In effect, they will cease to communicate, and the unresolved issues will force them further and further apart, psychologically if not physically.

That is not to say that therefore the notion of one party conceding authority to the other needs to be restored; as already suggested, that would not now be either acceptable or workable. But it is to say that in a situation where each partner expects to have equal authority in all areas of decision-making (and neither acknowledges that they are bound together under the jurisdiction of divine authority) the chances for sustaining a harmonious, long-term relationship are much reduced. Their situation is rather like two people in a rowing boat, each with an oar, neither in control of the tiller. They may hope that they will keep a straight course and eventually arrive at some mutually-agreeable destination. But if one begins to get disheartened and fails to co-operate, the boat starts to go round in circles, going nowhere.

No doubt the tradition of marriage will survive for the time being, despite the mounting odds against lasting success. Young people – though probably at an increasingly later age – will continue to enter into the commitment hoping that they will be able to make it work and that they will be happy ever after. And there will continue to be older people whose first marriages have failed who will choose to marry again in the belief that they will not make the same mistakes again.[68]

Probably the most enduring influence in favour of the continuation of marriage is that it is still widely-believed to be the most suitable context in which to beget and raise children. Sociologists endorse this view on the grounds that children brought up without the benefit of stable, two-parent influence tend to be prone to greater psychological disturbance. However, as more and more children experience unhappy parental relationship, broken homes, divided loyalties, single-parent unbringing, having to adjust to step-parents, and so on, the less confident they in their turn are likely to be when they themselves consider or undertake the commitment. A vicious circle indeed.

Overall, there can be little doubt that the chances of a long-term, contracted relationship enduring happily until the death through old age of one of the partners (usually the husband) are now nowhere near what they used to be. Even if it continues to be accepted that marriage is the best context in which to raise a family, one may well begin to wonder whether its continuation through a post-family phase of two or three decades is necessarily as beneficial as it is generally maintained.

Social consensus promotes the belief that the endurance of a marriage is in itself proof of its success. The lasting of it from one decade to another is regarded as cause for congratulation and celebration. This is understandable in the left-brain sense where survival through time signifies success. The long-lasting marriage fulfils the criteria of continuity and stability. And the couple will gain some sense of security from the comfort, familiarity and predictability of the relationship. But what of the marriage in the right-brain sense? That side perceives and evaluates success by different criteria – to do with quality, not quantity; to do with finding self-fulfilment, not the number of children and possessions acquired. During the first decades, sense of fulfilment may be found in working, running a home, raising a family; but what of the decades when the family has moved on? There may still be the home and for some there may still be work; but what of the marriage? Is there fulfilment enough to be happy? Or is it simply continuing in default of preferable alternative, in fear of loneliness and the unfamiliar?

In the past, marriage has been looked upon as an integral part of progression through life, a *modus vivendi* that mature adults of both genders will naturally expect to undertake. Social conditioning assumes and strongly persuades that all members of the community will enter into it for the sake of the continuity and welfare of the group to which they are beholden. It is at the same time also assumed that living permanently with one member of the opposite sex is physically and psychologically the most beneficial arrangement for the individual. No doubt it can be an arrangement which may well provide for sense of security and stability, and for the sharing of pleasures and problems, of hopes and fears. In more recent times – perhaps due to growing awareness of certain limitation in the above scenario – greater emphasis has been placed on the notion that the married state is also the best vehicle for the self-development of each partner.

That sounds on the face of it a reasonable and laudable proposition. But, to say the least, it presents a formidable challenge. It rather depends on what is meant by 'self-development'. Let us assume that it implies exercise and evolution of the right side of the mind, given that the married state caters well enough in theory for the needs of the left side of the mind (continuity, security, stability, etc). Social conditioning in favour of the latter means that the right side will have to learn self-discipline, responsibility to others, putting the interests of others before one's own, and so on. But that does not constitute self-development, even if it makes one a nicer person for someone else to live with. Evolution of one's right-side powers and talents requires a medium for creative self-expression; and that has little or nothing to do with being married. Ideally, therefore, one's working occupation should provide it. That occupation may provide something of a vehicle for the gaining of wealth, status and power; but these days it is less and less likely to be a medium for creative aspiration and inner self-fulfilment.

Self-development implies self-motivation, independence as an individual, pursuing initiatives, taking risks, exploring opportunities, being adventurous, devoting oneself with passion to that which provides inspiration. Needless to say, none of these criteria fit comfortably with the precepts of marriage – which is no doubt why creative individuals in the past have frequently either eschewed it or made a hopeless mess of it. The fact is that the terms appropriate to describe the requirements for self-development are all-too-likely to be fatally at odds with those for permanent relationship.

This problem has long been familiar enough to the male, well used to trying to meet his responsibilities as a husband and father and also trying to pursue his personal ambitions and aspirations. All too often he has ended up favouring one at the expense of the other. And now, in the wake of women's liberation, the situation can become doubly fraught. With the advance of the female right-brain and her gaining equal rights, authority and opportunity, she is now also well into the quest for self-development. If marriage was never that easy before, due to the male partner's having to come to terms with the conflicting motivations in his psyche, it is bound now to be even more difficult with the female in the same predicament. How can two aspiring individuals, each developing independently, realistically expect to live harmoniously together for the rest of their lives?

If long-term, inter-gender relationship is to have any future, there will have to be some drastic re-thinking of attitudes and expectations, virtually a complete re-negotiation of the terms on which the old tradition of marriage has been founded. Such mutual re-negotiation will have to be worked out primarily at the psychological level, with as full an understanding of each partner's creative aspirations as possible. The old socio-economic basis will no longer suffice.

I recall being told by my wife a few years ago of the presenting facts of a marital problem she was dealing with as a counsellor. The wife – a smart, assertive, efficient-looking, thirty-year-old, career woman – came to the first interview claiming that her husband was continually breaking their contract. Upon enquiry as to what contract she meant, the woman took a five-page, closely-typed document from her handbag. It proved to be a contract which she had drawn up and had asked her husband to sign when they had married a year or so previously. It listed in detail who was to do what in the home and how frequently, how the expenses of running the home were to be shared between them, what proportion of each one's salary could be retained for personal use, how often they would eat out, and so on. I do not know under which clause the husband had continually broken the rules; probably several. Perhaps he had failed to make love to her the stipulated number of times a month; or perhaps he had wanted them to have a baby and had kept, accidentally-on-purpose, forgetting to buy contraceptives. Whatever the catalogue of transgression, the odds are that the husband was fed up with the whole business of living their lives according to a set of rigid, fear-born rules. Love does not strike bargains.

If traditional marriage is not already foundering on the rocks of present realities, then it is drifting perilously close. Before the whole convention goes down midst a wreckage of disillusionment, young men and young, liberated women who are embarking on it, would do well to work out what of lasting value is worth salvaging.

9 The Hero In Trouble

If by asking the question 'But what about men?' there is implied enquiry as to the present situation and future prospects for the male, then the answer would have to be 'Not good'. In the light of what has been outlined in previous chapters, he seems to be well on the way to being thwarted in just about every way he has hitherto looked to justify himself. In virtually all the roles through which he has in the past sought to exercise and prove his 'maleness' – warrior, hunter, procurer, explorer, inventor, lover, husband, father, leader, sage, priest – he has become increasingly redundant, impotent, dispensable, compromised.

The young man of today in modern society is better educated[69] and on average possibly more intelligent and aware than his forefathers. And yet crisis arises for him because he is still born with the same biological programme, still fired by the same ancient-brain compulsions and still fundamentally conditioned by the same social ambitions as his predecesssors, right back to the emergence of *homo sapiens* thousands of years ago. Programmed into the genes which have dictated his make-up, there is still the urge to compete and vanquish in order to gain status and power. And yet he finds himself in a technologically-developed world where such ambition is increasingly difficult to accomplish in the traditional manner. No wonder he feels confused and divided in his mind. How now is he to succeed? If the old conventions which once moulded his image of himself are now becoming inappropriate, how is he going to be able to maintain his gender-identity (if indeed such embassy itself is still appropriate)?

The male was once encouraged to prove himself as hero – one who did good deeds, conquered evil, accomplished feats of bravery, rescued imprisoned maidens, and the like.

But it is not easy to embark on heroic embassies in a world where good and evil are far less distinguishable (and less fashionable), where there is little scope for courageous enterprise and where there are few maidens who have not already liberated themselves. The restless and uncertain young man on the threshold of adult life can feel himself faced with a disheartening prospect in which opportunities for self-fulfilment look somewhat limited, unattractive and uninspiring. Success in gaining status and power today is all-too-likely to be seen in terms of gaining wealth and position within the hierarchies of large corporations or institutions. And all-too-often the most remunerative occupations can be those which are the least rewarding where the development of creative talents and sense of self-worth is concerned.

In the past, even if a man did not manifestly succeed in gaining wealth, status and power in the world at large, he could find purpose in earning a living through being able to support a wife and family. But even in this respect his prospects today look much less reassuring than they used to be. With the gaining of economic power by the liberated young woman, and thus the gaining by her of status and independence, he cannot necessarily be confident in pinning his self-respect on the indispensability of his roles as husband, father and breadwinner.

At the same time as the male is becoming less sure of his image in the eyes of the liberated female, she is becoming not only less dependent on his view of her but also more able to rely on the emerging new image of herself. As role-differentiation diminishes and the male's roles lose their definition, the female appears to him to be more of a competitor than a complement. As the male feels himself increasingly on trial, and dispensable if found unworthy, he may well now begin to wonder as he sets out in life just what is really worthwhile doing with it. If the female no longer needs heroes, where lie the incentive and inspiration in his relationship with her?

That is not to say, of course, that unattached young men and women cannot much enjoy each other's company, be stimulated and reassured by each other, and have a great time together in pursuit of mutual pleasures and interests.

Obviously, they can and do. But the above question can all-too-readily loom as soon as there is the prospect and attempt by them to enter into an exclusive, one-to-one, permanent commitment to each other.

Where there is no definition of 'territory' in relationship, occupation of 'common space' can soon become a rights free-for-all. Defence and attack, those most primitive of instincts, become synonymous – just as they were before rights of ownership were invented. Attack is reinstated as the best means of defence. What is claimed by one to be assertion of rights looks like an aggressive takeover bid to the other. The more frustrated the male, the more defiant the female; the more assertive the female, the more aggressive or withdrawn the male. A vicious circle of suppressed anger is set up which can all-too-readily be triggered into charge and counter-charge. And beyond a certain point, that confrontation can only result in a breakdown of communication and hence dissociation; or in an eruption of physical or psychological abuse.

Not a longer-term prospect that the modern young person of either gender is likely to relish. Such commit-ment begins to look like too much of a risk. And yet many will attempt it. Why? Because (left-side) social condition-ing, based on millennia of precedence, promotes the idea that any loss of (right-side) autonomy will be more than compensated for by the prospect of long-term comfort, stability and security. And commitment to one member of the other sex seems, in the throes of enchantment, to promise just that. Fear of loneliness can be alleviated by stable companionship. What is more, such commitment has long been promoted by secular and religious authority as being the best arrangement for group cohesion and continuity, shared responsibility for offspring being the paramount purpose and fulfilment. That group-biased scenario may have served society and its members in the past; but is it relevant for individuals of either sex today?

The women's liberation movement, as suggested in the first chapter, has brought about considerable change in social institutions, change which in general men may have been able to accommodate precariously for the time being through ignoring their longer-term implications (except in the case of the religious establishment). But the accompanying changes of attitude within heterosexual relationship, especially those now adopted by the female, are becoming extremely difficult to negotiate at a personal level. It becomes all-too-apparent very quickly that room for manoeuvre is very limited when both partners are in competition, have no agreed areas of authority and no overriding adjudicator. It may be that the women's revolution – essentially a bid for self-authority by the female – has only brought to the surface problems which have always existed but which have in the past always been suppressed and masked by the necessity for social cohesion and continuity. It may be that the old conventions were once expedient but are now only being perpetuated out of habitual conditioning and the propaganda of institutional authorities whose continuation depends on maintaining the *status quo*. (That is undoubtedly how large numbers of young people growing up in post-World-War-II societies have viewed the situation.) It may even be that the fundamental flaw or illusion in such ancient convention is maintenance of the pretence that the genders are entirely complementary when in reality they are not so.

What the women's liberation movement is in fact saying, especially the feminist wing of it, is that the female is an individual in her own right. In which case, the genders are not complementary – a word which implies that the female has characteristics and qualities, etc., which the male does not have, and *vice versa*. Extrapolation of that is that each can provide the other with what is lacking in himself or herself and that therefore together they constitute a whole. The notion that male and female are dependent on each other for their sense of completion entirely contradicts the precepts for becoming and being an individual. In which case, it would be sensible at this juncture in human history to make a clean sweep of some long-espoused and -cherished illusions. If the liberated female is saying that she has woken up to the fact that she is not dependent on the male for her fulfilment, then the male would be wise to consider the possibility that he is not dependent on the female for his realization of individuality either. That is not to advocate that they should go their separate ways; but it is to say that, having realized that they are not indispensable to each other, each may help the other in the quest for individuality and fulfilment without either being beholden to the other.[70]

The young liberated woman may well be fully occupied at the moment with trying to resolve the dilemma of pursuing independence versus fulfilling her traditional social responsibilities, expecially those biological ones deriving from her maternal instincts. In this situation the male cannot expect the female to pay him the attention he has been used to receiving. It is really up to him – if he is not too preoccupied with the pursuit of wealth and trying to sustain his outmoded 'macho' image – to undertake a considerable re-think as to what image of himself he wants to create for himself. He will have to envisage some radical, new initiatives if he is to experience a renaissance of confidence in himself.

Given that there has not been such a shift in the conventions of inter-gender relationship since patriarchy was superimposed on matriarchy several millennia ago, it would be hazardous to predict the outcome of present trends and to propose what the male might do about the erosion of his traditional functions in society. Perhaps the best one can do is to examine the present situation as objectively as possible and then take time to visualize and contemplate the possibilities and options. This would be to put the right-side powers of the mind to good use and should avoid the dangers of over-reaction – some signs of which are already apparent as outbursts of senseless behaviour in modern society.

Of the several features of the situation touched on in this book, three salient and closely-interlinked ones emerge as central to the male's image of himself – work, sex and long-term relationship with the female. All three are essential to his sense of 'maleness', how he sees the purpose of his life and how he gains sense of self-fulfilment and self-authority.

Traditionally, it has commonly been upheld that while the female may gain her sense of self-fulfilment through her maternal roles, the male has always needed to look primarily to his work-occupation to gain his. This may be seen as a reflection or consequence of the original, pragmatically-based differentiation of roles in mixed-gender society. Gradually, as the basic requirements for physical survival become increasingly well catered for in developing societies, the popular criteria for gauging male success became the degree of wealth and status gained. However one may view the use of such criteria for the measuring of success, and whether or not they are truly fulfilling, a number of factors are now making the gaining of them more and more difficult for the majority.

Technological advance shifted emphasis from muscle-power to brain-power and machine. Saving labour – one of the main purposes of technology – means that it becomes more difficult for the less intelligent and less educated to find work. Paradoxically, therefore, whilst on the one hand society promotes the need for its members to work and succeed, it is on the other hand reducing the amount of work available. Furthermore, the work available becomes less creative, more administrative. Even further, women are now competing for and taking their share of it. At one end of the workforce spectrum, there are those gaining wealth and improving their status complaining that they are overworked; at the other end of the spectrum, there are those with menial or no work finding that they are being denied access to wealth and status. In between, the great majority are either striving to move towards the former end or striving to avoid drifting towards the latter end.

All this is taking place as the result of an educational process which predominantly prepares young people to perform specialized functions in a technologically-based, commercially-oriented economy. It instils expectations of wealth- and status-gain, persisting in promoting the expectation that attainment of qualification will ensure a certain and lasting working life. It further assumes that this prospect should provide a sense of self-fulfilment.

As has become all-too-apparent, for the majority much of the above promise is not realized in practice – if the amount of debate, discontent and anxiety relayed by the media is anything to go by. There are clearly numerous aspects of this disillusionment, but let us take one which patently contradicts the promoted promise – that of a 'lasting' working life.

Some years ago – when unemployment was starting to increase and much was beginning to be heard of 'the right to work' and 'the need to create jobs' – a leading British economist[71] was pointing out: 'The way things are going, by the 1990's the traditional workspan of 47 hours per week times 47 weeks per year times 47 years will look more like 35 hours times 45 weeks times 32 years, thus cutting the total working life from 100,000 hours to 50,000.'

In other words, such a considerable reduction of likely work-span combined with increased life-expectancy means that 'the average person' will find himself or herself 'redundant' for the third third of his or her life. What is more, curtailment of working life is likely to take place when – if they have been developed during the work phase – the right-side powers of the mind are fully mature and probably at their highest potential.

None of this bodes well for the male's sense of self-fulfilment in his work-occupation. He may succeed in gaining wealth and he may find that gratifying to some extent – though the chances are that success in that respect will only engender appetite to gain even more. And he may succeed in gaining status which will also give him some satisfaction – though it is likely to be limited status only recognized within the ranks of his particular occupation. But to be faced with curtailment of further potential through 'voluntary redundancy' or 'early retirement' with a third of his life ahead is likely to be considerable threat to his confidence and morale. It can only threaten the image he has built up for himself, undermine his sense of self-worth, exacerbate 'mid-life crisis', detract from his prestige, and so on.

How can these demoralizing trends be reversed? The crux of the matter seems to be that earning a living has now come to mean simply earning money. Money represents power, especially the power to employ. Since a young person starting out in working life is now unlikely to be rich enough to be an employer, the educational process places emphasis almost entirely on the young adult needing to find employment. He or she is thus persuaded to accept that wealth and status can only be achieved through being a successful employee within an organization, corporation, institution, established profession, etc. So far, so good. The disadvantage, however, is that the terms in which the employee can succeed are entirely dictated by the aims, practices and disciplines of the organization. Even if he or she succeeds in climbing to the top of the pyramid and becomes nominally 'the employer', that status and power still has to be exercised in accordance with the same parameters. All may still be well and good – providing the employee fulfils his or her requirements and the organization meets its aims; otherwise, unemployment. But the chances are that, in order to maintain income and position, the employee will have either to discipline, compromise, under-employ or even deny his or her right-side talents. And that can mean discontent and frustration. In the above shift towards the necessity 'to be employed', emphasis has moved away from the 'self-employment' option – which, in reality, is the only status which is likely to offer full potential for self-fulfilment in self-generated terms.

Self-employment in a world committed predominantly to material gain is not, of course, an easy option. The pressure is there to make money in order to survive and the early years of self-enterprise for the young person, espcially in creative occupations, can be lean indeed. And even then, eventual success can all-too-often mean having to compromise, even the debasement of talents. Even though an increasing minority may now be taking the risk, it is not one that the majority will be able or dare to take. They will not see themselves as realistically having the option. And yet, if asked, the majority of that majority will most likely admire and envy those who have taken it. They would themselves like to have the relative freedom to be self-reliant, to have the challenge to succeed in their own terms, to have the opportunity to exercise their creative talents to the full, to fulfil themselves as individuals more or less independent of the dictates of others.

Interestingly, out of the juxtaposition of 'premature redundancy' in middle-age and the frustration of self-fulfilling talents during employment a challenging possibility arises.

Supposing each person's working-life, earning-a-living prospects were recognized as having two distinct phases, each of two-to-three decades. The first, following formal education, would be earning a living in the conventional sense, being in paid employment, contributing to the welfare of the group through taxation, etc. During this period, young couples, as mutually-desired and -agreed, would devote themselves to each other and to the shared responsibilities of home and raising a family. Jobs would be structured to allow full- or part-time working for both men and women so that the latter could be relieved of the career versus motherhood dilemma.

At the end of the paid-employment, family-support phase, both would embark on the second phase – as 'self-employed' individuals. Leaving the first phase with a degree of earned resources shared between them (plus some continuing pension or insurance income), each would begin a new and challenging career dependent on self-generated initiatives and enterprise. Here there would be a wide range of possibilities but each would choose an occupation in which skills and talents realized during the first phase could be further developed. Such occupation would not necessarily be connected with that undertaken during that first phase; in fact, it would most likely be something quite different.

There is a definite reason for this option of total change of direction. When having to make up their minds what to do with their lives, young people often experience indecision due to divided motivation. Typically, there can be a (right-side) ambition, often in favour of some adventurous enterprise or creative occupation, which they would love to pursue. But (left-side) caution combined with social pressure persuades them that such a course would be too risky, too insecure, from an economic survival point of view. They therefore take up a conventional, 'mainstream' occupation which will provide a more reliable and predictable basis for earning a living, marrying, supporting a family, etc. Enterprise is circumscribed and creative talent suppressed, remaining undeveloped unless pursued as a sideline in an amateur fashion. This denial of creative self-expression and -development, can then erupt as a feature of mid-life crisis, especially where there is also disillusionment with the career actually followed. That crisis would be much alleviated if there were definite prospect of a new and creative phase of life ahead.

The two-phase system would be appropriate and beneficial in other ways. As suggested above, it would permit development of creative and self-fulfilling aspirations at a time when right-side powers are mature, tempered and still full of potential; when the person is 'life-wise', experienced and less likely to be tempted by diversions. Also as touched on above, a woman if she so wished would feel reassured in giving time and attention to her children knowing that, after they have left, and she is experiencing the disturbances of menopause, she will be starting a new and challenging phase of her life – switching, as it were, from the procreative to the creative. And as far as inter-gender relationship is concerned, the family-support phase in which a couple will have been inter-dependent in meeting their shared responsibilities would give way at mid-life to a phase of 'mutual independence'. Each would be free to pursue their own initiatives as individuals. Apart from anything else, this would present the relationship with a clear and positive challenge in which each would need to examine its virtues and drawbacks, seeking positively to build on the former and resolve the latter in the light of promising, new opportunities.

This would have the effect of either revitalizing the relationship or terminating it, instead of letting it drift on unhappily out of habit and social convention. It would be better for the couple to more or less part company and lead independent lives than to remain in a stale and possibly acrimonious alliance which allows neither scope to develop and express themselves as individuals. If the couple elect to stay together, their lives will be the richer for having creative occupations rather than limping along filling time with what pleasures and entertainments can be afforded. What is more, the arrangement would mean that the couple entering the relationship for the first phase, whether formally married or not, would know that it was not necessarily a till-death-us-do-part commitment. This in turn would help prevent the partners from taking each other for granted and preclude their feeling trapped in a once-and-for-all situation. They would be more inclined to negotiate rather than attempt to establish and defend separate territory.

Thus, in the third third of life emphasis would be on self-employment, self-expression, self-development – via a 'vocation' which might have financial implications but not necessarily so. Either way, earning money would not be the principal motivation. Emphasis would be on individuals 'doing their own thing' for the purpose of self-fulfilment, having by then fulfilled their social obligations and responsibilities. They would then be 'earning their living' in terms quite other than those commonly associated with that expression.

Although to an extent some aspects of the above already happen, they are still regarded as unconventional, anti-social, irresponsible, etc. For such re-structure of life-expectation to become widely appreciated and acceptable, there would have to be a major overhaul of social conditioning. And that would have to include a radical shift in the present premises of the educational process.

At present, as mentioned earlier, great emphasis is placed in modern education in technologically-developed society on assimilation of specialized information in order to obtain qualification to earn money through being employed. During secondary and tertiary stages, encouragement given to the development of right-brain talents is heavily loaded with expectation that such talents will be applied to economically-viable occupation. Fair enough, up to a point. The trouble is that moulding talents to fit group-prescribed careers is likely to become such a preoccupation that there is little or no room for the individual to develop and use them in the realms of higher aspiration. Self-expression and self-development become channeled and limited by the constraints and purposes of a particular discipline – which may but, more likely, may not in itself be entirely self-fulfilling. Any student who wishes to explore the full range of his or her talents has to do so with spare energy through ancillary interests in his or her spare time – if he or she has any energy and time to spare.

For the two-phase prospect to be viable, the present left-brain bias of inculcation and specialization would have to be adjusted to give much greater scope for right-brain exploration and development. (At present, such interests as the creative arts, religion, spirituality, psychology, philosophy, etc, tend to be increasingly shunted aside or omitted altogether because they are viewed as irrelevant to the serious business of qualifying for a job.) It would have to be understood that the responsibility of education would not only be to prepare young people for the first phase of paid employment but also to prepare them for an equally-important second phase of self-employment. This would mean that the student would not be viewing the first-phase job as the be-all-and-end-all of his or her working life. He or she would see it as an intermediate phase with certain rewards leading on to a phase promising quite different and self-fulfilling rewards entirely self-generated and self-realized.

One of the major drawbacks of the present system, as touched on earlier, is that it leads to an unnerving full-stop. The common expectation is that when paid employment comes to an end, now at an increasingly lower age, people will move gracefully or protestingly into retirement. Those who still have years of work-potential in them are likely to be the protestors because to them the prospect is not earned retirement but enforced redundancy. But, because their right-side talents have not in their past been sufficiently encouraged and developed, they tend not to have the confidence, vision, initiative, enterprise and capacity to motivate themselves into subsequent self-responsible venture. If they had been educated into such possibility, their prospect would be quite different.

The advantage of the two-phase scheme would be that each person would pass through middle-age not with the depressing prospect of soon being useless but of looking forward to a stimulating challenge. What is more, after the employed phase during which an 'arbitrary' monetary value has been put on the person's services, he or she would have the opportunity to put a self-realized worth on himself or herself. To prove oneself to oneself is the really heroic task. Of course, society would need to reorganize itself to accomodate and facilitate the scheme; it may in the initial stages have to support it to a degree. But in the longer run it would undoubtedly become the richer for its investment, especially in terms of social morale. Even from the financial aspect, there would be considerable saving on the cost of helping to support the rapidly-escalating population of 'retired' people.[72]

This is not to say that people in the second phase would necessarily be earning to support themselves; as stated earlier, that is not the point of the exercise. Some may do so, some may not. But there would be economic benefit in general. A proportion would see their talents and skills most beneficially being used in social welfare in one form or another, a development which would reduce pressure on the taxpayer and the welfare state. (Not to the extent and in ways which would put first-phase employees out of work.) Apart from that aspect of economic benefit, those who are self-motivated and have purpose in life are themselves less likely to be ill and a burden on others than the employee, the under-employed and the unemployed.

Which brings us to the heart of the current problems with work. A fundamental fact has become obscured by the development in technologically-based society of what might be called the employer-employee-unemployed syndrome. The fact is that every person has been, is and always will be self-employed. But technology brought about specialization of function and concentrations of wealth; hence the syndrome (regardless of whether a society's ethos happened to be dominantly capitalist, socialist, communist or whatever.)

The employer is one who employs himself or herself in the business of employing others, the employees. The employee is one who employs himself or herself by hiring his or her muscle, skills and services to another, the employer. The unemployed is one who is not in a position to employ himself or herself as an employer or an employee. The employers' authority is limited by the amount they can afford to pay to hire employees; the employees' authority is limited by the amount for which they can hire their skills and services; the unemployed are limited through the loss of their power either to employ or gain employment. In this syndrome, everyone loses to some degree sense of self-authority because everyone can only evaluate themselves in terms of their command of wealth (which is not how people really want to measure their worth).

Needless to say, this syndrome produces a situation full of potential for discontent and conflict, especially where it is really impossible to put a market-value on a particular function. In the interests of economy or profitability, the employer is looking to minimize the fee paid to an employee. In the interests of self-gain, the employee will look to maximize the fee he or she can command. The stage is set for continual confrontation. And such confrontation can do nothing but demean both the respect each may have for the other and, more importantly, the self-respect of both. (In the male case in particular, a man may respect another for having superior muscle-power, skill, intelligence; but he will not respect the other's having authority through wealth alone.)

Arising out of the above contention come all manner of false assumptions and claims ... and absurdities. For example, 'the right to work' – which instead of meaning the right to employ oneself becomes the right to be employed. Or, the need to 'create jobs' – which means putting the responsibility to provide work on others instead of taking initiative oneself. Unemployment, instead of meaning the failure to find the means to employ onself becomes the failure of the employer to provide employment. The individual's option to 'withdraw (his or her) labour' escalates into the 'right to strike' collectively – the most pernicious off-shoot of all since, taken to extreme, it is likely to bring about collapse of the employer–employee alliance resulting in increased unemployment.

It would be as well to add hastily that none of the above is anyone's deliberate 'fault'. It has simply come about because technologically-based society has slipped into the error of believing possession of wealth represents entitlement to authority. Neither the employer nor the employee is particularly to blame for this conflict (whether the former be an individual, a corporation, an institution or a state authority.) The fault lies in their mutual conspiracy – just as capitalist and communist ideologies depend for their justification and distinction on the common ground which makes them appear to be in opposition. Anyone who has the intelligence and wit to recognize this conspiracy cannot help but realize that the only way out is to reinstate the virtues of self-development, self-responsibility and self-authority.

And the means to that end has to be restitution of the underlying self-employment principle. That is not to say that there ought to be an abandonment of the employer-employee syndrome, an equal distribution of all wealth, a rejection of technology and all its apparatus, and so on. Such a revolution would destroy a great deal that has been beneficial and would probably end in anarchy and chaos. But it is to call for recognition and restitution of the fundamental premise on which the whole development and evolution has been based – that individual initiative is essential to group-progress, that self-cognized responsibility is more important than collective persuasion, that in the final analysis, just as it is unworthy to depend on the opinion of others as to one's value, so it is necessary to take authority for one's actions in every respect. Therefore, in whatever walk of life one happens to find oneself operating, that function is a result of having chosen to employ oneself in that manner. Whatever one's participation, in that work one is really self-employed. In that realization, the carrying it out has really nothing to do with anything other than self-development and self-responsibility, whether or not it appears to have any direct bearing on the wealth and welfare of society as a whole. In other words, in final analysis, there is no one to blame but oneself.

By the old criteria for heroism, the above self-motivated initiative might seem strange. Maybe there is no further need for heroes? But, if there is – and only the individual can decide that for himself or herself – then heroism in the above respect looks now to be the only feasible option, even if attempting it has to be left until the third third of a lifespan. As suggested earlier, proving oneself to oneself in one's own terms has to be the ultimate heroic task in anyone's life.

10 The Sexual Conspiracy

Where male self-image or 'maleness' is concerned, fulfilment through work-occupation has now become increasingly difficult. Fulfilment through the other two aspects – sex and long-term relationship – seem to have become equally difficult, if not more so. What reassuring prospect is there for the lover, husband and father in a world of liberated women? In view of the foregoing survey, none to be sure of.

As described in earlier chapters, sexuality has two distinct aspects – the reproductive and the erotic. This division is physiologically-based and is endorsed in practice, for example, by contraception. Contraception denies the reproductive element, thus enabling birth-control; but it also gives licence to the pleasures of the erotic without fear of unwanted pregnancy. The division can engender some bizarre anomolies. In the UK, for example, whilst one partner in an estimated quarter of married couples is making himself or herself deliberately infertile through sterilization, an estimated one in seven couples are seeking medical help because of infertility problems in one partner or the other.

The male's self-image as lover can be aligned with the erotic aspect of sex, and that of husband-father with the reproductive (though for him, of course, the erotic component cannot be absent in the act of 'fathering'). Furthermore, whereas the reproductive element conventionally implies the necessity for long-term relationship the erotic does not (though orthodox religious doctrine has usually insisted that it should). Characteristically, the erotic aligns with the 'masculine-right' side of the psyche, the reproductive with the 'feminine-left' – i.e., the former with power and status, the latter with continuity and security; the former with individual initiative, the latter with group responsibility.

In the aspect of lover and erotic sex, the male has lost much of his licence. His self-image diminishes as his initiatives are constrained by such factors as virulent sexually-transmitted disease and challenged by the changed attitudes and behaviour of the liberated female. She is as likely now to be interested in the pursuit of sexual pleasure as he is. At one level, the male may welcome increased opportunity; but, at a deeper, psychological level, having to share the right to take initiative reduces his image as hero. It is not so much that he now has less need to compete with other males because the female has become more promiscuous; simply that there is little point in his trying to be the heroic lover. The 'rescuing' role of the lover in the romantic sense is an embassy in which the male proves himself by liberating the 'virgin' female from parental authority and environment. In effect, he is in competition with her father and, through awakening her sexuality, frees her so that she can become an independent individual, ready to give her allegiance to a younger, dominant male. Needless to say, in the wake of women's liberation, all this has gone out of the window. There is now no need for such an heroic exploit. His role as lover in that sense has vanished; he is now likely to be just a young male looking to gain sexual pleasure here and there, now and again, as opportunity presents itself.

However – to add insult to injury, as it were – opportunity for erotic encounter is not the whole story. As pointed out earlier, implicit within the (masculine-right) erotic, there is competition for status and domination. As pointed out earlier, to meet initiative and challenge from the female, the male needs to be able to erect on demand. And, if he fails, his virility is in question. This may or may not be a problem for a young male; but it does mean that he can be put on the defensive when by nature he is programmed to be on the offensive. In the event, he can be put into the feminine role or position – physically represented by her taking the superior position whilst he lies supine, she being active, he passive. She adopts the masculine, dominant role, exciting herself to orgasm.[73]

Furthermore, if the female for one reason or another fails to gain sufficient satisfaction via an aroused male, she is encouraged by modern sex-therapists to please herself (which, re. the tendency for her to become more masculine, can mean self-excitation of the clitoris, her vestigial penis).

Further evidence for this 'masculinization' of the female in the context of erotic pleasure-gain can be inferred from the observations of biologists. According to such observation of other species, the promise of orgastic climax, 'the height of venereal excitement in coition', is not an incentive factor in the female's willingness to participate in sexual intercourse in any creature other than the human being (except, possibly, some other primates). 'Female orgasm is simply a by-product of (human) evolution. . . The couple has to work at it and whether they do so or not is a product of their social, not their evolutionary, history. . . Perhaps the most interesting thing about female orgasm is that it is so similar to the male's.'[74] Well, it may be a 'by-product', but that should not be to underrate its present-day importance and significance. The couple may 'work at it' or the female may prefer not to rely on the male to achieve it; the 'interesting thing' is the female's motivation and experience being 'similar to the male's'.

Divorce of the procreative aspect of sex from the erotic – by contraception or, in general, sexual intercourse without intent to procreate – is 'unnatural' in the sense that it defies the purposes of Nature. Given that a central feature of patriarchal-cum-matriarchal religious doctrine upholds 'marriage' of the reproductive and the erotic, wide acceptance in developed societies of licence to enjoy the erotic alone has probably done more than anything else to undermine religious authority and influence. At the same time, it has to be admitted that 'divorce' of the 'feminine-procreative' from the 'masculine-erotic' has also reduced gender-distinction making the marriage of female and male increasingly irrelevant, less necessary. As emphasis falls away from the notion that the genders are complementary, and they thus become competitive as individuals, one begins to wonder whether we are on the threshold of social disintegration or evolution. Given that women's liberation represents a development and awakening of the masculine right-side of her mind, it is inconceivable that she can revert to her former passive status. The development, therefore, has to be one or the other.

The old tradition upholds the belief that being in love is a prelude to committed relationship and intercourse for reproduction. The new dispensation accepts that being in love is in itself good enough reason for 'making love'. Modern society is still ambivalent in its attitude towards casual sex and payment for sex, wavering between thinking it immoral because love is absent and condoning it because it cannot be eliminated and because trying to do so might have dangerous consequences where the behaviour of frustrated males is concerned. But, when you stop to consider it, 'making love' is a strange expression; can love be 'manufactured'? The common view would surely be that being in love – at least in the initial stages of enchantment – is a fragile state and that making love, though a natural consequence, may well do more to threaten than secure it in the longer term. The fact is that the erotic alone does not prove love, no matter how frequently repeated. When the object is pleasure only, the act is all-too-often followed by sense of dissociation and depletion, the latter especially so for the male, even when mutual satisfaction has been achieved. After the intensity of conjoining, the reality of being separate reasserts itself.

Of course, there is more than the attraction of the erotic in the state of being in love. The sense of being together, being intimately in touch, having someone special to share with – all such benefit helps to alleviate the fears of loneliness and failure (feminine-left) and to stimulate and inspire sense of power and purpose (masculine-right). But making love can all-too-easily exacerbate the former and undermine the latter in either or both partners as time passes and the act becomes a ritualistic habit. The unconditional giving of each to the other may in the moment of ecstasy be a total commitment; but there is also within it an element of 'suicide' or 'a little death' (of oneself). In the 'making of love' there is a degree of 'giving oneself away'.

Is there any way of avoiding this deteriorating effect?

Possibly. The inspirational factor in the erotic carries the power of creativity – as has been (and is) evident in the lives of those devoted to creative aspiration in one form or another. Their passion for their form of self-expression has frequently sprung from and been related to the erotic aspect of their sexuality – in both genders perhaps, but especially so in the case of the male. Such men fall passionately in love, seeing the female as their source of inspiration. Their difficulty, however, has frequently been that as soon as one source has faded they have had to find another; or lose their creative momentum. That particular example apart, the fact is that all sense of motivation, enterprise and purpose, especially in the male, stems from passion, and that passion in turn stems fundamentally from erotic power.

The trouble is, particularly in Western society, that the creative aspect of passion has tended to be eclipsed or suppressed by social persuasion that it must be channelled primarily into the procreative. Even when the religious establishment has acknowledged the virtues of creativity, it has usually made sure through patronage that such aspiration has been directed towards enrichment and aggrandisement of the establishment itself, thus making sure also that sensuality did not raise its ugly head above the surface of religiosity.

The legacy of this centuries-old conditioning ensures that most Westerners still tend to be stuck with the view that sexual intercourse is a means either to procreate or to spend passion. And, even though there has been much greater licence given to the erotic from time to time, in recent times on a much wider scale, there is still some legacy of bias in favour of the procreative being 'good' and the erotic 'evil'. Consequently, there is little awareness that there may be a creatively revitalizing and spiritually enriching aspect in the erotic. In some Eastern traditions, such division and denial has not been so much the case. They have long regarded the erotic as being an intrinsic element in creative and spiritual aspiration. Due to the Western religious traditions' preaching that the erotic and the spiritual are incompatible and should be clearly divorced from each other, superficial report and evidence

of some Eastern practices have usually been condemned
and dismissed in the West as simply decadent and
pornographic.

However, if the male lover is now confused and at a loss
as to how to restore his image as heroic, one solution might
be for him to give some thought to Eastern concepts,[75] the
origins of which go back at least as far as the Western ones
he is familiar with, the persuasions of which are far less
dogmatic and divisive. The ancient Chinese spoke of the
'transubstantiation' of semen into the 'nectar' of immortality (not by denying sexual energy but by consciously
transforming it). Indian traditions speak of the act of sexual
union being translated into spiritual union with the
divine, by transmuting passion into transcendent bliss
(not the transitory ecstasy of orgasm). The act heals the
sense of separation – both of the lovers from each other and
of themselves from the source of their love. In other words,
earthly union is intimation of divine communion.

It would not be appropriate here to elaborate in detail
but, in principle, the sexual practices involved require
self-discipline, one feature of which is total devotion to the
giving of pleasure to the other, not giving in to the desire to
take it. The act is performed for the conscious purpose of
comforting, restoring, fulfilling and revitalizing the loved
one – not exciting each other into passionate frenzy and
orgastic climax (and, in the male's case, expenditure of
semen). Gentle intimate touch and pleasing stimulation
lead to 'mutual tumescence', the female fully willing to
receive, the male fully willing to penetrate (both being
'full-filled'). But with full control; no rapid and strenuous
movement; no convulsive activity which would lead to
what the sexologists call the 'plateau' or 'threshold' beyond
which male ejaculation is inevitable; no striving for the
crescendo from which point there can only be detumesc-
ence, withdrawal, separation and recuperation. Simply the
most intimate, 'passive', sensual interlocking, intertwin-
ing; one expanding into, the other containing, in embrace.
Being two-as-one, each so merged into the other as to lose
self-definition, exchanging subtle yet revitalizing energy
without eventual loss to either. This state can, with
practice, be maintained for hours; even then, only to drift

into refreshing sleep untroubled by fears and sense of
isolation.

Obviously, as said above, such practice requires
discipline; though, since the purpose is mutually and
consciously understood, it is a case of self-control, not
self-denial, a world of difference. For the vast majority in
the West, who tend to speak of having a 'sex-life' or not
having one, the above represents a totally unfamiliar
dimension of possibility. What is more, it is one which is
totally absent from the textbook repertoire of 'sex-experts'
who tend to regard anything short of mutual orgasm as
indicating the presence of some inhibiting 'dysfunction'.
Yet how refreshing – and something of a relief – it would be
if such a dimension of non-demanding sex were commonplace.

Apart from its implications where problems of contraception and sexually-transmitted disease are concerned,
sex would be reinstated as a vehicle for compassion and
inspiration instead of passion and competition, as more
conducive to health and healing than temporary relief of
frustration and anxiety. Confrontations over performance
and exploitation would vanish overnight. Above all,
sexuality would be reunited with spirituality because each
gender would be giving to the other the energy and
assurance to aspire and to transcend the mundane
demands of sheer survival and sensual gratification as
mortal creatures. With reference to the quotation as preface
to this book, the 'liberated' Ophelias of this world might
become less likely to jump to the conclusion that the
Hamlets requesting to 'lie in their laps' had nothing but
'country matters' on their minds.

Whether or not the concept of 'passionless sex' could
become a generally-accepted feature of inter-gender
relationship in modern society, the fact remains that
prospects for long-term relationship in present 'passionate' circumstances do not look promising. Since the
exhortation to 'go forth and multiply' cannot now be
viewed by either gender as quite the shared obligation that
it used to be, emphasis in their sexual relationship has
inevitably shifted from the procreative to the erotic. The
criteria for judging the success of such relationship thus

tend to focus on the negotiation of the partners' sex-life, in particular on success in achieving orgasm – frequently, simultaneously, and so on. To maintain good performance, especially consistently and over a long period, is asking a lot; hence the modern preoccupation with 'sex problems'. A whole industry of sex therapy, much of it of American origin,[76] tackles incidence of frigidity, erection failure, premature ejaculation, retarded ejaculation, impotence, orgastic inhibition, perversions, vaginismus, nymphomania – a catalogue of 'dysfunctions' and abnormalities which militate against a 'healthy and successful sex-life'.[77]

Given such emphasis on the erotic as measure of successful relationship, it is no wonder there are recurring problems. It is hardly surprising that large numbers of couples attempting to maintain a stable relationship come to the conclusion that they are failing to do so. Each may think such failure is his or her fault; or, more likely, think that it is the other's fault. The temptation then, of course, is to start looking for another, more fulfilling partner; the existing relationship disintegrates; morale is lowered and greater urgency and expectation is placed on making a success of the next engagement. The trouble is that neither passion mutually-spent nor passion eventually-blocked are conducive to lasting harmony and contentment. Neither satiation nor suppression of desire eliminate fear of insecurity and discontinuity. Even quantity of mutual orgasms is found to have little to do with maintaining loving respect.

Failure to nurture the creative, inspirational aspect of the erotic all-too-readily reveals its destructive aspect. Failure to build on the compatible elements in sexual intimacy exacerbates the incompatible – the aggressive, competitive, desire-to-dominate ingredients of passion. Failure to exercise the 'higher' powers of the forebrain to transcend the primitive motivations of the ancient brain (in sexual intercourse without intent to procreate) reveals just how incompatible the genders are at the level of self-survival instinct.

Scientific thought, like social conditioning, prefers to promote the notion of an ordered and lawful world. However, when considering some of the fundamental elements and their behaviour within a system, some uncomfortable and seemingly intractable problems arise. Consider, for example, the Black Hole phenomenon in the world of astrophysics. Thought to be caused by the collapse of a star, the characteristics of the resultant 'black hole' have to be accounted for by the use of some unfamiliar concepts which seem to turn our assumed view of the world upside down. Such explanations as 'massive curvature of space-time', 'time ceasing to exist or going into reverse', 'negative emanations' and 'anti-matter' are near-impossible for the conventionally-programmed left-brain to cope with.

'One way to understand the emission (from the Black Hole) is as follows. Quantum mechanics implies that the whole of space is filled with pairs of "virtual" particles and antiparticles that are constantly materializing in pairs, separating and then coming together again and annihilating each other. . . Now, in the presence of a black hole, one member of a pair of virtual particles may fall into the hole, leaving the other member without a partner with which to annihilate. The forsaken particle or antiparticle may fall into the hole after its partner, but it may also escape to infinity, where it appears to be radiation emitted by the black hole.'[78]

Supposing this account of the fate of particles were analogous to the 'mechanics' of human interaction. Could it reveal something unexpected about the genders and their relationship, something that usually we are socially conditioned to ignore?

'Materializing in pairs' begs association with birth out of the mother (mater) of the two genders. In considering the fact of gender-diffentiation, we tend to presume that both genders were spontaneously created and came into existence simultaneously. However, scientific, anthropological explanation that *homo sapiens* evolved through genetic mutation out of Cro-Magnon Man poses certain problems (for the logical left-brain). Was this a gradual emergence; or did *homo sapiens* 'suddenly' appear? If the latter, were there two 'sudden', coincidental mutations giving rise to one instant female and one male? If so, how was incestuous interbreeding of their offspring then avoided? To obviate the coincidental generation of two genders theory, we may prefer the Old Testament explanation that the female (Eve) was taken out of the spontaneously-created male (Adam). In which case, the incestuous interbreeding problem would have been even worse. (Biblical account gets round this difficulty by having Cain find a wife in the land of Nod, an event which seems to negate the spontaneous creation in Eden theory.[79]) Or we may prefer to look for an explanation in line with New Testament belief – that an original female might have given 'virgin' birth to a male (parthenogenetically). This possibility might be biologically more acceptable but it still does not obviate the interbreeding problem. On balance, in this scientific age, we are likely to have to settle for the origin of our species having come about through gradual evolution of other species and assume that several males and females 'accidentally' and coincidentally emerged.

In whatever way the coincidental generation of two human genders took place, the male would probably have to concede that the female would be the equivalent of the Black Hole particle and he the antiparticle – with the former's connotation of being positive and the latter negative. For biological reasons described earlier, the female takes precedence as the primary, constitutionally-stronger, regenerating gender. The male is secondary and only relevant for his power to introduce genetic mutation – being variously described by commentators as 'a modification of the female', as 'an aberration', as 'parasitic', and so on.

We may see clearly enough that the genders 'materialize' (are born), that they 'separate' (grow up as distinct genders) and that they 'come together again' (in sexual intercourse and relationship). But what about 'annihilating' each other? At first encounter, such notion may seem to be taking the Black Hole analogy too far. Human social arrangements have been for so long based on the belief that the genders are complementary and indispensable to each other that to suggest that they may also be fundamentally antipathetic to each other sounds heretical. And yet . . . how come the 'battle of the sexes'? Or why is it that the males and females of other species are so often antagonistic in their behaviour towards each other? Relationship between opposites requires that they are held in a kind of bond of tension caused by their being attracted to each other and yet, at the same time, rejecting each other. In relationship, an equilibrium is brought about in which the centripetal force moving the partners towards each other is counterbalanced by the centrifugal force keeping them apart. So with the genders, being attracted to each other by forces of sympathy (the aspect we prefer to emphasize) and yet kept apart by those of antipathy. There is a desiring each other (giving rise to love) and a fearing of each other (giving rise to aversion). The tension is called 'sex'. At the same time as there is a desire to merge into each other, there is a polarizing fear of losing separate identity, i.e. being 'annihilated'.

As far as the female is concerned, she finds herself attracted to the male for various reasons – because he excites her sexuality, because he is stimulating company, because she admires his character and abilities, because he will make a good father for her children, because he is someone she can care for, because he will relieve her sense of insecurity, and so on. At the same time, there will be an undercurrent of deep resentment, born of the subconscious, self-survival instinct alerted by the implications of such attraction. The attraction represents an incompleteness in herself, a lacking which causes her to see herself as needing the male to provide for her. Thus there is a resenting that she seems to have to depend on the male for support and fulfilment. As she invites his penetration, she will resent being violated. She will envy the powers he has which she does not (e.g., what has been called 'penis-envy').[80] She would prefer different fathers for her children and yet she has been socially-conditioned to commit herself to one. She has to live with the fear that she may have misjudged in her choice and that he may fail her, dominate her or abandon her. All such factors as these the female has traditionally had to live with, and suppress their attendant fears, because of her maternal obligations. If all the above sounds an unduly negative view, then what else has women's liberation been all about? All such resentment and frustration has surfaced in her bid for rights and independence – a bid which implies independence from the male and, in the case of the feminist, explicitly rejecting him, the 'anti-particle'. Even if she is not consciously wishing to annihilate the male, then she is certainly seeking to nullify him.

The female may not yet desire or feel able to dispense with the male altogether; but her bid for liberation is inevitably a move in that direction – moving closer towards, say, the circumstance of the legendary Amazons. This tribe of warrior women had only periodic, ritualistic encounter with men for the purpose of copulation. Resultant male babies were either killed or traded with other tribes. Girls reaching puberty were taught the arts of defence/attack, having their right breasts removed to enable better handling of bow and arrow.

Given the future possibility (as described earlier) of the female even becoming independent of male penetration for her procreative fulfilment, she could then, if she so desired, only need to tolerate the male for erotic stimulation, thus moving closer, say, to the situation of the Amazon molly fish.[81] This is a hybrid species – derived from two other, sexually-reproducing species – which has itself reverted to asexual, parthenogenetic reproduction. The female produces eggs which, unfertilized, grow into female-only progeny. However, the molly, although effectively a female-only species, retains a curious legacy of its ancestral, sexual past. The female still attracts the attention and emission of a male, not to fertilize her eggs but to stimulate them to start developing. Since there are no male molly fish, the 'emancipated' female 'seduces' the male of a closely-related species into a mating ritual. He gets nothing in the way of reproductive fulfilment out of his sexual embassy, all his expenditure of sperm going to waste. Bizarre though this evolutionary development may be, there are elements in it which are not that far removed from trends in modern human society where sexual behaviour is concerned.

The ultimate extrapolation of all the above would be to arrive at a situation where the fully-independent female would only tolerate continuing relationship with the male on terms entirely dictated by her. In effect, that would mean his having to sacrifice himself entirely to her (cf. the image of the crucified man on the cross). As the previously-quoted (p. 169) feminist clearly demands, women will then 'have it all'. If the male values his survival, he should not underestimate the power of the female's better-integrated brain, i.e. her determination.

All the above is not to suggest that the male has had it anything like all his own way up until now. He has had his own 'schizophrenic' ambivalence to contend with. He is attracted to the female for many of the same reasons as she is attracted to him. And he is equally as resentful that he is subject to her powers (especially her seductive sexual power) and is dependent on her in several respects – not least that of being dependent on her for the continuation of his own gender. For all the reasons he may admire her and feel gratitude towards her, he is subconsciously fearful that she will divert or obstruct his enterprise and prevent his development – i.e., dominate, smother, enslave or castrate him (psychologically, of course).

A particularly dramatic account of this fear is given by a traveller in Ladakh after encountering a tribal prophetess: 'Back in Leh, I realized that it was the Oracle's violence that had frightened me, her flashing brutal violence, far more than any power she may have had. In her savage wit and energy she had revived old fears within me, of my grandmother and mother, buried male fears of a female cruelty that no reason could restrain, of a female dark and crazy wisdom that no concern for ordinary justice could keep from its work of destruction. . .'[82]

This account highlights a deep, psychological problem for the male. He is born of woman and has his first intimate relationship with his mother. As an infant, he is bound to her, as in an embrace, by the power of her love for him. Yet as he grows up, he must 'reject' her if he is to find and establish his 'maleness', his gender-identity.[83] Hence 'the fight to be male'. Because this rejecting may engender in him a sense of guilt, he may seek in later life to make amends to the female at the same time as he experiences anger at having been emotionally blackmailed into his predicament. He wants to give love back but, at the same time, to keep a safe distance. Ordinarily, like the female, he will suppress his fears and control his anger. But, pushed to extreme, if he fears being annihilated, he may react with violence and seek to punish (cf. the image of the bound woman being whipped).

This male ambivalence is well illustrated in the account of Tiamat and Marduk (p. 140) where the divine mother-goddess is seen both as almighty creatrix and begetter of chaos. At the juncture in human history when such legends were originated, it is as if the male psyche had reached the age of puberty (sexual maturity), torn between worshipping the mother and the confusions of finding his own sexuality. The triumph of the young male god, Marduk, presaged the bid for 'maleness' over the proclivity to become female, the establishment of patriarchal authority over 'chaotic' matriarchy.

In view of all the above, perhaps the annihilation factor in the Black Hole analogy is not too far-fetched after all. The couple – as particle and antiparticle – gain a degree of mutual security through their relationship, having to keep a degree of separation however in case one annihilates the other. Both fear that if the relationship fails through the force of rejection becoming stronger than the power of attraction, they will become divorced and either or both may fall into the Black Hole, the void, the abyss of outer darkness and 'alone-ness'.

And yet, deep in the psyche, especially of the male, there is an innate urge to self-destruct, to surrender life through sacrifice or suicide. The void, the unknown, has its own attraction – perhaps because it is realized that the security of the familiar is limited, that death eventually annihilates all relationship. The fear of the unknown (left-side) competes with the desire to enter it (right side). The archetypal void is represented for the mortal male by the procreative womb, the original space or Black Hole in which he originated. During his sexual life, he attempts to re-enter it by erotic penetration of the vaginal passage, an act in which he is willing to sacrifice himself. As a Lancastrian friend put it, quoting a typically-north-country, blunt but succinct saying, 'You spend nine months trying to get out and the rest of your life trying to get back in.' Be that as it may, it is in these ancient-brain realms of self-survival instinct that the close association of love and death are rooted. And the attraction of the unknown, of the Black Hole, must ultimately be that death means 'escape to infinity', becoming 'anti-matter', immortality by 'a-voiding' death.

Such metaphysical flights, or psychological depths, are not of course in the forefront of people's minds in everyday life, even though in the background they will frequently influence thought and behaviour. Most people most of the time shelter on islands of familiar ground, relying on what pleasure and security can be achieved, hoping that no 'monstrous intervention from the depths' will threaten disruption. Hoping for the best is the only sane way of coping with fear of the worst.

As far as gender-relationship is concerned, in the main we still rely on the sexual conspiracy born of social expediencey which has served the species well enough as a survival strategy – i.e., committed relationship, role-differentiation, responsibility to the group, and so on. If there is now a monster from the deep threatening to disrupt this whole system, then it has to be liberation of the female. Her bid for independence steadily negates the point of role-differentiation and thus undermines the old basis for committed relationship. At the same time, the process reduces the traditional means by which each gender defined itself and distinguished itself from the other. In particular, the liberated female taking on typically-male roles becomes increasingly masculine in disposition, outlook, attitude, conduct, etc. The question is whether this transition denotes a change for better or worse. Is it a retrogressive or evolutionary step for the human species?

Among the scriptures not acknowledged by Christian orthodoxy as being acceptable doctrine, in a fragmentary testament called 'the gospel according to Thomas',[84] there is an enigmatic statement attributed to Jesus: 'See, I shall lead her (Mary) so that I will make her male, that she too may become a living spirit, resembling you males (his disciples). For every woman who makes herself male will enter the Kingdom of Heaven.'

A strange statement indeed. Could it have been a blatant

piece of male chauvinist propaganda; or was it prophetic
insight born of psychological understanding? It cannot
mean sex-change at physical level; it has to mean a
psychological transformation[85] – a liberation of the female
from her gender-image and maternal disposition. And 'the
Kingdom of Heaven'? At least true fulfilment in mortal life
– a fulfilment, what is more, that has apparently always
been available to the 'living spirit' in the male. Perhaps
even immortality in realms of eternal life.

However the statement may be interpreted, one of the
implications of present trends may be that as the liberated
female becomes more masculine there is the possibility
that both genders may – with equal footing on common
ground, as individuals – together aspire towards a spiritual
renaissance which will have little or nothing to do with
either conventional social expectation or the exhortations
of orthodox religion. Nor will it have much to do with
traditional criteria for successful sexual relationship, i.e.
maximum procreation of the species and maximum
pleasure-gain via erotic sex.

This in turn implies a radical shift in the male's
conventional view of himself, of his social conduct in
general and of his relationship with the female in
particular. What is more, it will need to be a shift as
revolutionary for him as women's liberation has been for
the female. How is this to be accomplished, constructively?

To attempt to answer such a question would be highly
speculative since we are here entering virtually 'unknown'
territory. The male has not been confronted with such a
challenge to change his ways, at least since the emergence
of patriarchy and establishment of the almighty male deity
four or five millennia ago. If that event, as suggested above,
was indicative of the male psyche having reached the age
of puberty, then this modern adjustment has to be the
equivalent of its having reached adulthood. In other
words, he has got to be grown up about it, and not behave
either like a rebellious boy or a wayward teenager. As any
intelligent male who has passed from adolescence to
adulthood will recall, this transition invokes considerable
self-questioning and change of viewpoint. This collective
transition will most likely be no less confusing and

demanding. There may not be, at the moment, any clear answers; but there may be pointers in certain directions.

'Crisis' (from Greek) means decision, and 'decision' (from Latin) means 'cutting off from'. The implication for the male in his present crisis of confidence in himself would then be that he will probably need to look to 'cutting off from' a number of conventional attitudes and habitual courses of conduct rather than expect to see clearly what new direction to take. Indeed, he might do well to consider this cutting-off-from less as a possible denial to himself, more as a means to liberate himself from his conventional view of himself.

For example, he might adjust his attitude to his work-occupation, seeing it less as a means of acquiring wealth for its own sake and for supporting wife and family; instead, more as a medium for self-development, especially through 'self-employment'. After all, where does commitment to acquisition of wealth lead – to compulsion to gain yet more, to hoarding it, to gambling with it, to spending it on pleasures and accumulating possessions. . .? Such accomplishment may benefit the group indirectly to a degree; but is it self-fulfilling as distinct from self-satisfying? He might also direct his enterprise less in pursuit of technological advance for its own sake; instead, more towards creative aspirations in the realms of self-expression. Apart from obsession with technology having created a situation where we have become increasingly slaves to mechanical apparatus, there are now clear warning signs that in many areas technology has advanced as far as it can usefully and harmlessly go. For example, rather than seeking to invade and exploit the 'outer space' of the universe, humanity might be more sensibly employed discovering the 'inner space' of its own mind. In other words, if we are not to stumble from one crisis to another, there must be a backing off from the compulsions of our ancient-brain programming – to proliferate and procure to the maximum.

As far as his relationship with the female is concerned, the male might begin to see her less as a sex-object and a source of comfort and nurturance; instead, more as an individual also aspiring to self-development in her own terms. His responsibility (or response-ability) towards her in committed relationship would be not to allow the build-up of compensations and dependencies but to encourage her to make the most of her opportunities, talents and experience. Each would need to become stimulation and inspiration to the other in their individual quests for self-fulfilment. In other words, emphasis in the relationship would need to move from the procreative and pleasure-gain aspects of sex towards the creative and spiritual aspect. Translated into present-day circumstance, this would mean that though the first half of marriage might still be devoted to mutual- and family-support, the second half would be devoted to self-development as independent individuals. In the latter phase, 'sex would make no difference'. In the process, the male may regain the respect of the female – which he is not likely to do by trying to maintain his old image, or by becoming more feminine in response to her increasing masculinity, or by dissociating himself from her.

On what grounds might be male presume to take such initiative and responsibility? Apart from the obvious one of self-survival, there would seem to be two further good reasons.

The first is because the women's movement has of late begun to show some signs of running out of steam.[86] After the initial surge of enthusiasm for the cause, some erstwhile champions of it are evidently having a few second thoughts born of some disillusionment.[87] Misgivings are expressed that the movement may have lost momentum. Blame is laid partly on male resistance, partly on the disappointing fact that far too few women have wholeheartedly rallied to the call. Regret is expressed that liberation has not as yet brought much of the anticipated improvement in women's lives. What is more, it has caused many of them considerable stress – usually as a result of anxieties caused by the conflicting demands of success in career versus responsible motherhood.

For all the reasons given for the movement's deceleration, the fundamental reason must surely be that the initiative was made simply as a bid for independence and power for their own sakes. No real thought was given to post-revolutionary implications and consequences. There was no real vision of how the 'promised land' would be, of what would replace the conventions destroyed in the process. Thus, what has happened is that the female has simply moved into traditionally-male territory and is now discovering what it is like, and has always been like, to be male – i.e., that it is not the bed of roses that they thought it was. They have found that the grass is not, after all, greener on the other side. Having to compete is not an easy option, as many a liberated woman is realizing to her discomfort. Resultant stress (compounded by menstrual disturbances) are, for example, increasing her appetite for alcohol and making her vulnerable to illnesses previously primarily associated with the male. (Recent report by an Italian research scientist even suggests that career women are losing their hair through stress. Does this mean that bald women will become as commonplace as bald men?) Apart from liberated women becoming subject to the pressures and difficulties that men have always had to contend with, their disillusionment is throwing into sharp relief their stronger (left-brain) fear of failure, increasing their vulnerability to depression.

The first reason, therefore, for the male's needing to take responsibility is that the female is going to need help if her understandable quest for liberation is to succeed. The signs are that she is not in the end likely to prefer to 'go it alone'. The second reason, linked with the above, is that, whereas in the past the male needed to use his superior muscle-power to support her, he is now going to have to use constructively his only other superior asset – his more advanced right-brain powers, especially those of creative imagination and objective consciousness. He is the one who will have to envisage and initiate a spiritually-inspired renaissance, if there is to be one.

To put it another way, the male needs to restore his self-respect, a restoration which would be incomplete if it did not include retrieving the respect of the female. At the moment, he could be said to have two rather limited options where achievement is concerned. He can direct his ambitions into the procurement of wealth. The female may be pleased to share and spend that wealth; but that does not necessarily mean that she will respect him as a man. And, in the process, he may achieve some fame and status – as, say, a sports champion, a popular entertainer, an entrepreneur; or through rising to the heights of his profession. The female may be pleased to bathe in some reflected glory through association with him, and may admire or be amused by his public performance. But in the privacy of intimate relationship with him, she will again not necessarily respect him as a man. It depends on whether his achievement provides him with self-respect. This it will not do if it does not engender within him sense of self-integrity and self-authority – which is what the female does respect in a man.

Self-authority requires the finding of self-respect in one's own terms, not those dictated by others. A common problem for the male arises out of his failing to develop and use his right-side power of objective perception. For example, he easily falls into the trap of trying to gain female respect by seeking to please her. Up to a point, fair enough; but not if it means gradual capitulation into her assumption that he thinks like she does – an erroneous assumption because her better-integrated brain means that she is less aware of contradiction than he is. The male's giving in to compromise blocks his right-side powers and thus reduces his self-confidence. The paradoxical result is that he never really succeeds in pleasing her. To try to do so continually is doomed to failure – including his failure because the endless commitment eventually wears him out.

A typical, conventional marriage scenario runs as follows. A (usually) dominant-left wife, motivated by her need for security and continuity, fulfils her biological programme, bearing children and nurturing both them and her husband. Her (usually) dominant-right husband uses his enterprise and talents to procure and to support and protect his wife and chidlren. They share the family and the familiar. The children grow up, leave home and the couple return to living alone together. As the male ages and his sexual potency declines, he passes through 'mid-life crisis' and gradually becomes left-brain dominant – preferring security to risk, preferring habit to change, the attraction of ease and comfort being preferred to the stresses of competition. Perversely it seems, the wife, at the menopausal end of her procreative commitment, can experience a male-hormone, right-brain surge of power. But her opportunities for taking initiatives are traditionally limited, especially by her continuing marriage commitment, and she has to confine them mainly to domestic and social activities. (All such interaction was once the mainstay of music-hall comedy – domineering wives, interfering mothers-in-law, hen-pecked, peace-at-all-costs husbands heading for the pub, and so on.) The marriage alliance becomes an uneasy bond, each partner in effect becoming cut off from the other. (As an octogenarian American husband, celebrating with his wife their sixty years of marriage, confided when asked the 'secret' of their long relationship, 'Frequent separations and going deaf at sixty.') The implication is obvious enough – that two separate halves never succeed in making a genuine whole.

This may sound cynical; but only so in relation to a popular myth, born of ages of social conditioning, which is only partially valid. Such conditioning, in the interests of group-survival, promotes the belief that the genders are toally compatible and that lifetime commitment by one member of one sex to one member of the other is the best means to ensure the fulfilment of both. That may be valid in left-brain terms, i.e. as conducive to sense of security, stability and continuity (even though it ignores the fact that it is no insurance against fatal intervention). But it ignores a deeper reality, accessible to right-side perception, that long-term familiarity masks the fact that couples in relationship never really know each other as private individuals. In other words, each has a self-projected image of the other; but neither ever truly knows what the other means to himself or herself.

I recall meeting a woman a few years ago who described to me how she had unexpectedly met her ex-husband at a party. She had neither seen nor spoken to him during the seven years since their divorce. The image she encountered in the room was still immediately familiar in appearance but it was as if she was being introduced to a total stranger, even though she had previously lived with the man for fourteen years. She was greatly shocked and felt disconcertingly schizophrenic. She was aware of one side of her mind (the left) trying to reassemble the old, familiar picture of the man and to recall something of the common ground they had once shared. At the same time, the other side (the right) was perceiving that the man was a stranger no more known to her than any of the other guests she had met for the first time that evening. She then realized that she had deceived herself into thinking that she had ever truly known him.

The reality of any relationship is that people meet and communicate in a dominantly left-side sense – seeking to establish common ground and mutual interest. Behind this outer performance of public expression, the right side, in its inner, private world, will be vigilant and scheming – seeking to evaluate advantages to be gained and disadvantages to be resisted. Whilst the outer is engaged in exchange of information, the inner is engaged in visualizing a kind of self-gain, self-defence strategy. During the initial stages of intimate relationship, when each partner is committed to making it work to mutual advantage, there will be honest attempt to divulge as much as possible of the inner world's heartfelt fears, desires and highest aspirations. But as time passes, communication tends to become more and more left-side biased, settling for the familiar, common ground which gives each partner sense of security and continuity. Each tends to think that he or she knows the other's inner game well enough. In reality, neither can continuously keep track of the other's inner world and private thoughts. Neither knows how one really sees the other nor how the other sees himself or herself; in short, neither ever really knows the other at all. One is only familiar with how the other usually behaves. One only knows 'all about' the other.

As an upshot of the above, in the interests of the relationship's security and continuity, each wants the other to remain constant and not to change. Thus, if one does something unexpected, 'out of character', the other is likely to be disconcerted. 'It's just not like him/her. . . (to say this, or do that).' And if it is something disloyal, the other will be offended, 'How could he/she . . . (do this, that or the other) . . . to me?' The above-mentioned wife, on seeing her ex-husband with whom she had lived for fourteen years, said, 'I did not know him;' her past illusion was her once thinking that she did. In the ordinary, everyday conduct of human affairs, perhaps the illusion does not matter most of the time. But the danger of it is that it can beget deep undercurrents of frustration and anger. Thinking one knows the other and not expecting the other to change can mean not allowing the other to develop as an individual in his or her own right (i.e., on the right side). And that will destroy the potential of the relationship.

The maintaining of mutual right-side stimulation (based on either the sensual or inspirational aspects of sexual eroticism) between partners in long-term relationship is difficult, if not impossible. Alleviation of fears of insecurity tends with the passing of time to take precedence over the risk of pursuing desires which might endanger continuity of the relationship. In a way, the female needs two males – a husband for her left-side security and a lover for right-side stimulation. It is asking too much of one man to fulfil both roles continually. Likewise, a man needs two females – a wife and a mistress. But left-side bias in traditional social conditioning does not allow such leeway. It is perhaps in defiance of such constraint that in modern society fidelity in marriage is becoming less normal than infidelity.[88] People 'having an affair' are usually assumed by consensus to be looking for sexual gratification. That may well be partly so; but, at the same time, to greater or lesser extent, they will be looking for mental stimulation, inspiration and restoration of sense of self-confidence and independence.

Although the above may strike the traditionalist as being indicative of social degeneration, it may also hold the potential for positive, evolutionary initiatives. Human intelligence and consciousness may now have reached the point where it can objectively dismantle an illusion or two. The sexual conspiracy has long upheld the belief that the genders are one hundred percent complementary. The fact is that they are on average fifty percent compatible and fifty percent incompatible. If that were fully understood, each would see the other not just as 'the other sexual half' but also as a 'genderless' individual in his or her own right.

11 So, What About Men . . . and Women?

Taking into account all that has been assembled in previous chapters, it is difficult to avoid the conclusion that the old conspiracy of complementary genders is well on its way to being discarded. The fact that both are now less confident in finding lasting happiness through the long-term contracting of themselves to each other is causing widespread anxiety and suffering – and not a little depression and desperation. A lot of people, especially the young, are of course still falling in love; but a large number are also falling out of it – midst blazes of accusation and counter-accusation.

I once heard a spiritual teacher pointing out one of the commonest illusions about marriage. He said that couples having gone through a ritualistic wedding ceremony then think of themselves as being married. They do not understand that what they have actually done is make a mutual contract *to* marry. Marrying has to be worked at over a long period, perhaps a whole life-time – and even then it may be that marriage has not been truly accomplished. Sexual consummation and physical cohabitation for a long time under one roof are one thing; psychological integration quite another. Which is perhaps what Shakespeare had in mind when he spoke of 'the marriage of true minds'.[89]

The popular concept of marriage being the coming together of two halves to make a harmonious whole – in which state each is dependent on the other for a sense of completion – has become increasingly discredited. It implies that neither male nor female can be fulfilled without bonding with the other and that a good marriage should ideally be a steady and blissful state of 'static equilibrium'. But, if continuous giving of love must depend on the constancy of the other, it is not likely to be that 'love which alters not when it alteration finds.' the only way in which the concept of marriage can now be viable would seem to be through mutual recognition by the partners that their relationship must be one of 'dynamic flexibility' – each allowing and supporting the other in becoming self-fulfilled as independent individuals. Not an easy challenge; 'mutual independence' is close to seeming a contradiction of the marriage concept.

Individuality means, at root, 'not being divided'; and that in turn implies self-integrity, self-authority, and so on. Rather than militate against individuality, the advantage of long-term relationship could be that it is the best circumstance for a person to come properly to terms with himself or herself – and thus understand the meaning of being individual, i.e. not being divided within oneself. Eve is described in the Old Testament story as having been created a 'help-meet' for Adam. Sexist bias apart, there is no reason to suppose that Adam was not capable of being a help-meet for Eve also. The point is that each may help the other meet himself or herself, being as it were a mirror to the other. Blaming the other is an easy option; admitting fault in oneself far more difficult. Yet achieving self-authority has as much to do with perceiving self-deception as with exercising one's power. In the previous chapter it was suggested that one partner never truly knows the other; but it may be that each may know himself or herself through the other. The Old Testament story later states that Adam 'knew' Eve. A strange expression since they had evidently been together for some while. In its context, the statement is generally assumed to mean that they were sexually consummated. But supposing, since Eve was created out of him, it means that Adam knew himself through her being a reflection of himself? Or that the masculine-right side of the mind came to understand the feminine-left side?

In this reciprocating reflection, each partner's mind would become 'true' through an inner resolving of conflict between the two sides of his or her own mind. This would be a quite different outcome from the process which usually takes place. 'The working relationship between the left and right brain is developed much the same as any partnership develops. A slight advantage for one hemisphere is magnified with time as its partner increasingly stands back to let it handle a particular task. Ideally, each hemisphere does what it is best equipped to do, but bad habits develop in which the wrong hemisphere prevails and prevents abilities being expressed.'[90] In other words, compensations for imbalances in the mind of one partner are projected as demands on the other. Reciprocating projection is quite the opposite of reciprocating reflection. It makes all the difference between taking and giving. Putting onus on the other is the opposite of self-responsibility; and putting responsibility for one's own imbalances on the other detracts from self-authority. In this confusion, neither party is likely to understand the meaning of self-integrity and individuality.

As a consequence of the confusion – well and truly brought to the surface by the implications of women's liberation – many young people contemplating marriage (and many in the married state) fear that the commitment will deplete them, not complete them. They fear that the likelihood of their having to change themselves to meet the expectations and dependencies of their partners will compromise their potential for self-development. They are apprehensive that becoming interdependent will diminish their valued independence. Such misgivings used to be the fate of the bridegroom, the jokes of his surviving-bachelor friends echoing in his ears as he walked to the altar. Now such doubts are the fate of the 'liberated' bride also, convinced that at least she should not be required to surrender autonomy by promising to obey her husband. She, once only too willing to become well-and-truly married, has of late undergone quite a change of mind.

If the role-differentiation which over the ages has given each gender distinct identity is now disappearing, and therefore gender-distinction itself is now diminishing, a possibility quite unprecedented in human history presents itself. If the female is liberating herself from her old, socially-imposed image of herself, the male has no option but to abandon his also. If the human being is reaching the end of the road where the gaining of advantage through genetic mutation is concerned, then sexual differentiation begins to lose its point. The implications of that may be the inception of a psychological evolution in which gender difference is increasingly transcended. Becoming an individual in one's own right would then take precedence over the performing of specially male or female roles in accordance with the procreative dictates of conventional society (and Nature). Self-authority would be more important than obedience to either patriarchally- or matriarchally-biased authority – just as attainment of adulthood should mean becoming free of the governing influence of father and mother. Only as individuals can the genders transcend through forebrain intelligence those antipathetic, ancient-brain powers which bind them in states of tension and contention. (This is not to suggest, as indicated in the previous chapter, that the genders would need to forego the beneficial aspect of erotic sex.)

The heroic vision of renaissance pursued in Europe several centuries ago emphasized developing the potentialities of the individual, being a quest for 'the complete man'. It could be that the germinating seeds of that 're-birth' have gone through their period of gestation and are now coming to fruition. Just as, in the act of conceiving, a couple will have no clear image of what their offspring will be like, so those progenitors of the cause of individuality will not have had any vision of where their initiatives might eventually lead centuries later. Just as parents may wonder at the fact that the adult son or daughter standing before them is connected with their passionate intercourse many years ago, so those initiators of renaissance, who expressed themselves in a Catholic-dominated world, would be astonished to witness the bid for individualism in our modern world. Apart from anything else, they would not have envisaged then that women – whose liberation has ironically been much facilitated by contraception – would ever be involved in such quest.

If we are indeed on the threshold of spiritual renaissance, then initiatives will only come from 'the living spirit' and authority of the self-generating individual (and, most likely in the first place, from the male's superior powers of creative and objective visualization). It will not evolve out of the prevailing consensus based on old-fashioned, no-longer-relevant belief-systems. Nor will it arise out of a women's liberation movement concerned only with gaining equal share of socio-economic power.

What then, one might well ask, would the purpose of such renaissance of the Individual be? Ideally, of course, greater happiness all round. Happiness is commonly thought of as depending on circumstance of many kinds. But one thing is for sure – that it will not be a secure and lasting happiness if it is not rooted in sense of self-fulfilment and self-integrity. And, in the final analysis, that sense itself will not be securely well-founded if there has not been a coming to terms with the inevitability of death. It is no good persuading oneself that all is well if there is an avoiding of that which will end it all. 'Lay not up for yourselves treasures upon earth. . .' And all that.

The feminist may accuse the male of being an unrepentant killer and of 'loving death'. But the facts of life-as-survival are that the male is biologically-programmed to kill and he has in the past been well-and-truly conditioned by society to be ready to face death. The other side of the equation is that the female is biologically-programmed both to kill and give birth. But, due to role-differentiation, her social conditioning has excused her the former in favour of her furthering the latter. Consequently, she tends to give her attention to regeneration and generally prefers to ignore the inevitability and possible imminence of discontinuation of life. If the male is to take responsibility for initiating an 'internalized' spiritual renaissance, then it must be in constant mindfulness that death is inevitable and impending. And that it is the individual's responsibility to come to terms with it consciously, here and now, every day. Only then will he or she behave wisely.

Meanwhile, orthodox religion can do no more than offer comfort, promising a heavenly after-life for the faithful (and a hellish one for the recalcitrant). Such promise has lost much credibility in a world putting its trust in scientific guarantee. But science itself, once confident that it would find the elixir of life, has been unable to do more than delay the inevitable, often prolonging lives beyond the point of their being worth living. As a result, society at large seems to have become quite schizophrenic about death. On the one hand, it puts it aside and hides it away, pretending that it will not or should not happen. On the other – judging by the news content of the media – it seems obsessed with it. Day after day, we are fed with reports of fatal event, the more shocking the incident, the more sensational the coverage. Such fascination with death could be construed as indicative of a widespread morbid condition in modern society. But it could also indicate an urgent need in that society to come to terms with its fears, especially of death. This prevailing ethos of fear finds its ultimate poignancy in the haunting threat of horrendous man-made disaster – ironically perhaps, a threat most likely created by that science which originally set out on noble quest to find the elixir of life.

Needless to elaborate, any threat of massive destruction of humanity has an insidiously depressing and dispiriting effect on every 'self-conscious' human being. He or she feels helpless to counter the relentless presence of threat, much of which he or she can see no hope of controlling or avoiding. Being able to do nothing about it can only undermine his or her sense of self-authority. No wonder that society at large presently suffers the effects of continual, underlying uncertainty and anxiety.

If that sounds unduly negative, why else the massive consumption of drugs of various kinds, both medically-approved and officially illegal? Doctors are prescribing pills by the million to tranquillize and induce sleep; millions more to stimulate and restore confidence. Even more millions are prescribed and bought over the counter to alleviate the pains of stress, especially in the head.[91] And, as far as illegal drugs are concerned, the tide of demand obstinately refuses to ebb. For example, in the U.S.A. in 1985, an estimated twelve million people were taking cocaine, a number rising at the rate of five thousand a day at that time. Whereas in the 1960's in the UK only a few thousand were using hard drugs, the number had risen to an estimated sixty thousand by 1985. Alongside the drug problem, thousands seek psycho-therapeutic help to ease mental stress and to combat possible breakdown, while thousands more unable to carry on drop out of social participation either partially or fully. Can all this really be the culmination for a species which presumed to call itself '*sapiens*'?

Generally-speaking, whilst institutional authority tolerates mind-numbing drugs, it frowns upon the mind-blowing kind, partly because of the latter's possible threat to social responsibility, partly because of their destructive effect on the user. But, apropos of earlier suggestion concerning the self-destruct compulsion built into the biological system, is not the drug-user's attempt to penetrate the Black Hole of oblivion also indicative of the desire to 'escape to infinity', to make a bid for immortality?

As we witness the heightening sense of precariousness in human society today, we will be aware of the continual attempt to identify the cause of problems so that it is then possible to target blame. Filtered down to personal level, this becomes something like, 'If you will do this . . . or stop doing that . . . I will be happy.' Yet, really, anyone willing to contemplate their situation and own state of mind, knows perfectly well that their happiness, ultimately, is their own responsibility. What is more, it is always the requiring and blaming which destroys it. No one can be responsible for another's suffering or happiness any more than one can do another's dying for them. If a truly spiritual renaissance is to emerge, it will have to be born of each person's determination to reconcile the split-motivations within his or her own mind – i.e. to become 'non-divided', individual. Realization that the cognitive powers of the forebrain can transcend the self-survival of the ancient brain has to be the evolutionary point of our having been created capable of being objectively conscious of ourselves. Fear of death can only be properly transcended by fully-conscious preparation for it. It has to be the only wise way out of what otherwise becomes an increasingly vicious circle of diversion and tragedy.

The days of the human being's commitment to maximum procurement and maximum proliferation are surely numbered. Apart from the fact that the planet cannot go on being expected to sustain it, it is patently obvious now that the strategy has not brought about the degree of security and happiness that was once envisaged. It has to be time for less getting and having, more being content and grateful. Time for less (sexually-generated) competition, more (spiritually-inspired) contemplation. Which is what Hamlet, having assured Ophelia that he did not have 'country matters' on his mind, perhaps meant when reflecting that her 'thinking nothing' was 'a fair thought'.

If such potential for renaissance is to become realized, then men had better start seriously reflecting on their image of themselves – not in the eyes of women, but in their own. The heroic attempt by Orpheus to rescue Eurydice from the Underworld of the Dead failed because, having been forbidden to look at her on the way back, he was tempted to turn round to make sure she was still following him. As a result, he lost her for ever. So inconsolable was he at his loss, that he would not look at another woman. This so infuriated the women of Thracia that they tore him to pieces. His severed head floated across the sea to the island of Lesbos where it became a famous oracle . . .

Notes and References

1 The term 'feminist' is used in this book to denote that lobby of the women's liberation movement which regards men as intolerably arrogant, exploitive, oppressive, dangerous, etc. The extreme militant wing of feminism goes so far as to advocate dissociation from men, even their 'elimination'. Although ardent feminists were vociferous and gained much publicity in the 70's and early 80's, their aggressive stance has become far more muted (unpopular?) in recent years. Nevertheless, their views are brought into account in the following text, partly because of what they reveal about the female psyche, partly because they have had considerable and continuing effect on women's current attitudes towards men and on men themselves, and partly to distinguish that lobby of opinion from the mainstream conduct of the women's liberation movement. The great majority of women directly involved in, supporting or affected by the movement are mainly concerned with gaining rights and opportunities equal to those held by and available to men, seeing themselves meanwhile as remaining in continuing relationship with them.

Literature consulted to obtain a representative selection of views, attitudes and concerns expressed by the feminists and the mainstream liberation movement include: Lee, C., *The Blind Side of Eden* (The Sexes in Perspective), Bloomsbury, London, 1989; Eisenstein, H., *Contemporary Feminist Thought*, Unwin, London, 1984; Greer, G., *The Female Eunuch*, Granada/Paladin, 1971; Holland, J. (ed), *Feminist Action 1*, Battle Axe Books, Middlesex, 1984; Strachan, E. & G., *Freeing the Feminine*, Labarum Publications, Dunbar, Scotland, 1985; Eichenbaum, L. and Orbach, S., *What Do Women Want?*, Collins/Fontana, London, 1984; Collins, W., Friedman, E. and Pivot, A., *Women* (A Directory of Social Change), Wildwood House, London, 1978; French, M., *The Women's Room*, Penguin/Sphere, London, 1978.

2 Research survey in the mid-80's by Drs. Holmes & Rahne, published under the title *Modern Maturity*.

3 In his report 'Body Pleasures and the Origins of Violence',

published in 1975, James W. Prescott, a neurophysiologist working at the U.S. National Institute of Child Health and Human Development, described research demonstrating the reciprocal relationship between physical pleasure and violence; in brief, deprivation of the former precipitates the latter.

4   *Feminist Action 1* (note 1); p. 96, quoting Higginbottom, J. and Roy, M.

5   'When women disengage completely from their traditional role, they become more ruthless and savage than men. Men and male animals fight to show off their prowess . . . with women and female animals there is no game. When they fight, it is fierce and to the death. Women are naturally suited to kill for survival . . . much more than men are.' Dr. Margaret Mead, quoted (p. 126) by Goldberg, H. in *The New Male-Female Relationship*, Coventure, London, 1984.

6   *Social Trends*, annual publication by the Central Statistical Office, H.M.S.O., London, 1986 edition, estimated that the number doubled from 2½% of total households in 1961 to 5% in 1983.

7   *Holy Bible* (AV), Genesis, ch. 2 and ch. 3.

8   The biological basis for human sexual and social customs and practices is surveyed in some detail by Cherfas, J. and Gribbin, J. in *The Redundant Male*, The Bodley Head, London, 1984. A number of points in the following text derive from this source.

9   Sagan, C., *The Dragons of Eden*, Hodder & Stoughton, London, 1977.

10   In an assault such as rape, sexual satisfaction may well, of course, be involved. But the fact that there is growing incidence of the rape of elderly women, for example, corroborates the suggestion that such satisfaction cannot be the only motivation, perhaps not even the principal one. The modern male can become frustrated by the messages of a glamour trade encouraging women to flaunt their sexuality – an invitation to which a large proportion of younger women are happy to respond. Desire is thus continually aroused in him; but he is then not allowed or may not be able to satisfy that desire to anything like the extent that the arousal demands. As in a shop window, the goods are on tempting display but it is forbidden to touch them. No doubt, such customs as those in the Middle East where women are more confined, required to keep their bodies well covered, their eyes veiled in public etc., are intended to negate the female's power of seduction. It is thus that, behind the male's aggressive assault on the female, sexual or otherwise,

being 'mother-headed') had by 1987 risen to about one million, caring for about 1.6 million children. A report published this year (1989) by the Family Policy Studies Centre, under the auspices of the Common Market Commission, estimates that one British family in seven is run by one parent, the 'overwhelming' majority of them being women.

23   The figure given in *Social Trends*, Central Statistical Office, H.M.S.O., 1987 edition. The Family Policy Studies Centre report (note 22) puts the figure at nearly one in four (double the rate at the beginning of the 80's).

24   *The Redundant Male* (note 8), p. 146.

25   *Feminist Action 1* (note 1), p. 92.

26   Cf. note 5.

27   *The Redundant Male* (note 8), p. 7.

28   Research by Dr. C. de Lacoste-Utamsing at the University of Texas.

29   A fuller account of the possible implications of the consciousness factor in human psychology is given in a previous book: *Being In Your Right Mind*, Element Books, Shaftesbury, Dorset, 1984.

30   'Brain/Mind Bulletin', Los Angeles, September 1984, reporting on research findings at the Naval Ocean Systems Center in San Diego.

31   Sources of information for this chapter include: Dimond, E.J. and Beaumont, J.G. (eds), *Hemisphere Function in the Human Brain*, Elek, London, 1974; Eisenberg, H., *Inner Spaces*, General Publishing Co., Ontario, 1977; Blakeslee, T.R., *The Right Brain*, Macmillan, London, 1980; Lishman, W.A., 'The Two Hemispheres', published in 'The Teilhard Review', June 1977.

32   The link between fear and habitual ritual may be discerned in those who suffer compulsive-behaviour disorders (estimated to number at least one million in the U.K. and between four and six million in the U.S.A.). Obsessively repeated habits – e.g., excessive washing or cleaning due to fear of contamination, continual checking of security, that objects are in exactly their usual place, and so on – are attempts to relieve tension due to imagined threat.

33   *Handbook of Anatomy and Physiology* (note 35), p. 59.

34   A fuller account of these alignments and their effect as divided motivation in the human condition are given in a previous book: *Sexuality, Spirituality*, Element Books, Shaftesbury, Dorset, 1980.

there lies resentment at her power over him, a resentment which triggers impulse to take revenge.

11 An Office of Population and Census Surveys estimated (in 1986) that by the year 2025 one in four people in the U.K. will be over 60.

12 World Wildlife Fund report (1985) using figures given by The World Conservation Strategy authorized by the United Nations.

13 World Wildlife Fund report (1987): current world desertification, 80,000 square miles per year; deforestation, 50 acres of tropical rain forest per minute.

14 Even if this may not be regarded as already happening. In a UNICEF report in December 1988, it was estimated that 14 million children a year (40,000 per day) are presently dying from disease and malnutrition.

15 In China, with its population now in excess of a thousand million, the state regime has sought – not, it seems, with unqualified success – to reduce the rate even further: to one child per couple.

16 The U.K. Office of Population and Census Surveys estimated that by 1986 the average number of children per family had fallen to 1.7, well below the 2.1 required for long-term replacement of population.

17 The above Office also estimated in 1986 that, whereas 11% of British women born in the 30's did now have children, 20% of those born in the 50's will not do so.

18 One such challenge now (1989) being the practice of implanting ova donated by younger women in the wombs (primed by appropriate hormone treatment) of infertile, post-menopausal women (possible, it is thought, up to the age of 55). Needless to say, such medical ingenuity creates a host of attendant physical, social and ethical problems which others will then have to try to resolve.

19 *The Redundant Male* (note 8), p. 59.

20 Research at The Medical Research Council's Reproductive Biology Unit in Edinburgh; report in 'Nature', May 1983.

21 Social Security Statistics, D.H.S.S., 1984, reported that single-parent (female) families receiving financial support from the state increased from 212,000 in 1970 to 417,000 by 1982.

22 The National Council for One Parent Families estimated in 1987 that the number of single-parent families (the vast majority

35 Sources of information for this chapter include: Bevan, J., *Handbook of Anatomy and Physiology*, Mitchell Beazley, London, 1978; Zilbergeld, B., *Men and Sex*, Fontana/Collins, 1980; Phillips, A. and Rakusen, J., *Our Bodies Ourselves*, Penguin Books, London, 1978; Bourne, G., *Pregnancy*, Pan Books, London, 1975.

36 *The Redundant Male* (note 8), p. 51.

37 ibid., p. 6.

38 Reported in 'The Listener', May 1979, in an article by Edward Goldwyn under the title 'The fight to be male'.

39 ibid.

40 Research by Prof. G. Geschwind of Harvard University reported in BBC/TV programme 'Horizon', February 1985.

41 *The Right Brain* (note 31), p. 152.

42 Sources of information include: Brown, M., *Left-Handed, Right-Handed*, David & Charles, Newton Abbot, Devon, 1979; Corballis, M.C. and Beale, I.L., *The Psychology of Left and Right*, Lawrence Erhbaum Associates, 1976; *The Right Brain* (note 31); report on the research carried out in Switzerland (Dr. P. Irwin) and USA. (Prof. M. Fink), 'New Scientist', August 1984.

43 *The Right Brain* (note 31), p. 95.

44 *The Redundant Male* (note 8), p. 51ff. The information and statistics in the following text depict the situation and trends recorded until recent times. A Family Policy Studies Centre report in 1987 reveals that the disparity in gender numbers is reversing. In the U.K., there is now an outnumbering of females by males in all age groups except the over 60's. In the 29–50 age group, there are presently almost half-a-million more men that women. The reversal is attributed to improved standards of health care, medical advances and fewer males being killed in war, risk-taking occupations, exploits, etc. For the theme of this book, the reverse trend is significant in several ways, not least that it implies increased male redundancy in all aspects of heterosexual relationships.

45 ibid., p. 53.

46 For example, research carried out by the Italian Association of Democratic Education (reported in 'The Daily Telegraph', 25th February 1988) found that 52% of wives committed adultery against 40% of husbands. One in ten wives questioned claimed to have had at least ten extra-marital affairs, mainly 'one-night-stands'. The common reason cited was sexual dissatisfaction. (See also note 61).

47 In an article in 'The Standard' (London) in January 1983, alcohol was described as enabling 'reduction of anxiety' and as 'augmenting the creative process in the right or "image" side of the brain'.

48 Laing, R.D., *The Divided Self*, Penguin Books, London, 1965.

49 *The Redundant Male* (note 8), p. 51.

50 Exception might be claimed in the case of literature in particular, there having been a number of acclaimed women authors over the past century or so. This would accord with the female's left-brain strength and hence her facility with words. Their work, however, has mainly been confined to report, description and fictional representation of their social and domestic environment (comparable at a more creative level with their reputation for relating gossip). Left-brain strength is also conducive to their capacity for biographical and historical works (the latter sometimes imbued with right-side influence in the form of romantic imagination). It should be added that much of the above applies, of course, to a large number of male authors also.

51 *Feminist Action 1* (note 1), p. 96.

52 Downing, C., *The Goddess*, The Crossroad Publishing Co., New York, 1984 (p. 12).

53 Dr. J. Jaynes, in his book *The Origin of Consciousness in the Bicameral Mind* suggests that, until some 5000 years ago, the human mind had probably not developed 'ego-awareness'. This would equate with the idea that, at that stage in history, increasing brain-hemisphere differentiation in the male precipitated in him growth of personal ambition, rejection of the matriarchal *status quo*, patriarchal initiative, challenge to the goddess cult, and so on.

54 Various attempts to reinstate the divinity of the female principal (e.g. deification of the Virgin Mary) or to establish the concept of God as female (e.g. by Julian of Norwich) have been made throughout the history of the Christian Church. For nearly two thousand years without success; but present initiatives and pressure to permit the ordination of women into the priesthood and hence to gain senior office within the hierarchy may be seen as prelude to renewal of initiatives in that ultimate direction.

55 In the U.K., membership of the Anglican Church, estimated to have been about 2.5 million in 1970, had declined by the late 80's to about 1.8 million. In the Roman Catholic Church (in the U.K.), over the same period, the respective numbers were 2.6 million down to 1.9 million.

56 Jung, C.G., (tr. Hull, R.F.C.), *Aspects of the Feminine*, Routledge & Kegan Paul, London, 1982 (p. 124).

57 For instance, I have a conventional assessment, based on learned data and historical evidence, as to who I am. I was told the date of my birth, I was given a name and, in retrospect, I can recall images and incidents experienced in my youth and beyond, all of which I can fit into chronological sequence. Although all that may have influenced the way I now conduct myself, it seems to have no relevance to the immediacy of my being conscious of myself here and now. I know I am not just an historical phenomenon with a particular name-tag; in truth, that really is what I am not. My private, inner (right-side) self is who I really am; not the public, outer (left-side) performer who is identified by others. Searching for the true identity of the former is the spiritual quest.

58 The risk may be seen (generously) as genuine concern that change may be detrimental to the welfare of the group. But, just as likely (if not more so, given the power of self-interest), the resistance will be born both of those in authority not wanting to lose their status and power and the majority preferring the security of the familiar.

59 Matthew, 6:24 or Luke, 16:13; and Matthew, 8:22.

60 In the U.K. in 1984, one in six spinsters marrying was a teenager; a decade earlier, the figure was one in three.

61 In a recently published survey (Lawson, A., *Adultery: An Analysis of Love and Betrayal*, Blackwell, Oxford, 1989), only 25% of British wives and husbands interviewed (600, white, middle-class) claimed that they had never been unfaithful. (The findings are similar to those carried out in the U.S.A.) What is more, wives tend to be unfaithful earlier (after 4.5 years of marriage) than husbands (5.2 years). This is a 'complete reversal' of figures compiled twenty years ago. Even further, interviewees were far less reluctant to divulge their infidelity than in earlier surveys (presumably because they felt far less guilty about it).

62 Betty Friedan (quoted by Penny Perrick in 'The Times', December 1985.

63 Following forecast in *Social Trends* (note 6), 1987 edition: marriages in the U.K. in 1985, 393,000; divorces, 193,000. Interestingly – in relation to the initiatives of women's liberation – three times as many wives are divorcing their husbands as *vice versa*.

64 See note 22.

65 Adler, G., *Dynamics of the Self*, Coventure, London, 1979.

66   Goldberg, H., *The New Male-Female Relationship*, Coventure, London, 1983.

67   ibid., p. 34.

68   In the U.K. in the mid-80's, more than one third of the total number of marriages involved the re-marriage of one or both partners. At the same time, one in five divorces involved partners who had already been divorced at least once before.

69   Albeit, in a left-brain sense – i.e. memorization of factual information, logical processing and extrapolation of accumulated data, the disciplining of it into historical perspective and practical applications, and so on.

70   Nevertheless, there has to remain the possibility that Individuality – in the full, transcendental and spiritual reaches of its meaning – may still as yet be unattainable by the female. It may be that she is psychologically still too committed (as most males are) to the actuality of the phenomenal world. It would then be that her power of objective consciousness cannot yet be raised to the level where she is able to understand and realize the abstract Reality which requires renouncement and liberation from the illusory reality ascribed to the physical world. In other words, due to the procreative aspect of her biology, she is still too identified with and attached to her body as being her only and real self. Esoteric, Eastern, spiritual traditions refer to the indispensibility of a male incarnation in this aspiration towards spiritual liberation. It is as if potential for spiritual 're-birth' (renaissance) is the male's equivalent of the female's potential for physical regeneration. And it is thus that the female may still be dependent on the male to lead the way where spiritual fulfilment is concerned.

71   Professor Charles Handy of The London Business School.

72   In the U.K., 9 million at present; probably 13 million by the end of the century. Present retirement rate: 500,000 per annum. (BBC/TV 'Brass Tacks', June 1988.)

73   A procedure recommended (for example, in *Men and Sex*, note 35) for maintaining a successful 'sex-life'. Clearly the acceptability of such techniques takes some pressure off the male to take all the erotic initiative.

74   *The Redundant Male* (note 8), ch. 7.

75   As in Tantric, Kundalini and Taoist traditions (described, for example, by Huard, P. and Wong, M. in *Chinese Medicine*, Weidenfeld & Nicholson, p. 54f.). The emphasis in such teachings is not on passionate orgasm and male ejaculation but on transformation of sexual energy. There are also intimations

(cf. note 70) not only that the transmutation is of male 'seminal essence' but that the female cannot herself experience 'spiritual orgasm' without surrendering herself to male 'penetration'. As suggested by Singer, J., (in *Androgyny* [Towards a New Theory of Sexuality], Routledge & Kegan Paul, London, 1977, p. 182ff.), actual transubstantiation of semen cannot be meant. Transformation of energy which would have been used to produce semen may be implied; but it is the psychological transformation of sexual potency from outer expression in passion to inner aspiration towards spiritual ecstasy which is essential.

76　E.g., Kaplan, H.S., *The New Sex Therapy*, Brunner/Mazel Inc., New York, 1972.

77　According to a report in 'The Guardian' (19th May 1988), 'one in ten women between the ages of 35 and 59 regard themselves as having a sexual problem. However, the number may be as many as three in ten given that what doctors define as dysfunction many women seem to accept as normal' (being regarded as due to ageing, menopause, etc.).

78　S.W. Hawking of Cambridge University in 'Scientific American', 1977.

79　Genesis, ch. 4.

80　But such envy may have more to do with the implications of notes 70 and 75.

81　*The Redundant Male* (note 8), p. 42.

82　Harvey, A., *A Journey in Ladakh*, Jonathan Cape, London, 1983.

83　As described, for example, in *What Do Women Want?* (note 1), ch. 5.

84　Guillaumont, H. and others (tr), *The Gospel According to Thomas*, Collins, London, 1959 (log. 114).

85　Cf. notes 70 and 75.

86　Re. note 1, especially the aggressively critical campaign of the militant feminists whose stance now seems to have become unacceptable to most women, including those who regard themselves as liberated.

87　For example, Germaine Greer in *Sex and Destiny*, Secker & Warburg, London, 1984.

88　Cf. notes 46 and 61.

89　Sonnet 116.

90　*The Right Brain* (note 31), p. 16.

91　In the U.K., 2,000 tonnes of aspirin (enough to make 6,000 million tablets) are consumed each year.

Index